CONFERENCE ON BRITISH STUDIES
BIOGRAPHICAL SERIES
Editor: PETER STANSKY
Consultant Editor: G. R. ELTON

G. D. H. COLE

G. D. H. COLE

AN INTELLECTUAL BIOGRAPHY

L. P. CARPENTER

ASSOCIATE PROFESSOR OF HISTORY
CITY UNIVERSITY OF NEW YORK

CAMBRIDGE
AT THE UNIVERSITY PRESS
1973

Published by the Syndics of the Cambridge University Press
Bentley House, 200 Euston Road, London NW1 2DB
American Branch: 32 East 57th Street, New York, N.Y. 10022

Library of Congress Catalog Card Number: 72–88614

ISBN 0 521 08702 3

© Cambridge University Press 1973

Printed in the United States of America

PREFACE

Although Dame Margaret Cole kindly read and commented on an early version of this book, it is not an authorized biography of Cole, nor does it represent Dame Margaret's opinions. I should like to thank the following people for talking with me about Cole, as his friends, his colleagues, or as people interested in Labour history and politics: Mrs Jane Abraham; P. W. S. Andrews; Robin Page Arnot; A. L. Bacharach; Mrs Rosamund V. Broadley; D. N. Chester; Colin Clark; Sir George Clark; Hugh Clegg; F. C. Cummings; Paul Derrick; W. N. Ewer; Richard Fletcher; Michael Fogarty; A. H. Halsey; Geoffrey Hancock; Christopher Hill; H. D. Hughes; E. M. Hutchinson; J. G. K. Kennedy; Marcus Lower; William Lowth; R. B. McCallum; Frank Matthews; John Mogey; John Papworth; John Parker, M.P.; Jack Pavey; Henry Pelling; Maurice B. Reckitt; Miss Eva Reckitt; Professor W. A. Robson; and John Saville. I should like to thank the Warden of Nuffield College for giving me access to the Cole Papers and to papers relating to the Nuffield College Social Reconstruction Survey, and the Librarian of Nuffield College and her staff for their assistance. The Trustees of the Passfield Papers gave me access to Beatrice Webb's diaries. Maurice B. Reckitt kindly allowed me to use an unpublished manuscript, 'G. D. H. Cole, the N.G.L. and the L.R.D.'. Special thanks go to John Clive, who was my thesis adviser, and Peter Stansky, who helped me prepare the book for publication. My research was partially financed by a Harvard University Travelling Fellowship.

L. P. C.

ACKNOWLEDGMENTS

The author and publisher are grateful to the following for granting permission to reproduce material first published by them: to the Macmillan Press Ltd. for extracts from G. D. H. Cole: *Self-Government in Industry, The World of Labour, The Next Ten Years in British Social and Economic Planning, Principles of Economic Planning, Economic Tracts for the Times, Essays in Social Theory, Persons and Periods* and from Asa Briggs and G. Saville (ed.): *Essays in Labour History*; to J. M. Dent & Sons Ltd. for extracts from Maurice B. Reckitt: *As it Happened*; and to Nuffield College, Oxford, for material from the *Social Reconstruction Survey* and from the Cole papers.

CONTENTS

INTRODUCTION

As interest revives in G. D. H. Cole, scholars find themselves questioning his motivation. What made him devote so much time and energy to socialist commentary and research? To many, his activity appears abnormal, implicitly requiring a psychological explanation. I do not give a psychological explanation, because I believe none is called for.

The most promising psychological models for historical and political analysis are developmental. Early Freudian developmental models placed much emphasis on the first five years of life. We know very little about Cole's early years. But this is not as great a handicap as it would appear. Erik Erikson places his greatest emphasis on the 'identity crisis' of adolescence, and argues that the identity shaped then must bind together and satisfy personality characteristics formed earlier.[1] In order to argue that early developmental stages uniquely shaped Cole's intellectual development, problems arising in these early stages would have to remain visible in adolescent and adult behaviour. Reading backwards from Cole's adolescence, revealed in his conversion to socialism and in his undergraduate essays and articles, we do not find him having to deal with awkward residues of previous developmental stages. He does not appear crippled by mistrust, or agonized by guilt, or overwhelmed by his relations with father figures. His relationship with his father apparently stayed amicable, and he did not go through a period of hankering for messianic religion. His relationship with the Webbs did culminate in Cole's storming out of the Fabian Society in 1915, but Cole surmounted this crisis and managed to preserve friendly relations with them. As a Guild Socialist, Cole was antagonistic to the state. This may owe something to adolescent rebellion but it stopped short of a romantic urge to create revolution, and was offset by his appreciation of the importance of community. The suspicion of centralized power which Cole carried over from his

---

[1] Erik H. Erikson, *Childhood and Society* (New York, Norton, 1950); Erik H. Erikson, *Gandhi's Truth* (New York, Norton, 1969); E. Victor Wolfenstein, *The Revolutionary Personality: Lenin, Trotsky, Gandhi* (Princeton, N.J., Princeton University Press, 1967).

earliest days fell within the liberal tradition and was healthy. Thus a developmental approach does not seem necessary to explain how Cole's socialism developed, or able to reveal a crisis that 'made'him a socialist, although a developmental approach might shed light on how Cole became receptive to socialism.

Through interviews and in his large output, it becomes clear that Cole was a highly sublimated person who put little energy into sexuality after the age of forty. But I do not feel that this indicates a major psychic disturbance that would explain the content of his socialism. Unlike Gandhi, Cole did not take a vow of chastity, or develop an ascetic position either in private life or in his view of human needs. In connection with his sublimation of sexuality, one should mention his serious illness in 1930; but the more basic point is the combination of satisfactions and disturbances coming from the objective world. Teaching was obviously something Cole did well, as were journalism and popular political writing; all were creative and rewarding. Large-scale public events – depression, the agonizing experience of the MacDonald Government, the need for creative rethinking of socialism, and the rise of Fascism – round out the picture.

The identity that Cole formed was not a rigid 'purified identity', an intolerant sense of right that artificially blocks out the perception of awkward facts and sources of claims.[1] Cole's identity was pluralist. He was a socialist, but not simply or monochromatically socialist. As a young socialist, at Oxford and in the Guild Socialist movement, he mixed research and propaganda with sheer fun and with teaching for the Workers' Educational Association. His later life resembled an ellipse with its foci at Oxford and in the London of the *New Statesman* and Labour politics – with a bulge for the writing of murder mysteries. The same pluralism marks his socialism. Guild Socialism attempted to reconcile claims of workers' control with consumer and community participation, and grew as new claims were brought to Cole's attention. When Guild Socialism became unwieldy and failed to keep step with British political reality, Cole looked for a less confining picture of the world. From 1920 onwards, he tried to mediate between left-wing opinion and the bulk of the Labour movement, rather than developing

[1] Richard Sennett, *The Uses of Disorder: Personal Identity and City Life* (New York, Alfred A. Knopf, 1970).

a rigid policy all his own and insisting that the movement accept it. But this flexibility did not mean that his identity had come unstuck. His Socialism continued to function as a backbone, rather than fragmenting or solidifying into a ramrod.

Thus we come to the picture of Cole given in this book. We see a socialist responding to his world. His socialism was humanistic, emphasizing major liberal values such as democracy and freedom, integrating them into a value structure that was comprehensive without being rigid. His value structure and his personal experience in the Labour movement gave him an understanding of human needs. Interlocking with that value structure was his perception of human needs. His background – St Paul's School, Oxford, and the Webbs – taught him the importance of research. Any policy that Cole considered had to satisfy both his values and his practical side. A third factor, closely related to these two, was his desire to serve the Labour movement. Service was heavily stressed in the late Victorian professional bourgeoisie, the social stratum in which he was educated. It was reinforced by his awareness of others' claims to freedom, respect, and basic necessities, and by his research and experience. All this helps explain why Cole was often considered as a 'secular saint', for they prevented him from developing an inordinate desire for fame or power. Cole is noteworthy for his understanding of the limits on the intellectual within the working-class movement. Finally, his prolific output may seem compulsive; but compulsive people usually are much more out of touch with reality. A nearly-compulsive level of output was necessary to express the varied parts of his identity. Academic scholarship alone, politcial research alone, propaganda alone, teaching alone, would not have satisfied him. In a passage about William Morris, Cole revealed how his voluminous output related to the pluralist identity he had formed:

. . . though a man's work may fall short of greatness if he attempts too many things, it does not at all follow that he would do better in attempting less. For the truth may be that he wants to do and say so much that he is much more concerned to get it done and said than to do one thing, or a few things, supremely well. He may have the power of expressing himself, and of serving his fellow-men, rather in many things than in a few; and though no one thing mark him out as master, his mastery may appear none the less plainly in all . . .[1]

[1] G. D. H. Cole, 'William Morris and the Modern World,' in *Persons and Periods* (London, Macmillan, 1938), pp. 288–289.

3

CHAPTER I

JOINING THE LABOUR MOVEMENT

I became a Socialist as a schoolboy a year or so before the General Election of 1906, which first put the Labour Party firmly on the parliamentary map ... My conversion to Socialism had very little to do with parliamentary politics ... I was converted, quite simply, by reading William Morris's *News from Nowhere*, which made me feel, suddenly and irrevocably, that there was nothing except a Socialist that it was possible for me to be ... I became a Socialist, as many others did in those days, on grounds of morals and decency and aesthetic sensibility.[1]

This conversion placed Cole on the road which he was to follow all his life. Not that socialism was Cole's whole life; his work in education, and the murder mysteries he wrote in his spare time, testify to his versatility. He tempered the strength of his conversion to Socialism through his participation in non-political activities. He sought to avoid fanaticism: 'I distrust the man for whom the Socialist ideal, or any other ideal, looms so large as to cover the whole of life.'[2] As a political man, he often avoided taking a stand that would limit him to being a partisan of one fragment of the Labour movement. Yet in a broad sense he was converted to socialism. What he meant by socialism lay behind all his public activities, and pervaded his personality. Socialism formed his academic interests in trade unionism and Labour history, his democratic educational practices. As he wrote in 1956, 'I can still feel the glow of that conversion ...'.[3] Socialism united Cole's life and attitudes in the same way that Morris's socialism united his.

At a first glance, one would not have expected Cole to become a socialist. Socialism was still in its heroic infancy in many parts of England, and especially in the South where Cole grew up. The impetus given to trade unionism by the strikes of 1889 had petered out during

---

[1] G. D. H. Cole, 'British Labour Movement – Retrospect and Prospect', *Ralph Fox Memorial Lecture, Fabian Special, No. 8* (London, 1952), pp. 3–4.
[2] G. D. H. Cole, 'The Inner Life of Socialism', *The Aryan Path*, I, No. 2 (February 1930), p. 7.
[3] G. D. H. Cole, 'World Socialism Restated' (*New Statesman* Pamphlet, London, 1956), p. 5.

his childhood. Meanwhile, socialist ideas had only made sporadic inroads into the middle classes and the intelligentsia. Cole appears to have had little direct contact with the effects of industrialization while he was young. G. N. Clark, one of his oldest and best friends, said very aptly, that 'Cole became a Socialist from the back seat of a car' rather than from direct experience.[1]

Cole was born on 25 September 1889, the youngest child of a rising self-made man. George Cole was an estate agent, whose firm in Ealing Broadway still prospers. By the time that G. D. H. reached adolescence, his father had become a Tory and a member of the Church of England. There is no evidence that Cole became a socialist in reaction against this traditional background. While he found Samuel Butler's protests against late Victorian family life appealing, Cole always took care to explain that his father did not resemble Canon Pontifex.[2] The Coles stayed reasonably close as a family. Margaret Cole recalls that they were kind to her when she married Douglas in August 1918, at a time when her father largely broke off social relationships with Douglas and Margaret Cole, and with her brother Raymond Postgate, who had also become a Guild Socialist.[3] Even in the 1930s Cole continued to visit his father, and they would argue politics without acrimony.[4] They had much in common. Cole shared the *laissez-faire* liberal's strong belief in liberty, while differing from his father in his application of the principle. Cole failed to learn the traditional middle-class identification of freedom with the right to property. Despite his radical politics, his personal tastes remained conservative. He especially enjoyed Victorian fiction, even having a good word to say for Charlotte M. Yonge; he never enjoyed motion pictures. The presence of these traditional elements in his beliefs and habits kept Cole from developing the bitterness one sometimes sees in left-wing Socialists. Although he disliked many aspects of capitalist society, his was not a socialism of hatred, but one which emphasized what had to be done to liberate the tendencies he loved in English society.

[1] Interview with G. N. Clark.
[2] G. D. H. Cole, *Samuel Butler* (Writers and Their Work, No. 30, London: Longmans Green, 1952), p. 41.
[3] Margaret Cole, *Growing Up Into Revolution* (London: Longmans Green, 1949), p. 77.
[4] Interview with J. G. K. Kennedy, Cole's nephew and the owner of Cole and Hicks, the estate agency founded by Cole's father.

Cole was educated at St Paul's School. It provided him with an urban and intellectual environment, in which the traditional values of 'empire' and social position were not as overwhelming as they were at other public schools. In 1913, he wrote that Compton Mackenzie's *Sinister Street*, with its descriptions of mental and social adventures outside of the heavy academic curriculum, was a realistic description of the school. Cole emphasized that 'St Paul's draws on a mixed urban population that is predominately professional and artistic or literary'. He contrasted the atmosphere of 'spiritual adventures' with Harrow's 'empire building'.[1] Unlike Mackenzie's protagonist, Cole belonged to the University Sixth form, and his advanced education consisted almost entirely of Greek, Latin, and classical history. From the beginning, however, Cole wished to investigate a great variety of subjects on his own. He won prizes in English verse, history, and English essay, in addition to Latin prose and elegiacs. He edited *The Pauline*, the school newspaper, and became a prefect; he mocked both activities in *The Octopus*, a humorous paper whose distinguished ancestors included one edited by G. K. Chesterton. An anonymous reviewer in *The Pauline*, perhaps even Cole enjoying the chance to criticize his own efforts, said that *The Octopus* 'dealt blows on tender spots with a persistence which is not generally credited, even to the most savage of marine monsters . . . the humor was crude, the cynicism immature. . . .'[2] The judgment will certainly stand the test of time. Cole contributed some savage remarks about himself and others, a variety of short stories (one of which is a parable in the fashion of Morris), some doggerel and parodies,[3] and mockery of the cant of moral theology.

[1] G. D. H. Cole, 'School Stories', *The Northerner* (Newcastle, December 1913), 42–3. He compared Mackenzie's book with Arnold Lunn's *The Harrovians*.

[2] *The Pauline*, Vol. xxvi (April 1908), pp. 48–9. Surmaster F. C. Commings of St Paul's allowed me to consult the St Paul's Union Society Minute Book and *The Pauline*, and discussed Cole's curriculum and prizes with me. Copies of *The Octopus*, ed. A. L. Johnson and G. D. H. Cole (London, November 1906–June 1907) are at Nuffield College.

[3] Cole's parodies were generally the best of his poetry. Many of them were written for and with the Guild Socialist movement. See *The Bolo Book*, ed. G. D. H. and M. I. Cole (London: Labour Publishing Co. and Allen & Unwin, 1921), which includes the songs from 'The Mysterious Homeland', a musical comedy about Soviet Russia conceived and presented at the 1920 Fabian Summer School. 'The Striker Stricken', a musical written about the 1926 General Strike, is at Nuffield College, and one hopes that it will be published. It has been sung privately, at meetings of the Cole Group in Oxford, but has been considered libellous. Cole published two volumes of poetry

He appears to have developed a taste for shocking the bourgeoisie which he never lost.

At St Paul's, Cole and his friends considered themselves 'the brainy', and waged war on the athletes. His interests at this time lay chiefly in literary and artistic subjects. In the Union Society, of which he became president, Cole was often to be found debating topics such as 'That this house considers modern drama degenerate'. Cole moved that resolution, and supported his stand by arguing that Shaw was a great author but not a great dramatist.[1] The Union Society offered opportunities for the aspirant to fame and public office, even one who developed as unconventionally as Cole. One debate, on the House of Lords, even drew Chesterton as a spectator. In his column in *The Daily News*, Chesterton commented that Cole (who drew the assignment of defending the Lords' existence) and his opponent 'were learning to be a politician – that is, they were being taught not to care about politics'.[2] Cole only learned part of the lesson; he came to take political ideas more seriously than Parliamentary politics.

Cole's circle at school appears to have been politically progressive; it approved minimum wage legislation and included several socialists. However, Cole was hesitant to commit himself publicly to socialism; no record exists of his intervening in Union Society debates on municipal socialism and the Progressive Party, the Webbs' effort to permeate London municipal politics. He was also slow to realize the connection between his socialist ideals and existing political institutions. The success of the Labour Representation Committee in the 1906 elections does not seem to have impressed him. He first joined a socialist organization in the spring of 1908, just before going up to Oxford; yet he had first read Morris late in 1905.

Cole was introduced to William Morris by one of his friends at St Paul's. He began with *The Defense of Guenevere*. He felt the appeal of the 'rich, luscious beaker of Victorian medievalism'. He pursued this

[1] St Paul's School Union Society Minute Book, 24 October 1907.
[2] G. K. Chesterton, *The Daily News* (5 October 1907).

before the First World War: *The Record* (Oxford, Basil Blackwell, 1912) and *New Beginnings* (Oxford, Basil Blackwell, 1914); and *The Crooked World* (London, Gollancz, 1933).

8

spirit in the pictures of Rossetti and Burne-Jones, 'made pilgrimage to Kelmscott Manor and to Hammersmith Hall, and set out to read every work of or about William Morris on which I could lay hands'.[1]

The picture of the place of the artist in society which Morris associated with the middle ages formed the bridge between the aesthetic interests which he outgrew and his developing social consciousness. He was ready to agree that art grew out of society, and that the separation of art from craftsmanship was morally and psychologically wrong.[2] Starting from these premises, Morris's writings taught Cole

that the quality of work and the quality of living could not be dissociated, and that men whose daily labours were to them no better than an irksome round of toil, and satisfied no part of their natural impulses, could by no means live happily or fruitfully in the rest of their existence. The quality of their working hours would penetrate and poison their lives, making them worse and less happy as friends or lovers, as citizens and as men. Can anyone deny that this is true, or that the irksomeness and strain of much modern factory labour are powerful causes of unhappiness, ill-temper and thwarted or twisted personality in the world of to-day. The happiest of us, I verily believe, and the most at peace with the world – however much we find ourselves at war with its abuses – are those who are able to enjoy our work.[3]

This argument was of infinite importance to Cole for all his political life. It gave him a purpose for which he could fight. Morris taught Cole that a whole life depended upon the expression of oneself in work; Cole built his faith in industrial democracy and Guild Socialism around this perception. He associated the meaning of work with another phrase from Morris which he loved to quote: 'Fellowship is heaven, and lack of fellowship is hell.'[4]

[1] These quotations are taken from an article on William Morris, published in *Revisions and Revaluations* (1931). There is a galley proof in a volume of Cole's articles at Nuffield College; I have not been able to locate a published copy.

[2] Cole avoided the crudities that can come out of the argument that art reflects the society in which the artist works. He would not have agreed fully with Morris that good art could come only out of a good society. See 'Art and Socialism: A forgotten incident of the Paris Commune and other matters', Manuscripts and Proofs, Box 7, folder 93, Cole Papers, Nuffield College. Probably written in 1911.

[3] G. D. H. Cole 'William Morris and the Modern World', in *Persons and Periods* (London, Macmillan, 1938), p. 293.

[4] William Morris, 'A Dream of John Ball', in *William Morris: Prose, Verse, Lectures and Essays*, ed. G. D. H. Cole (London, Nonesuch Press, 1934), p. 212.

These beliefs, to which Cole responded in Morris, became the basis of his attempts to improve the world. From Morris, he learned what a good society felt like and what values were involved. Thus Morris's egalitarian, energetic, and libertarian spirit exerted more influence on Cole than the details of *News From Nowhere* or 'A Factory as it Might Be'.[1] Morris himself remained a figure of veneration for Cole. He owned one of Morris's best cretonnes, 'The Woodpecker', and kept a marble bust of Morris in his library. Cole responded to Morris's goodness; and in many ways he came to resemble Morris. Thus, in one comment on Morris, he offered the definitive answer to those who rebuked him for having written too much:

... though a man's work may fall short of greatness if he attempts too many things, it does not at all follow that he would do better in attempting less. For the truth may be that he wants to do and say so much that he is much more concerned to get it done and said than to do one thing, or a few things, supremely well. He may have the power of expressing himself, and of serving his fellow-men rather in many things than in a few; and though no one thing mark him out as a master, his mastery may appear none the less plainly in them all. This, I think, is true of William Morris. He is greater as a man and as an influence than in any one part of his work.[2]

Cole, converted to socialism by reading Morris, entered the Labour movement in a most idealistic fashion.

I became a Socialist because, as soon as the case for a society of equals, set free from the twin evils of riches and poverty, mastership and subjection, was put to me, I knew that to be the only kind of society that could be consistent with human decency and fellowship and that in no other society could I have the right to be content. The society William Morris imagined seemed to me to embody the right sort of human relations, and to be altogether beautiful and admirable ...[3]

He suddenly saw an entirely different, morally superior way of living, and called it socialism. 'Socialism presented itself to me, not as an

[1] G. D. H. Cole, untitled paper on Morris, in 'Manuscripts and Proofs', Box 7, folder 91, Cole Papers, Nuffield College. Dated 17 November 1910.
[2] 'William Morris and the Modern World'. Cole wrote a similar passage at the start of his career: 'William Morris', *The Blue Book* (June 1913), 355–66. The decision to do a workmanlike job on many things rather than an artful one on a single task was one of the most important he ever made.
[3] G. D. H. Cole, 'World Socialism Restated' (*New Statesman* Pamphlet, London, 1956), p. 5.

economic or political doctrine, but as a complete alternative way of living – as I still regard it'.[1] Thanks also to Morris, Cole saw socialism as a truly free way of living. One might argue that Cole could never have become a socialist without discovering that his own firm belief in freedom could be expressed through socialism. In this important sense, Cole's socialism was the heir of the Edwardian Liberalism in which he grew up. He argued that socialist measures were necessary to bring freedom, and the argument clearly carried tremendous weight with him. But Cole did not resemble the majority of the Liberal recruits to socialism. He lacked the classical Liberal's paramount belief in the 'principles of the English constitution'. For Cole, freedom was a basic human demand, a way of treating people and of providing them with all the opportunities they needed to govern and express themselves. In his conversion to socialism as Morris had described it, Cole entered the socialist movement on the libertarian wing.

That Cole was converted by Morris, rather than by Marx or by the speakers of a particular political sect, had another important effect on his socialism. He always devoted himself directly to the socialist movement as a whole, above and beyond any particular manifestation of it. While choosing to support certain sections rather than others, he never developed a narrow sectarianism. He spread his efforts across the movement's activities; even when he was attacking the Webbs in his early days, he could see the usefulness of groups opposed to the ones he formed or joined. He often felt that dissension was a sign of growth, not of weakness. And so he was above the sectarian politics of 'divide and conquer'. He would go to tremendous lengths to create unity by a brilliant composite resolution, or disband his own organizations when he felt that two organizations could not serve in the same functional area. This devotion to socialism as a whole placed him in awkward, and from some perspectives even naïve, positions at certain points in his career; yet one could argue that sectarianism would have entailed even worse dangers. Thus he never questioned Russia's claim to be socialist, and he refrained from responding viciously to the British Communists' taunts. Even after the Russians suppressed the Hungarian revolution, he refused to be drawn into anti-Communist

[1] 'British Labour Movement – Retrospect and Prospect', p. 5.

crusading although he condemned the Russian invasion.[1] He saw one overriding ethical imperative, that socialists had to unite to remake society, and this led him to disregard behaviour which violated his beliefs.

Cole could understand and at times condone non-libertarian tactics because he found the transition to socialism hard to outline definitively. His conversion left him knowing two worlds, socialism and capitalism. The gap between these two worlds could scarcely be bridged; an undefined change of the whole of society had to occur somewhere in between. This change would be revolutionary, although Cole usually refused to say that the revolution had to be violent. The socialist revolution might resemble the industrial revolution rather than a *coup d'état*. The suddenness, the complete re-creation of society involved in a revolution, had an emotional appeal to Cole which was rooted in his initial conversion to socialism. He chafed at having to think about economic and social problems before men could come to live fuller lives.[2]

This desire for a radical transformation that would make the world live up to his ideals often found full expression in Cole's work. Much of his Guild Socialist writing can usefully be considered a kind of utopian socialism, and at other times in his career Cole served as a custodian of socialist values. If this had been the only side to Cole's personality, he might even have turned his back on the existing world, insisting that his ideals be kept pure and transcendent. But Cole was not that single-minded. Another mental factor interacted with his ideals. Maurice Reckitt's perceptive triolet gets at the duality:

> Mr G. D. H. Cole
> Is a bit of a puzzle;
> A curious role
> That of G. D. H. Cole,
> With a Bolshevik soul
> In a Fabian muzzle;

---

[1] See G. D. H. Cole, 'World Socialism Restated' (*New Statesman* Pamphlet, rev. ed., London, 1957), pp. 47–8; 'Socialists and Communism', *New Statesman*, LI (5 May 1956), 472–4.

[2] 'British Labour Movement – Retrospect and Prospect', p. 5.

Mr G. D. H. Cole
Is a bit of a puzzle.[1]

In 'Bolshevik soul', Reckitt was pointing to the complex of values that made up Cole's idealistic understanding of socialism. If one looked at Cole exclusively from the stand-point of his highest ideals, one would say that these ideals were held in check by another aspect of his personality. Reckitt called this his 'Fabian muzzle'. The adjective is revealing. The 'Fabian muzzle' included many of the traits Cole had in common with the other great Fabians. Like them, he insisted upon 'getting the facts'. Much of his considerable energy went into the Fabian Research Department, various study-circles, social history, the New Fabian Research Bureau, and the Nuffield College Social Reconstruction Survey. Cole had a tremendous capacity for facts, and insisted upon honesty and accuracy. He combined these empiricist traits with a Fabian insistence upon efficiency and expertise. His emphasis upon facts often offended others who were equally idealistic. For example, he infuriated some members of the left of the National Guilds League in 1917 by demanding that the League study all proposals for post-war social reconstruction 'on their merits' – while the League was energetically pressing for Guild Socialism.

Another crucial component of Cole's 'Fabian muzzle' was his practicality. He was a pragmatist in his choice of means and in decisions concerning his own activities. He sought theories and facts alike for specific purposes connected with the formulation of Labour policy. Study had to reveal what was likely to happen and what Labour could do. It was useless to maintain an impractical position out of sheer doctrinal consistency, and useless to ignore the factors already at work in a situation. He was a prophet who sought to identify and work with the progressive forces, rather than a dogmatic utopian who stated an ideal without regard to the means to be used in obtaining it.

The 'Fabian muzzle' could even affect Cole's interpretation of his basic beliefs. 'Belief, in the sense here relevant, is a compound of factual judgment and of value judgment, in such a way that the two

[1] Maurice B. Reckitt, *As It Happened* (London, J. M. Dent & Sons, 1941), p. 123; *The Guildsman*, No. 31 (June 1919), p. 3.

are merged into a single act of faith.'[1] Moral principles and facts were both components of social obligation. Cole committed himself deeply to both. Both morals and reason entailed duties in given circumstances; either might be the factor which determined right or valid action.[2]

Cole's practicality thus was more than a muzzle for his idealism. A basic constituent of his personality, it was on the same level as his idealism. Reckitt wrote that when he showed the triolet to Mrs Cole, she 'declared that it was really a Fabian soul in a Bolshevik muzzle, and there is certainly a case for this interpretation too'.[3] Reckitt saw that either aspect of Cole's personality might dominate. Yet it was not a question of a basic dualism, in which 'idealism' and 'practicality' fought for control. Rather, an idea or policy had to satisfy two sets of criteria as much as possible. Each set of criteria could be modified by arguments from the other side. At the same time, both the 'Bolshevik soul' and the 'Fabian muzzle' were 'sticking-points', establishing limits beyond which Cole could not go without being uneasy. The major positions that Cole adopted were equilibria that tried to satisfy both his idealism and his practicality, even where one side of his personality dominated. Thus Cole developed his Guild-utopian speculations at a time when he felt they were practical. At other times he appears to swing towards the other extreme, a full endorsement of reformist political action; yet even then the ideal still comes through. When he concentrated upon short-range policies, he insisted that they had to prepare the way for more fundamental reconstructions of Britain.

The fact that socialism had to satisfy both Cole's 'Bolshevik soul' and his 'Fabian muzzle' helps account for Cole's slowness to convert his instinctive, idealistic socialism into socialist practices. Trying to go beyond Morris's ideas, Cole was not greeted by a strong, self-assured Labour movement. The Labour movement as a whole had much to do to make its demands precise, to clarify what its ends were and to link them to short-term measures. Looking backward from 1958, he wrote, 'We could advocate Socialism all the more easily because we did not really expect it to come about at any early, or anticipable, future date;

[1] This quotation comes from a proof, entitled 'What I Believe', and dated March 1953, in 'Manuscripts and Proofs', Box 8, Cole Papers, Nuffield College, p. 116.
[2] G. D. H. Cole, 'An Essay on Social Morality', *Essays in Social Theory* (London, Macmillan, 1950), p. 72.
[3] Maurice B. Reckitt, *As It Happened*, p. 123.

and our Socialism was all the simpler because we had no expectation that we should soon be called upon to put it into practice.' As far as actual demands were concerned, British socialism before the First World War was extremely mild. Politically it was subservient to the Liberal Party – hardly inspiring to a young militant.

Our immediate objectives hardly went beyond the minimum wage, the eight hour day, and the 'right to work' – by which we meant essentially the right to public maintenance in default of employment. We did, indeed, advocate the socialisation of the means of production, distribution, and exchange . . .; but we hardly expected this to come about at all soon, even in relation to [coal and the railways]. Certainly, we did not expect an early supersession of the capitalist system by Socialism . . .[1]

Thus Cole's instinctive socialism, and the movements that were at his disposal in developing it, left much for him to work out. Instead of there being a ready-made body of doctrine for him to absorb, he had to participate with others in creating the doctrine. The Ealing Branch of the Independent Labour Party, which Cole joined early in 1908, apparently did not fit his needs. He required a group of friends with whom he could think out a consistent, realistic socialism. He needed to create simultaneously study groups and research organizations, magazines and propagandistic associations. In the autumn of 1908, when he went up to Oxford, Cole found the necessary friends and the seeds of the necessary organizations.

'I celebrated my first week in Oxford by joining the University Fabian Society . . .'[2] This was the scene of much of his early intellectual development. It introduced him to many of the leading socialists of the day, who came to lecture under its auspices. Keir Hardie's speech in March 1909, at one such meeting, provided the kernel for a legend which gives something of the spirit of the times. The Bullingdon Boys, a group of local Tory toughs, planned to break up the meeting. Getting wind of their plans, Cole enlisted the support of quarrymen from Headington, the eastern part of Oxford, to serve as 'ushers'. According to the legend, they asked Cole to march with them from Headington into the centre of Oxford. Cole then stationed himself on the platform,

---

[1] G. D. H. Cole, 'Socialism Now and Fifty Years Ago' (Webb Lecture, London, Athlone Press, 1958), p. 2.
[2] 'British Labour Movement – Retrospect and Prospect', p. 4.

and, when a Bullingdon Boy entered the hall, Cole pointed him out to the quarrymen. A quarryman stationed himself directly behind each of the Bullingdon Boys. The meeting was raucous, and when a Bullingdon Boy rose to challenge Hardie in the middle of his speech, the quarryman behind him rose and pressed him down into his seat. The meeting passed without serious incidents, and the Society voted profuse thanks 'to all those gentlemen who served as stewards'.[1]

In the Society, Cole made two sorts of friends who were to stand him in good stead. One set comprised the older socialists and socialist sympathizers of the University, men like A. D. Lindsay, Gilbert Murray, and the Rev. A. J. Carlyle. Carlyle was to be especially important; he sat on the committee which selected Cole as University Reader in Economics in 1925, thus allowing him to return to Oxford. R. H. Tawney fell into an age group all his own, just outside Cole's immediate group of friends, but younger than Lindsay, Murray and Carlyle. During Cole's years and to a large degree because of his activities, Oxford nourished a large number of young, active socialists. William Mellor, with whom Cole collaborated on many Guild Socialist articles, was an officer of the Oxford University Fabian Society when Cole arrived. The younger group of Oxford Socialist friends included Ivor Brown and A. L. Bacharach, and they stayed together as they moved into Labour politics. Along with younger Oxford men such as Raymond Postgate and J. Alan Kaye, they provided the personnel for the Labour Research Department and the National Guilds League. These friends helped Cole gather his facts and criticize his ideas. His first book, *The World of Labour*, arose directly out of discussions of Syndicalism held by the Balliol College Group and the Political Science Group of the O.U.F.S. Cole did much of his best work when surrounded by a group of energetic thinkers and researchers; the O.U.F.S. must be given credit for speeding up his development.

After joining the O.U.F.S. – in fact, in his second week at Oxford – Cole started the first of his many ventures into Socialist journalism. The *Oxford Socialist*, edited by F. K. Griffith and Cole, appeared in his first term at Oxford; it and its successor, the *Oxford Reformer*,

---

[1] Entry for 5 March 1909, 'Minutes of the Oxford University Fabian Society', Ms. Top. Oxon. 465–6, Bodleian Library. I first heard this story from Marcus Lower, of the Oxford W.E.A., who heard it from Cole but was inclined to date it as 1912.

appeared for seven terms. Here Cole found a forum for his broad conception of socialism. It allowed him to express himself on the aesthetic, moral, and philosophical problems which bothered him, as well as on socialist strategy.

Cole enjoyed academic success at Balliol. He received a coveted double first, in Classical Moderations and Literae Humaniores, and a seven-year fellowship at Magdalen upon graduation. The fellowship brought no obligations, and gave him an Oxford base for his excursions into Labour politics. But, while academic success gave him standing and something to fall back upon for contacts and for a livelihood, it did not determine his patterns of thought. From the beginning his intellectual development took place outside the traditional world of classics. J. A. Smith's lectures on Idealism attracted him for a while; A. D. Lindsay's lectures exerted a more substantial pull upon him. It is very likely that Lindsay introduced Cole to political pluralism and to a functional conception of the State which emphasized the roles of economic and social associations. G. N. Clark put Lindsay's influence upon Cole in its proper perspective when he said that Cole found Lindsay's frame of mind more congenial, more in tune with the way in which he was already developing.[1]

Cole's interest in philosophical Idealism, while transitory, is of some interest to the historian of socialist thought. It offers some solace to the historian who likes to argue that socialism owes much to English non-conformism. Cole turned to Idealism as his religious faith, which apparently had had some impact on him, waned.[2] His short spell of hankering after a substitute for religion, however, provides no support for those who argue that socialism is a substitute religion. He never felt that socialism would provide an answer to all questions, and suspected those who did think so.

An Idealist conception of God provided him with short-term answers to questions on the foundations of morality and the source of creation.[3]

---

[1] Letter from G. N. Clark to the author.

[2] This may be inferred from the articles he wrote on religion in *The Oxford Socialist* and *The Oxford Reformer*. In 'Faith-Making', *The Oxford Reformer*, No. 1 (November 1909), pp. 12–15, Cole approached the problem of religion from the point of view of a person who has given up faith but is considering what to replace it with.

[3] See G. D. H. Cole, 'God the Child', *The Oxford Socialist*, No. 3 (Summer 1909), pp. 15–18.

Soon he discovered that he could live without these supports and threw them away. He never regretted having done so. In a paper entitled 'Theism and Freedom, or the One and the Many',[1] Cole presented a fascinating personal and philosophical argument against God on political grounds:

... our preference will be either for an autocracy or a democracy, or if that is possible, for a mixed constitution – for God, for man (or individuals), or for God, Man Ltd ... A few of us ... irrationally, experience a sort of French Revolutionary ardour in which he figures as the arch-tyrant, the last of the hated Bourbons. I myself belong temperamentally to this last section ... [1]

He sought to demonstrate that a democratic view of the universe which gave real importance to human wills had no place for God. In this way, Cole's philosophical interests from the normal adolescent questioning of the nature of the universe and focussed upon social and political theory. He reacted against spiritual and philosophical claims to provide a comprehensive account of the world. He replaced them with a strong set of political beliefs, and with the determined use of common sense and empirical methods to turn these beliefs into a realizable picture of the 'good life'.

Meanwhile another intellectual influence had crossed his path, to be accepted briefly and then rejected. Cole's discovery of the Webbs coincided with their campaign on behalf of the Minority Report of the Poor Law Commission, which brought them to Oxford to lecture to the O.U.F.S. Sidney Webb also contributed an article to Cole's *Oxford Reformer* in February 1910, and the minutes of the O.U.F.S. reveal that Cole started a branch of the National Committee for the Abolition of Destitution. He accepted the whole of the Webbs' Report, including ideas about treating the poor which he was soon to find repulsive. Among these were the call for Detention Colonies for the forcible restraining of those unemployed who would not undergo voluntary training, and an outcry against promiscuity in the existing workhouses.[2] The Webbs, however, had much more substantial and lasting material to contribute to his education. Above all, they brought him into contact with the empirical side of social questions. They

---

[1] In 'Manuscripts and Proofs', Box 7, folder 92, Cole Papers, Nuffield College.
[2] G. D. H. Cole, 'The Reform of the Poor Law' (London, 1919). Reprint of articles that appeared in the *Middlesex County Times* (January–February 1910), at Nuffield College.

intensified his growing distrust of pure theory, and brought him to realize that there was more to socialism than ideals. In February 1910, after his first contact with the Webbs, Cole wrote in the *Oxford Reformer*:

One thing which forces itself more and more to the front in our discussion in Oxford is the increasing technicality of Social Reform. As each question comes nearer to practical solution, it becomes harder to talk airily around subjects, or to generalise from the instance to the theory. It becomes continually harder to relate in words the political creed and the specific knowledge ...[1]

The Webbs also provided the institutional means by which he could convert this growing awareness of the need for technical knowledge into social research: The Committee of Inquiry into the Control of Industry, and the Fabian Research Department.

It is very likely that Cole's early relations with the Webbs did much to establish the political role which he played all of his life. In May 1910, we find him approving the Webbs' policy of permeation.[2] He never really lost his belief in permeation, treating the Labour Party itself as a foreign body to be permeated; in fact, it actually took Cole longer than the Webbs to decide that the Labour Party had to be the main instrument of progress. Like the Webbs, Cole conducted pressure-group politics rather than trying to become a leader within the formal political process; he was the archetypal 'outsider', choosing to influence rather than to wield power.

Thus he learned the principles of Fabianism from the lips of the 'Old Gang'. But despite his debt to the Webbs, he remained their disciple for two years at the outside. Without pushing the analogy too far, one could say that the Webbs were Cole's 'Socialist parents'. He learned much from them, but soon reacted against them, escaping from their tutelage. The Webbs seem to have regarded him as their heir almost from the beginning of their relationship,[3] and Cole soon tried to claim that inheritance, i.e. the leadership of the Fabian Society. Throughout the difficult years which followed they were generally on friendly terms. But not until Cole gained independent stature

[1] No. 2 (February 1910), p. 4.
[2] *The Oxford Reformer*, No. 3 (May 1910), p. 4.
[3] Beatrice Webb, 'Diary of Beatrice Webb', vol. 32 (15 May 1915), 113; Vol. 32 (May 1914), 57, Passfield Papers, London School of Economics.

within the Labour Movement was he ready to acknowledge their greatness.

Cole's discipleship came to an end because the Webbs failed to articulate some of his deepest beliefs. Essentially, Cole reacted against the paternalistic and statist elements of Webbian collectivism. Hilaire Belloc's *The Servile State* made a strong impression on him by arguing that collectivism would not abolish classes and increase tyranny. The Webbs' faith in officials was irritating, and in the period just before the First World War they had not given the libertarian side of their thought adequate expression.[1] And so Cole's generation, believing strongly in libertarian socialism and in trade unions as the instrument of reform, collided with the Webbs, whose philosophy had room for these things but had not emphasized them. The collision was fully as much a conflict of generations as a conflict between 'freedom' and 'bureaucracy'.

By 1912, the Webbs were definitely *passé* as far as the younger generation of Labour enthusiasts were concerned. Their policy of slow advance dissatisfied those who wanted to leap the gap separating socialism from capitalism. Those with whom Cole associated were impatient, feeling a new impulse to creativity and radical change. Cole, in a paper he wrote at the end of 1912, described their mood as a 'new romanticism'.[2] He used intuitionist phrases derived from Bergson and Sorel, and called for a new alliance between the heart and the brains of the Labour movement. But, while it was romantic, their state of mind was also hard-headed. Maurice Reckitt brings this out well:

Our confidence was founded on no evolutionary optimism, but on a belief that there were no problems to which man could not find the right answer if he looked in the right direction and worked on the right lines – but we always insisted that he had got to look very carefully and work very hard.

[1] See G. D. H. Cole, 'Beatrice Webb as an Economist', in *The Webbs and Their Work*, ed. Margaret Cole (London, F. Muller, 1949), p. 280, where he says that Beatrice Webb had 'natural sympathies' with voluntary organizations that her leaning towards bureaucracy concealed. See 'Diary of Beatrice Webb', Vol. 33 (1 June 1916), p. 56, where she considers the Guild Socialist ideal valuable as a corrective to trends destroying freedom – a belated sign of sympathy. For Cole's criticisms of the Webbs, see G. D. H. Cole, *The World of Labour* (London, G. Bell & Sons, 1913), p. 4; G. D. H. Cole, 'The New Statesmanship', *University Socialist* (1913), p. 108–10.

[2] 'The Romantic Movement in Modern Life, 'Manuscripts and Proofs', Box 7, folder 94, Cole Papers, Nuffield College. George Dangerfield, *The Strange Death of Liberal England* (New York, H. Smith and R. Haas, 1935) conveys this well.

There were plenty of places in which to look, however, and no serious reason to fear that our work would be interrupted.[1]

This optimism has a different tone both from the evolutionary faith of the Webbs and from milder, more querulous surges of optimism in the 1940s and 1960s. Reckitt again gets at the source of the difference.

I am happy to think that I lived and was young in what my friend and contemporary, G. D. H. Cole, has aptly described as 'that prehistoric age before 1914'. No doubt, as our young prophets, whether Christian or Communist, enjoy reminding us, it was an age of illusion; no doubt its hopes were dupes, and if its fears were liars it was only because they so grotesquely underestimated the scale of the disasters that were to befall. No doubt . . . we deserved that gigantic blow to human confidence – the First World War . . . We had had plenty more such blows since the post-war deflation (alike of the pound and of the whole reconstruction hope); the economic crisis, the Nazi hypnosis, stupefying the Europe it planned to destroy, so that the arrival of the second period of military operations seemed almost like a piece of good news. But we guessed nothing of all of this before 1914, and were always prepared to meet the unknown with a cheer. In view of the welcome we gave it it is very difficult for those of us who are over forty [in 1940] not to feel that the unknown has treated us very badly. Common decency demanded something better.

This sturdy optimism did not end with the war; it revived strongly with the cry for post-war reconstruction, and stoutly resisted the overwhelming blows of the inter-war period. For Cole and his friends, the 'prehistoric age before 1914' did not end until the collapse of the building guilds in 1923. One aspect of pre-war optimism stayed with Cole for all of his life – the moral security of a settled society. This was the aspect of Edwardian security which impressed Orwell most in *Coming Up For Air*:

It was that they didn't think of the future as something to be terrified of . . . More exactly, it was a feeling of continuity . . . Their good and evil would remain good and evil . . . They didn't feel the ground they stood on shifting under their feet.[2]

In this way, Cole believed that he knew what values were right, without having to ground them in a metaphysic. On this moral security depended the strength of his efforts to change the world, to make it

[1] *As It Happened*, pp. 111–12.
[2] (New York, 1950), pp. 124–6.

fit his conception of good, a conception which guided much of his life and gave him influence.

This optimism was powerfully reinforced when the young militants discovered a new force which they felt would be their ally in attaining socialism. By 1912, a major wave of strikes was well under way. The miners, dockers, and railwaymen all held regional or national strikes which gained their objectives by an impressive show of strength. These strikes had a special significance for socialism. Many of those who sought to articulate the feelings behind the strikes took their conceptual apparatus from French Syndicalism or American Industrial Unionism, and thus broadened the vocabulary of English unionism. The Syndicalists argued that trade unions were to be the instrument for bringing socialism; reformists on the other hand had seen them simply as alliances for defending the workers' standards of living. The Industrial Unionists in particular argued that trade unionism could only be strong enough to win when there was only one union to an industry, linked to create a massive striking force. The pure Syndicalists took their departure in a more libertarian direction, arguing that industrial organization had to supplant the state. Both doctrines, despite their potential incompatibility, led to the substitution of industrial 'direct action' for political socialism. The Syndicalists gained much of their appeal by arguing that the Parliamentary Labour Party's failure to do more than support the Liberals was inevitable; the economic power of capitalism would always control political institutions until the workers smashed capitalist economic power.

To Cole and his friends, the strike wave and the theories associated with it had great attraction. They liked the new militancy. The new claims advanced on the behalf of the producers seemed to provide an answer to the 'servile state', and fitted in with the pluralistic theories then becoming academically influential. Cole in particular was attracted by the potentiality offered for ideas which he had found in Morris. The workers seemed to be asking for a form of organization which would give them room to exercise creativity in their work; they were asking for workers' control.

With his friends at Oxford, Cole plunged into the study of this labour unrest. Much of the discussion and study took place under the auspices of the Political Science Group of the O.U.F.S. Out of them grew *The World of Labour*, which Cole published in the autumn of 1913. It was an immediate success among the young intellectuals, perhaps the most successful socialist book Cole ever wrote. It continued to sell throughout the war, with a fourth edition coming out in 1917.[1] It met the obvious need felt by intellectuals who were attracted by the strikes and theories loosely called Syndicalism, and by articulate trade unionists coming out of the W.E.A., Ruskin College, and the Central Labour College. '. . . it was obvious that Cole was the man who, if anyone could, might establish relations between "the world of labour" and the theorising that was developing in Chancery Lane and the Domino Room of the old Café Royal.'[2] Because of its success, *The World of Labour* expanded Cole's circle of associates, helping to create the nucleus of the National Guilds League and attracting people to the Labour Research Department.[3]

The World of Labour deserved this success; it still remains the best description of Syndicalism and Industrial Unionism in Britain, comparing them with European and American counterparts. It was a surprisingly mature book for a young man of 24, just down from Oxford. It approached the wave of militant acts and theories in the best pragmatic fashion. Faced with strikes on one hand and cloudy theorizing on the other, Cole asked the crucial question:

. . . 'What can be made of the Labour movement, taken as it is?' or still better, 'What is the Labour movement capable of making of itself?' What, in fact, are its practicality and its idealism respectively worth?[4]

In this way, he attempted to judge militant ideals and practices together, asking how they supported each other and what sort of a world they could create. He did not lose track of his democratic ideals, but asked how current tendencies in Labour could further them. He followed his

---

[1] Publication figures unfortunately are not available. There was a fifth edition in 1919, and publication rights were transferred from G. Bell & Sons to Macmillan in 1928, after which Macmillan brought out another edition.

[2] Maurice B. Reckitt, 'G. D. H. Cole, the L.R.D. and the N.G.L.', unpublished manuscript (1961) kindly lent by Mr Reckitt. The *New Age* circle of intellectuals especially used the Café Royal.

[3] In 'G. D. H. Cole, the L.R.D. and the N.G.L.', Maurice Reckitt says that *The World of Labour* made him anxious to meet Cole, who apparently had not impressed him while Reckitt was at Oxford before; Robin Page Arnot told me that he met Cole after Cole gave a speech in Glasgow shortly after publishing *The World of Labour*.

[4] *The World of Labour*, p. 2.

penetrating question with solid, realistic analysis, the first intellectual analysis of the British trade union movement since the Webbs' *Industrial Democracy* of 1897. He skilfully set British developments against similar movements in other countries. And he knew when to draw a careful distinction between modes of organization and aspects of theory, so that he could come to a reasoned, balanced judgment.

Cole welcomed the Syndicalist and Industrial Unionist emphasis on the producer and on the trade union. Syndicalism 'demands that men be regarded not as "citizens" or "consumers", but as "producers", that their work be recognized as the central fact of their lives, and that industry be reorganized in their interest rather than that of the consumer'.[1] These emphases had positive value, both in themselves and for the way they forced a reconsideration of the Webbs' emphasis on the State. He welcomed the claim advanced on the workers' behalf to control the conditions under which they laboured. In this claim he recognized the voices of Owen, Morris, and Ruskin, calling for 'Pleasure, joy, interest, expression in the works of a man's hand . . .'[2] In this way Syndicalism appealed to his basic reasons for being a socialist.

But his acceptance of the claim for workers' control of industry did not lead him to endorse all the Syndicalist corollaries. He rejected the general strike, for the time being, on pragmatic grounds: it was a poor way of attracting new unionists, and an inefficient way of fighting a revolution when a revolution would come to be possible.[3] He disputed the claim that industrial direct action alone could destroy capitalism and substitute a democratic way of life. In 1913 he clung to political action more tightly than he would in 1917:

Expropriation is the State's business; and the development of the new forms of industrial control must be under State guidance and direction. Nationalisation, therefore, retains all the importance assigned to it in Socialist theory; but it becomes a means, and not an end in itself.[4]

He instinctively opposed the extreme French Syndicalist desire to build the new society solely around the trade unions.

It is, on the face of it, improbable that either producer or consumer ought to have absolute control; it is unlikely that either the State or the Unions should

[1] Ibid., p. 7.
[2] Ibid., p. 9.
[3] Ibid., pp. 201–4.
[4] Ibid., p. 391.

take the place of the exploiter entirely; for then either the State would be in a place to exploit the worker, or the worker would be in a position to exploit the community – just as the capitalist exploits both at present. The solution must surely lie in some sort of division of functions, allowing both producer and consumer a say in the control of what is, after all, supremely important to both.[1]

With this argument, Cole came very close to declaring himself a Guild Socialist. Later I shall examine his development as a Guild Socialist; as such he penetrated most deeply into the nature of the functions and interests which should belong to men as producers and as consumers.

Guild theory itself was in its infancy in 1913, and Cole was to be much involved in its growth. Towards the end of 1912, S. G. Hobson had started to publish the series of articles in the *New Age* that became *National Guilds: An Inquiry into the Wage System and the Way Out*. He tried to reconcile consumer and producer interests in the assertion that the workers in each industry should run it on behalf of the community. In turn, Hobson had taken the word 'guild' from some of Arthur J. Penty's speculations. Penty, an old follower of William Morris, sought to return to medieval forms of production, in which all work would be done by craftsmen who united to govern their respective trades.[2] These arguments played a relatively small role in *The World of Labour*; Cole had just become able to use and develop them. Although he had been reading the *New Age* for some time, his uncertain handling of Hobson's and Penty's arguments shows that he reached Hobson's point of departure largely on his own, from his study of the strike wave. A. R. Orage, the brilliant editor of the *New Age*, protested that Cole had mis-stated their position,[3] and Cole introduced several changes into the second edition of *The World of Labour*. From Hobson's and Orage's point of view, the most important of these 'errors' was that Cole had given the State a direct role in

---

[1] Ibid., p. 352.

[2] *The Restoration of the Gild System* (London, Swan Sonnenschein, 1906). Penty used the word 'gild' to emphasize continuity with the middle ages; Hobson introduced 'guild'.

[3] 'Survey and Strategy', *New Age*, Vol. XIV (20 November 1913), 71–2. A. R. Orage started the *New Age* in 1906 with Holbrook Jackson, and made it into the most lively intellectual journal of the day; Arnold Bennett, among others, wrote for it. He pursued new intellectual fashions, espousing Social Credit after the First World War, and eventually ending up a follower of Blavatsky. See Philip Mairet, *A. R. Orage* (London, Dent, 1936).

deciding what was to be produced, and that he had not adequately discussed their systems of remuneration. Cole warily expressed the opinion that Hobson had not concerned himself enough with democracy.[1]

Cole did not merely take a theoretical interest in the wave of strikes; he sought to make practical use of his talents. Oxfordshire before the First World War was backward from a trade unionist's point of view. Only the railwaymen had any real strength in the district. It was still in the heroic age of trade unionism, the period of struggle to obtain recognition. Owners fought the unions savagely where they appeared, sacking 'fomenters of discontent', using the lockout, and forcing their workmen to sign agreements not to join unions.

The two strikes against these practices were effectively 'the first trial of Trade Unionism in rural Oxfordshire since the days of Joseph Arch'.[2] Of the first of these strikes, the Oxford bus strike, we know little. Cole and G. N. Clark made themselves available to the strike committee from the outside, and wrote a leaflet in defence of the workers.[3] The second strike, the Chipping Norton strike, took place while Cole was teaching in Newcastle, but when in Oxford he supported it actively. In November 1913 most of the operatives at Bliss' Tweed Mill, the only industry in Chipping Norton, formed a branch of the Workers' Union. The management immediately sacked three of its members for union activities, and 250 of the 380 employed at the mill came out in support of them. The plant did not close, but continued limited operations – with imported members of the Amalgamated Society of Engineers keeping the machinery running.[4]

The fight followed the archetypal pattern. The manager of the mill offered an 'Employee's Association' in his terms for settling the strike.

---

[1] *The World of Labour*, pp. 363, 366. There is no difference in pagination between the first and second editions.

[2] G. D. H. Cole and G. N. Clark, 'The Strike at Chipping Norton', in Cole and Mellor, 'Pamphlets 1913–1916', Nuffield College. Unless otherwise noted, the materials in the following four paragraphs come from documents collected by G. N. Clark, in Ms. Top. Oxon. C 523, Bodleian Library. They begin in January 1914, just before Clark returned from abroad, and continue through the relief work done at the end of the Chipping Norton strike.

[3] G. D. H. Cole and G. N. Clark, 'The Tram Strike' (Oxford, May 1913), in Cole and Mellor, 'Pamphlets 1913–1916', Nuffield College.

[4] Cole and Mellor, 'The Need for the Greater Unionism', *Daily Herald* (24 February 1914), p. 4.

The workers demanded recognition of their union, higher wages, and no victimization. By January it was obvious that the men would not get higher wages, and that the management would have to recognize the union. They concealed this important retreat by making one clause of the proposed agreement read that the workers had been wrong in supposing that the management had ever opposed the union! The crucial clause, however, concerned reinstatement. The men thought it meant that all would be back within a month; the company insisted that it meant they would be taken back as trade improved. So the men stayed out.

We do not know when Cole joined the strike committee; Clark joined it in February, as the strike dragged on. Early in March 1914, Cole and Clark sought to re-open negotiations between the strike organizers and the management, using as intermediary a local solicitor involved in the prosecution of strikers for rioting. By this time the management was determined to fight to the finish, and nothing came of it. Cole and Clark helped to raise funds for the strikers, and Cole and Mellor sought to give the strike wider publicity in the *Daily Herald*. The strike committee began to devote more of its time to finding jobs for men elsewhere, and finally had to abandon the strike at the end of May. The management had the last word:

To our late employees . . . you must, however, be prepared for a great many disappointments, as owing to your action in taking part in the ill-advised strike . . .[1]

Many of them were still out of work at the start of the First World War.

This experience undoubtedly strengthened Cole's predisposition to see the unions as the source of liberation from a cruel, unjust industrial system. The management and its supporters in the Oxford region appear in the most tyrannical and inhumane light. Take, for example, this letter from a man criticizing the opening of a relief fund after the strike had ended:

Do they deprive themselves of any pleasures, or are they still attending the cricket matches and pictures, dressing smartly, smoking, and generally

[1] Letter in the *Oxfordshire Weekly News* (date not given), folio 60 of Clark's file in the Bodleian.

enjoying life? When they answer those questions satisfactorily perhaps more people will believe in the distress which they say they are suffering.[1]

Class warfare on this scale simply could not be answered by the Webbs' policies.

The Webbs, of course, were temperamentally opposed to the strike wave; but they recognized its appeal. Late in 1912, they launched the Committee of Inquiry on the Control of Industry, in order to draw up an attractive alternate way of bringing democracy to industry. Mrs Webb wrote a brilliant memorandum, which perhaps showed too clearly how she intended to use the Committee. She was appalled by the lack of agreement within the Labour movement on industrial questions. The rapid spread of anarchic ideas seemed likely to drive away workers and middle-class people alike; the emotionalism of Syndicalist conceptions of industrial democracy would drive younger intellectuals from the socialist movement.[2]

The Webbs completely controlled the early stages of the inquiry; one rapidly gains the impression that they saw it as a way of getting young researchers to provide facts supporting their conclusions. Naturally, they drew up the scheme of organization, and even insisted upon a common system of note-taking. As far as the Webbs were concerned, the essential task was to develop counter-claims to the control of industry for professional people and for the consumers.[3] In their initial memorandum they assumed that the basic picture of trade unionism they had arrived at in the 1890s, allowing it at most negative control, was still valid. Here the group of young intellectuals, including Cole and Mellor, strongly disagreed, and the Webbs lost control of this part of the undertaking. No report ever appeared from the section dealing with the associations of wage-earners, for each side blocked the other's reports with savage criticism. But out of this section eventually grew the Labour Research Department, through a series of reorganizations which created the Fabian Research Department and ultimately separated it from the Fabian Society in 1918.

[1] Letter in the *Oxfordshire Weekly News* (date not given), folio 82 of Clark's file in the Bodleian.
[2] A copy of this memorandum is in Section IX, subsection 2, folio 1, of the Passfield Papers, London School of Economics.
[3] Section IX, subsection 2, folio 48–9 (mimeo letter 4 December 1914 from Beatrice Webb), Passfield Papers, London School of Economics.

Having begun to quarrel with the Webbs in the Fabian Research Department, Cole and his friends carried the battle into the parent society itself. It culminated in an effort to take over the Fabian Society in 1915, and kept matters in uproar for several years. In her diary, Beatrice Webb recorded the disturbance that Cole and his friends created at a session of the Fabian Summer School just before the First World War broke out. The young men from Oxford first struck against the Summer School's curfew. Defeated on this issue, they kept to themselves throughout the session, eating together and conspicuously sending out for beer. They disrupted the daily discussions on questions of research and politics, maintaining an uncompromising Guild Socialist position. Equally offensive in Mrs Webb's eyes were their antics outside the Summer School. They raised the red flag, and met the Great Keswick Evangelical Convention with revolutionary songs. This latter incident brought the police to Barrow House, to Mrs Webb's extreme discomfort.[1]

This experience illustrates some of the most important aspects of Cole's revolt against the Webb's influence. It was a clash of generations, of life-styles and of backgrounds. Cole and his group were in their early twenties, and acted the part. They sought to shock the respectable Webbs, who had had very little contact with the arrogance of the older universities. The Webbs could not understand the 'rag week' atmosphere which surrounded the 'fun' of the Oxford men. The latter found great pleasure in group singing and in group discussion; their humour helped keep the group together but it alienated the Webbs. The Guild Socialists made their group a fellowship in Morris's sense, rather than a Communist cell; there was much less emphasis upon power, but a strong desire to work out their ideas intelligently. As a consequence the struggles between the Guild Socialists and the Webbs lack the intense factionalism that the split with the Communists brought into the Labour movement.

In 1915, the group which centred around Cole, Oxford, and Guild Socialism made a pact with a slightly earlier group of Fabian Rebels. Henry Schloesser and Clifford Allen had led a challenge to the Webbs in 1912. They had sought closer affiliation with the Labour Party and the abandonment of Webbian attempts to influence the 'bourgeois'

---

[1] 'Diary of Beatrice Webb', Vol. 32 (31 July 1914), 59–61.

political parties. Cole knew Allen as the president of the Universities Socialist Federation, but Robin Page Arnot, Allen's room mate in London and an associate of Cole's in the L.R.D., seems to have been the 'broker'. The two groups agreed on a negative membership rule which would move the Fabian Society closer to the Labour Party. The Society, they said, should not include active supporters of the Liberals and the Tories. This obviously was the most Cole could grant; in fact, his own criticism of the membership rule had been that it implicitly limited membership to politically-oriented Socialists.

In return, Allen and some of his friends in the Fabian Society agreed to support the main demand of Cole's group. They sought to restrict the Society's activities to one function, research.

We maintain that the Society's true function is to be found in that part of its work upon which it largely concentrated in its early days, and to which it has shown a hesitating disposition to return . . . *Research* is not being undertaken by any other section of the Socialist Movement, nor is it at present carried out on anything like the required scale by the Fabian Society itself. Yet probably never in the whole history of the Movement . . . has there been such need for research as there is today, when many of the ideas of Socialists are in the melting pot.[1]

They directed part of their indignation against the attempts of the Fabian Society to sponsor candidates, and its general effort to act a political role. The argument has a sort of logical clarity, based on the allocation of functions within the Labour movement. There was no need for the Society to develop into yet another small socialist party. Cole always felt that middle-class intellectuals should place themselves at the disposal of the movement, and provide it with the long-range thinking guided by research which it so desperately needed. This argument clearly fitted Cole's interests, and the location of his group's power. They were the researchers, the lively and growing part of the Society. The Webbs effectively demonstrated the egocentric nature of the rebels' challenge. They pointed out that their argument, taken logically, would destroy educational work and lectures, which the rebels themselves wanted to be involved in. Without these activities, it could not survive; the subsequent financial problems of the Labour

[1] 'The Right Moment', *Fabian News*, vol. xxvi, no. 5 (April 1915), 27–9.

Research Department lend some credibility to the Webbs' point. Finally, the Webbs argued that the proposed membership rule would 'fetter . . . the freedom of members in their individual lives'.[1] Here the Webbs come off as the more liberal of the contending parties, with the rebels' logic and militancy making them more rigid.

In themselves, these points of disagreement could have been resolved. The real source of difference lay in the political styles of the two generations, which pushed the band of rebels into an extreme position from which Cole personally felt he could not retreat. At the climactic Annual General Meeting of May 1915, Cole reacted violently to the failure of his resolutions. Losing his temper, he accused his opponents of being fools. When he was censured, he strode from the hall and immediately resigned from the Fabian Society.[2]

The incident was superficial, but had unfortunate consequences for the Fabian Society, which sorely needed active young members, as well as for Cole, who placed himself in political limbo for a while. The incident is often cited against him, as proof that he was not fit for political action. However, it did not set a precedent for later actions. While he left the group writing *New Fabian Essays* in 1950, no acrimony was involved. Cole returned to preside over the Society in 1952. Both these resignations, and Cole's departure from the Labour Research Department, occurred after he had invested a large amount of energy in a course of action. They seemed to arise when Cole, through defeat, was reminded of the distance between his values and the exigencies imposed by the actual state of the Labour movement. Cole quickly learned to control the temper which he had displayed in 1915, and in the 1920s grew into one of the most tolerant of Socialists – a 'secular saint', in Kingsley Martin's phrase. This was the only time when he was not the apostle of Socialist unity, when he personally tried to take control of a group.

Cole's resignation from the Fabian Society acted as a sort of purgative, and did not interfere with his growing concentration upon socialist journalism and Guild Socialism. When he wrote *The World of Labour*, Cole had not been ready to declare himself a Guild Socialist, although we can see that he had already reached a position similar to

---

[1] 'Report by the Executive Committee', *Fabian News*, Vol. XXVI, No. 6 (May 1915), 40–1.
[2] 'Diary of Beatrice Webb', Vol. 32 (14 May 1915), 112–13.

that being propounded in the *New Age*. At the Fabian Summer School in August 1914, he strenuously and rudely upheld the Guild position; soon he moved towards more public support and agitation for Guild ideas. During the Christmas vacation of 1914, Cole and several of his friends, most of them members of the O.U.F.S., spent a week at the White Horse, an inn at Storrington, Essex. There they debated the ramifications of claims which had been advanced by the Syndicalists, and the Guild Socialist resolution of these with collectivist claims, in their typical energetic manner. They argued for several hours a night; and they spent much time walking and singing. Out of this fellowship came the Storrington Document,[1] which contained the points on which they had unanimously agreed.

Thus the actions and discussions leading up to the formation of the National Guilds League proceeded parallel to, and even slightly ahead of, the struggle against the Webbs in the Fabian Society. It appears unlikely that Cole and his friends wanted to make the Fabian Society their own propaganda body. The National Guilds League was actually inaugurated a month before the climactic Annual General Meeting of the Fabian Society.[2] George Lansbury and Will Dyson of the *Daily Herald* joined with Cole, Mellor, W. N. Ewer, Robin Page Arnot, Maurice Reckitt and Ivor Brown in calling for the new organization. But there were important resistances to overcome. A. R. Orage, whose *New Age* had been the vehicle for early propaganda for the Guilds, did not believe that the time had come for more active propaganda.[3] He may well have been suspicious of the young men, and jealous of their moving into his territory. S. G. Hobson, the author of the articles which provided the first definitions of Guild Socialism, proved more sympathetic, although he too had criticisms.[4] The war had made inroads into their potential membership, and threatened to consign the new organization to oblivion. On the other hand, the war probably crippled rival political associations even more; and ultimately the

---

[1] The Storrington Document was circulated among recruits to the National Guilds League. It exists in several forms with minor alterations; I am using the version in 'National Guilds League: Various Papers', Cole Papers, Nuffield College.

[2] 20–1 April 1915, while the Fabian meeting occurred on 14 May 1915.

[3] Maurice B. Reckitt, *As It Happened*, p. 132.

[4] S. G. Hobson to Cole, 30 March 1915, in 'National Guilds League: Various Papers' folder 'Formation', Cole Papers, Nuffield College.

radical atmosphere of reconstruction which grew out of the war made the N.G.L. prominent for a short time.

With the formation of the National Guilds League, the Guildsmen, as they called themselves, constructed another link in a chain of organizations which gave them a variety of useful approaches to different segments of the Labour movement. The fellowship and joy in work which mattered so much to Cole were part of their daily life, together with exhausting work and much gaiety. Reckitt outlined a typical day in his autobiography:

Morning at the department, a bus ride to lunch in Soho with others of the movement who might have the time and money to spare . . . Then back to the department for a bit, leaving early perhaps for the flat because an article had to be written, possibly for the N.G.L. journal, *The Guildsman,* or a speech prepared. After dinner there might be a N.G.L. executive, or one of its extremely thorough-going study circles, which would commonly finish up with every one round a piano singing, to some extemporised rendering of my own, one of G. K. Chesterton's lyrics from *The Flying Inn,* which became the song book of our movement.[1]

To these activities Cole added W.E.A. work and speeches on behalf of the Guilds movement.

The importance of this network of friendships and contact is two-fold. On the one hand, it gave Cole the criticism and intellectual ferment to encourage him. Guild Socialism was far from a static orthodoxy. At its best, the N.G.L. and L.R.D. sponsored a communal way of thinking, nurtured in study circles. Cole himself thought communally, trying to formulate a synthesis which would satisfy his friends and offer grounds for unity in the Labour movement. The results of this interchange of ideas are especially apparent in Cole's theory of the Guild Commune, in which he incorporated criticisms made from the standpoint of the co-operatives and the consumers into his earlier models of a decent society.

On the other hand, the multiplicity of activities in which Guildsmen participated meant that people met Cole in a variety of situations; people who did not sympathise with Guild Socialism still found him useful in gathering facts or in organizing for the Labour Party or for a trade union. Still others knew him through the Workers' Educational

[1] *As It Happened,* p. 138.

Association. For this reason, it is wrong to dismiss Cole and his friends as 'merely Guild Socialists', members of an interesting but ephemeral movement.

The organization that attracted the largest number of Guildsmen was the Fabian Research Department, which soon became the Labour Research Department. Cole stayed with the F.R.D. after quitting the Fabian Society; he became Honorary Secretary of the L.R.D.

The L.R.D's small overcrowded rooms became the nerve-centre of left-wing Guild Socialism, with Cole in ultimate command, Page Arnot in day to day control, Alan Kaye and Rose Cohen continuously and Eva and Maurice Reckitt more sporadically, at work.[1]

Despite this overlap in personnel and ideas, there was a functional separation of sorts between the N.G.L. and the L.R.D. The N.G.L. was a propaganda body, the L.R.D. was for research. The line was hard to draw, for research would be likely to yield results for propaganda, and communicating the results of research often becomes propaganda, but the distinction always carried significance for Cole. The L.R.D. amassed material on trade unions which no one had previously attempted to study. Its collection of clippings on strikes, pay, and industrial problems proved invaluable to the Guildsmen. Cole wrote a little book on *The Payment of Wages* for the L.R.D. which earned praise even from conservative economists.[2] Other material gathered by the L.R.D. found its way into *The Labour Yearbook* and into a gazetteer of trade unions which the British Government took over. And, as the years went by, trade unions found the researchers useful. They came in handy when it came to drafting resolutions or pamphlets, and in presenting a union's case to the public during a strike. This change of attitude is all the more significant because of the unions' resistance to the intellectuals.

The turning-point in this process, Arnot suggests, came with the passing of the Munitions Act in 1915 and the subsequent pressure on the engineering unions to allow infringements of their carefully guarded trade rules.

A record was made of all prosecutions and other cases under the Munitions Act: Questions were prepared for the House of Commons, followed by

[1] Maurice B. Reckitt, 'G. D. H. Cole, the L.R.D. and the N.G.L.'.
[2] See (G. N. Clark), 'Prof. G. D. H. Cole', *The Times* (15 January 1959), p. 13.

material to be used in debates; draft Amendments and Bills were circulated; and in other ways a campaign against the repressive clauses of the Munitions Act was carried on, in conjunction with the Executives of the Unions. In addition we were brought into touch with the shop steward organization and, in so far as it was desired, the services of the Department were used as an intermediary at certain moments of crisis.[1]

Cole and Mellor played important roles in these activities, and it is hard to separate Cole's individual contribution from what Arnot attributes to the L.R.D. He went to work for the Amalgamated Society of Engineers in 1915 as a research worker, operating in the twilight zone between the official and unofficial leadership. Cole and Mellor prepared at least two circulars for the Executive of the A.S.E.[2] These circulars played the dual role of telling the local negotiators what was the minimum they had to give up, and of making clear to politically minded people what sacrifices the Unions were making. Cole also wrote less official documents, presenting a militant approach to the problems of the dilution of labour and dealing with the government.[3] Margaret Cole comments ironically that Douglas 'secured exemption from military service by doing his best to make the Munitions Act unworkable.'[4]

Cole regarded the war primarily as a threat to the workers. 'Throughout, where business has been unable to go on 'as usual', business has been compensated. Labour alone has been expected to make every sacrifice without return or gratitude.'[5] He feared that business and reactionary interests would be able to regain some of the ground they had lost to Labour. He could find much evidence to feed his fears. Manufacturers accused unions of restrictive practices, while obtaining guarantees of high profits; middle-class people criticized

[1] Robin Page Arnot, *History of the Labour Research Department* (London Labour Research Department, 1926), p. 14.
[2] 'Safeguards for Dilution: What Circulars L2 and L3 Mean' (1915); 'The Price of the Dilution of Labour' (1915); 'Amending the Munitions of War Act, 1915; Record of Conferences and of the Interview with the Prime Minister and the Minister of Munitions' (1916).
[3] 'The State and the Engineers', *A.S.E. Monthly Journal and Report* (April 1915), 75–6; and many articles in the *Herald*, notably 'Dilution' (19 February 1916); 'Emergency Labour' (22 April 1916); 'Trade Union and Labour Notes: The Clyde Dispute' (6 March 1915).
[4] *Growing Up Into Revolution*, p. 60.
[5] G. D. H. Cole, *Labour in War-Time* (London, G. Bell & Sons, 1915), p. 114.

working-class habits on the grounds that they impeded the war effort.[1]

What annoyed Cole was Labour's slowness to defend hard-won rights in work and education against these attacks. The Labour movement did organize a series of public meetings against the outbreak of war, conforming to the traditional Socialist plea for international working-class solidarity to prevent a capitalist war. But as soon as Germany invaded Belgium, most sections of the movement dropped all resistance to the war and the practices that went with it. Trade Unions cancelled wage claims; the TUC cancelled its annual conference, and the unions engaged in creating the Triple Alliance suspended their deliberations. In effect, Labour declared an 'industrial truce' without demanding any *quid pro quo*, any guarantees of fair treatment. Cole, considering the war to be largely a capitalist affair, objected to this total acceptance of it.

It does indeed seem absurd to suppose that the class struggle can be altogether eclipsed by any national crisis. A national crisis means that the nation has many difficult problems to face, and a capitalist Government, left to itself, is hardly likely to face them in a manner agreeable to the workers. Surely at all costs the forces of Labour should have preserved their identity; but participation in an interparty recruiting campaign was hardly the best way . . .[2]

It was not until the spring of 1915 that rising prices and crises in the munitions industries provided an audience for what he and others had to say about the war.

For Cole, the war was not the polar issue; class warfare was. He thus neatly inverted the positions of both the militant pacifists and the ardent supporters of the war. The war was the dependent variable, not the independent moral issue of the times, and hence a pragmatic approach to it became possible for him. The criterion by which he judged the war effort was its effect on the Labour movement. His first objective was to preserve the power of the unions and prepare that power for the resumption of open class warfare after the international war ended. He both hoped for and feared the outbreak of this class

---

[1] Chapter IX, *Labour in War-Time*; Mary Stocks, *The Workers' Educational Association: The First Fifty Years* (London, George Allen & Unwin, 1953), p. 73.
[2] *Labour in War-Time*, p. 36.

warfare. He hoped for it although he personally disliked violence, because he felt that it was the only way to achieve socialism; at the same time he feared that class warfare would come in the form of a successful capitalist attack upon the workers' standards of living. The need to prepare for this offensive lay behind the scores of articles which Cole and Mellor wrote in the *Daily Herald*, analysing the weapons which various unions had at their disposal and the rights which they needed to defend. These articles were Cole's main literary endeavour during the middle years of the war. With Labour on the defensive, he did not find the time or the enthusiasm to carry his Guild Socialist speculations much beyond the positions reached by Hobson's *National Guilds* and the Storrington Document.

When Cole ventured to take the offensive, he treated the war as a possible source for new rights. In *Labour in War-Time*, he argued that the workers had a right to demand 'guarantees that their economic position would not be worsened by the war, that prices would be kept down, or, as an alternative, wages raised, and that the Trade Unions would be taken into the Government's confidence and used as the official means of dealing with the problems that arose with the workers'.[1] He also demanded that Labour prevent the Government from handing back to private ownership the industries which had been taken over for the war effort. But he did not have much faith that the Government would recognize these claims.

Pursuing his activities on behalf of the workers, Cole tried to ignore the war. Maurice Reckitt tells a story which illustrates how vigorous his personal disregard could be:

This contemptuous indifference to the irrelevance of war on the part of philosophic spirits was apt to impose something of a strain on less exalted souls. I remember my sister telling me that she was once on the way to a N.G.L. meeting with G. D. H. Cole. They had just turned the corner out of Aldwych when the maroons went off. Eva declared that Cole's pace at once perceptibly slacked (as, knowing his characteristic cussedness, I can well believe). She felt the impossibility of even suggesting the desirability for haste, and they maintained a measured tread until the hall was reached. Never, she said, had the length of Kingsway so much impressed itself upon her before.[2]

[1] *Labour in War-Time*, p. 48.
[2] *As It Happened*, p. 140.

37

Very likely this indifference to the war could have been broken by events – either a German invasion or a revolution. In the last resort, in the event of a total conflict between carrying on the war and carrying on class war, Cole said that he would choose class war. He told the National Council for Civil Liberties that 'The Trade Union must claim allegiance, if necessary, against the State'.[1] But in the war, such a breaking-point was not reached, and Cole did nothing to force it. At the time of the German spring offensive in 1918, he joined W. H. Hutchinson of the A.S.E. in an appeal against strikes.[2] Since a breaking-point did not arise, Cole could recognize the plurality of allegiances owed by the average person, and incorporate them into the advice he gave. Members of the working class were more than workers; they were English.

> The unity of all the inhabitants of Great Britain is not the merely artificial unity of legal subjection to a common sovereign. Nations are real persons, and the individuals who compose them are conscious of their part in the national life.[3]

This allegiance was a fact, in Cole's life as well as in the workers'; it could not be wished away by chanting phrases of a false internationalism or cosmopolitanism. The war was a fact, and an outright rebellion against it was simply bad politics. It would fragment the Labour movement if it failed; if it succeeded, it still would not advance the workers' cause. The problem therefore was to find a *modus vivendi* which would recognize nationality, yet keep class loyalty alive.

Cole tried to determine this *modus vivendi* empirically. He ascertained the moral and practical limits which loyalty to the workers and to Britain imposed upon each other. 'At the most the worker is only bound not to hamper wantonly the work of the war – that is, not to take the offensive against capitalism where such action is likely to be hampering to the State.[4] Labour's position had to remain essentially

---

[1] Syllabus of lecture on 'Labour and Civil Liberties', in 'Manuscripts and Proofs', Box 6, folder 81, Cole Papers, Nuffield College.

[2] Raymond Postgate, *The Life of George Lansbury* (London, Longmans Green, 1951), p. 179.

[3] *Labour in War-Time*, p. 3. Cole had a strong cultural nationalism, which often surprised his friends. See Hugh Gaitskell, 'At Oxford in the Twenties', in *Essays in Labour History*, ed. Asa Briggs and John Saville (London, Macmillan, 1960), p. 12, and G. D. H. Cole, *Life of William Cobbett* (London, W. Collins, 1924).

[4] *Labour in War-Time*, p. 19.

defensive, in the face of capitalism's inevitable encroachments. Cole himself appears to have employed his negotiating skill and contacts with the unofficial leadership in the A.S.E. to prevent the unofficial strike wave from moving on to the offensive – a measure which would have called forth repressive action by the Government. He informally helped create opportunities for the shop stewards to back down when they were caught in an exposed position.[1]

Cole's pragmatic approach to the war tended to irritate many people in the Labour movement. For most people, the sudden coming of war totally changed the patterns of existence; they were for the war, or against it. In calling an 'industrial truce', the unions made the war the overriding issue of the times. A section of the Labour intelligentsia made the war the central issue in the opposite sense, by actively demanding peace and opposing conscription. To the convinced on both sides, Cole's indifference to the war seemed an evasion of moral responsibility. Reckitt wrote that 'I thought then, and I think still, that he evaded the essential issue and he did so not uncharacteristically by tending to treat it as beneath his notice.'[2]

Personally, Cole was a pacifist; but he was a different sort of pacifist from those who organized the Non-Conscription Fellowship. Clifford Allen and Bertrand Russell tended to argue from 'the sanctity of human life'; Cole was suspicious of such a sweeping, and potentially sanctimonious, argument. He agreed with them in not wanting to take life himself, but he recognized that there were circumstances in which he would approve the use of violence. Mrs Webb cruelly and inaccurately used this point to argue that Cole was not a genuine pacifist because he had defended violent action by the workers.[3] However, while Cole had considered a general strike a possible, although unlikely, way of trying to obtain socialism, he had not urged civil war. Mrs Webb's more general argument was that the Guildsmen would have

[1] See G. D. H. Cole, *Trade Unionism and Munitions*, Economic and Social History of the War, British Series (Oxford, Clarendon Press, 1923), pp. 145–6; 'Diary of Beatrice Webb', Vol. 33 (4 April 1916), 44.

[2] 'G. D. H. Cole, the L.R.D. and the N.G.L.'

[3] 'Diary of Beatrice Webb', Vol. 33 (9 March 1916), 34–5. Her cruelty appears in the evident pleasure she derived from watching Cole and his friends escape conscription. Yet here, as so often, Mrs Webb revealed her ambivalence towards Cole – disapproving of his position, she nonetheless helped him gain exemption from conscription, and paid tribute to his work for the Labour movement.

supported the war if it had not been for their hatred of the British Government. She related this charge to her well-known dislike of 'anarchists and aristocrats', by accusing Cole of hedonistically indulging his wish to avoid fighting.[1] Her frequent accusation of hedonism only applies to Cole in a very limited way. Cole did like his creature comforts, good food, a bottle of wine, and cigarettes, but Mrs Webb always tended to make too much of this. She argued that he was ruining his health by these habits; if anything, he ruined it by excessive work for the Labour movement. Cole, while healthily hedonistic in a range of pleasures close to him, did not let them dominate his life. 'Hedonism' cannot adequately explain Cole's indifference to the war.

Mrs Webb was right on one point – Cole's form of pacifism would not have complied with the legal requirements for being treated as a conscientious objector. He obtained a deferment partly through a peculiar combination of favouritisms. The A.S.E. supported his claim for exemption on grounds that his work was of national importance. The Government appears to have been anxious not to create petty disturbances which would upset the war effort and Cole, as a link between the official and unofficial leadership in the A.S.E., did have an important role to play in maintaining production. The President of the A.S.E., W. H. Hutchinson, made a personal appearance before his tribunal; Cole's work for the Workers' Educational Association was also cited on his behalf. Mrs Webb recorded a piece of gossip in her Diary which indicates the benefits Cole reaped from belonging to the fringes of the intellectual establishment. Apparently the College authorities who controlled the Oxford Tribunal did not want to humiliate a Fellow of Magdalen by rejecting his plea.[2] Having received his exemption, Cole was freed from the need to choose formally between war and outright pacifism; he could maintain his indifference. Consequently, while he joined the Non-Conscription Fellowship, as so many of his friends did, he took no part in its public actions.[3]

The problems created by the war allowed Cole and his friends to work with the trade unions in ways which generally had been closed to middle-class intellectuals. Page Arnot recalls that when he addressed

[1] Ibid., Vol. 32 (3 May 1915), 105.
[2] Ibid., Vol. 33 (18 March 1916), 36.
[3] Ibid., Vol. 33 (8 April 1916), 48.

a District meeting of the A.S.E., he was the first intellectual to have done so since the Webbs in the 1890s. The Webbs themselves realized the success which the young Guildsmen were having; Beatrice wrote in her Diary that the Guild Socialists were penetrating to the heart of the trade union movement and making the Labour Research Department an intellectual centre for trade unionism.[1]

The Guildsmen did hope to constitute an intellectual centre for the Labour movement; they argued that the Fabians had failed to do this. Like the Webbs, they saw their task as one of permeating the groups which had strategic importance in their picture of what society needed. Thus they were drawn into seeking influence. But we should not raise to unrealistic heights our expectations of the amount and kind of influence they could have had, only to conclude that they had no influence at all. Above all, we should not construe influence as a mechanistic relation between them and the unions, in which the young intellectuals designed dramatic policies and forced them on the unions. Influence is inevitably conditioned by what the influenced party is able to make use of; in a very real sense, it often consists of the 'influencer' doing work for the people he is trying to influence.

Mrs Webb, whose own influence has come under strong attack recently,[2] understood this point. In 1915, perhaps with a tinge of personal jealousy, she accused Cole and his friends of trying too hard to permeate the unions and win them over to Guild Socialism. She held Sidney up as a model:

If the young intellectuals would serve as unpaid civil servants of the Labour world and consent to remain unrecognized they could do splendid work. But young men with vigorous opinions and healthy ambitions very naturally want to hear their own voices and see their own names.[3]

This criticism applied most to Cole and Mellor's articles in the *Daily Herald*, and Mrs Webb felt that it was damaging their effectiveness. They rapidly learned their lesson, and Cole in particular performed many tasks for the unions in a quiet fashion, without seeking to ram Guild Socialism down everyone's throat or obtain public renown.

[1] Ibid., Vol. 33 (9 March 1916), 34–5.
[2] In E. J. Hobsbawm, *Labouring Men* (London, Weidenfeld & Nicholson, 1964).
[3] *Beatrice Webb's Diaries 1912–1924*, ed. Margaret Cole (London, Longmans Green, 1952), p. 46. Taken from 'Diary of Beatrice Webb', Vol. 33 (9 September 1915), 7.

For a short time after the revision of the Labour Party's Constitution in 1918, Cole appeared to be moving towards an influential position within it. He was probably the author of an election manifesto in 1918, 'Why Labour Left the Coalition.'[1] The new party constitution provided for the formation of Advisory Committees; Cole became the secretary in charge of them. This would have given him some voice in their membership and in bringing matters to their attention, but he does not appear to have been an ex-officio member of these committees.[2] At the same time, he obtained another foothold in the Labour Party offices, when the Labour Research Department moved to Eccleston Square in July 1918. Perhaps Cole hoped to use these connections as a means to informal personal influence. We find Mrs Webb alternately acclaiming and complaining in her Diary that Cole was succeeding in getting Henderson's ear. One of her reports indicates the misunderstandings which can intervene between one who influences, and the person he is influencing. Cole, in 1919, was advocating the idea of making each industry bear the charge of the unemployed who regularly worked in it; Mrs Webb asserted that he only confused Arthur Henderson.[3]

In seeking influence, Cole does not seem to have been moved to any noticeable degree by personal ambition. One cannot be absolutely sure of this, and Mrs Webb at times certainly would have thought him so motivated. But he was continually doing things which brought him no remuneration and no offices. Chief among these were his activities for the Labour Research Department. Early in 1920, the L.R.D. loaned Cole and Arnot to a group of minor professional societies, and they proceeded to draw up a model constitution for confederation. They ran into difficulties. *The Times* and the *Morning Post* denounced Cole and the Labour Research Department for trying to trick the technicians into joining the Labour movement, and some of the professional societies withdrew from the confederation.[4] When the job was finished, they returned to the Department; similarly, Cole did not seek office within the Building Guilds movement.

---

[1] A copy is in G. D. H. Cole, 'Articles 1913–1923', Nuffield College.
[2] Labour Party, 'Education: Advisory Committee', boxes 1 and 2, Transport House. I am indebted to the Labour Party for allowing me to see these materials.
[3] 'Diary of Beatrice Webb', Vol. 35 (24 September 1919), 89.
[4] 'Diary of Beatrice Webb', Vol. 35 (11 February 1920), 109–10.

Even as a young man seeking influence for his ideas, he thus appears personally disinterested. What ambitions he seems to have had just after the First World War are those which grew out of his identification with Guild Socialism and with a more militant trade union movement in general. There was no alternative to his directly taking a hand, especially since he mistrusted almost every Labour leader. At the most, he wanted only to play the role of an 'eminence grise'.[1] Such a role would have held an intellectual attraction for him, similar to his emotional attraction to the idea of revolution. But it would have been annoying to a person as uninstitutional as Cole, who was not prepared to be Machiavellian for long, and had an aversion to political manoeuvring.

Well before the end of Guild Socialism, Cole had lost any means of influence in Eccleston Square. In the summer of 1920, Cole resigned as secretary to the Labour Party's advisory committees. Arthur Greenwood replaced him, and took steps to ensure that the Parliamentary Labour Party would remain in full control of the committees.[2] Cole took some interest in both the Education Committee and the Local Government Committee after ceasing to be secretary, but this appears to have come to an end by 1922. Meanwhile, the L.R.D., which had been under attack for some time, was expelled from Eccleston Square in the summer of 1921. Personal antipathy towards Cole on the part of both influential trade unionists and the Labour Party's staff was undoubtedly part of the reason for this. According to Mrs Webb, Bevin, Bowerman, Bramley, and Shaw of the T.U.C. combined with Gillies and Tracey of the Labour Party's secretariat to break the connections the Labour Research Department had formed with both the trade unions and the Labour Party.[3] The growing support which members of the L.R.D. gave to the unofficial leaders who later formed the Communist Party undoubtedly hurt the L.R.D., making its advice suspect to leaders who would otherwise have made use of it.

Thus, by 1921, Cole found himself once more in a sort of personal political wilderness. He had lost his sources of influence, and was not to gain an institutional platform until he founded the New Fabian

[1] One interviewer felt that this was his ambition. 'Personalities and Powers: Mr G. D. H. Cole', *Time and Tide* (3 September 1920), 345.
[2] Labour Party, 'Education: Advisory Committee.'
[3] 'Diary of Beatrice Webb', Vol. 35 (18–25 June 1920), 126.

Research Bureau in 1931. Consequently, he developed an independent political style. Working from the outside, he soon lost much of the personal cantankerousness which had hampered him when he worked from the inside. He learned to separate his ideals from himself, so that he did not seek personal influence or grow angry at neglect or personal abuse. He was well on his way to becoming a 'socialist saint'. He would have influence, plenty of it; but it would be of a different sort from that of the person who makes or registers decisions within an institutional structure.

Even during the period surrounding the First World War, when Cole was able to work within the power structures of the A.S.E. and the Labour Party, his influence stemmed chiefly from his abilities as a writer and propagandist and from his personal energy and attraction. Cole's influence rested with his pen, his ability to write and think clearly about a variety of subjects, making them intelligible to a non-academic audience without being condescending. It rested with his ability to make himself the proponent of an idea broad enough to direct a major reconstruction of society. It rested with his inspiring energy. It rested with his power as a teacher, especially with his ability to liberate men's minds. And it rested with himself, with his peculiar charisma – the way his goodness impressed other people and was consonant with his ideals.

Between 1917 and 1923, Cole achieved a considerable reputation as the leading exponent of Guild Socialism. Guild Socialism had little direct, dramatic 'influence' of the sort which historians crave. But while high rates of employment and the enthusiasm for 'reconstruction' lasted, Guild Socialism was an important factor in British politics. It exerted a pressure that the defenders of the *status quo* had to consider seriously. The willingness of business leaders to talk about the Whitley Councils and other devices for broader consultation with the workers indicates the indirect influence wielded by the Guildsmen and other Labour militants thinking along parallel lines. Guild Socialism did not create the demand for self-government which an important minority of militant socialists felt; if it had had to create such a demand from scratch, it could not have had any influence at all. Its influence consisted in articulating this demand, making clearer and sharper the discontents that many workers felt with both capitalism and collectivist socialism. Some of these militants were so moved by Guild Socialism that they participated in efforts to obtain it through union activities and the formation of working Guilds. Many more were moved to a lesser extent, and acquiesced in adding self-government in industry to the list of demands that their unions presented.

This indirect influence possessed by Guild Socialism depended upon the contribution which it made to socialist and democratic ideals. Guild Socialism was an important restatement of the libertarian features of British socialism. Cole did far more than merely repeat these features. He embedded them in institutions, creating an important model of a decent society. In short, he created a utopia – perhaps the last socialist utopia – and gave it much more contemporary relevance than most utopias ever obtain.

CHAPTER 2

THE GUILD UTOPIA

No matter how one defines the word 'utopia', it applies to Cole's writings about the society which Guild Socialism would establish. Cole himself, as he looked back on his early thoughts, labelled them utopian in the Marxist sense.[1] He emphasized their visionary nature; the thoughts on Guild Socialism had gone far beyond what events showed to be practical. But the Guilds were not simply utopian in this sense of building 'castles in the air'; Mannheim's famous definition would also apply to Cole's work at this time. The principles Cole enunciated did demand a fundamental reconstruction of the social order, and they did, to some extent, represent an objective possibility.

Accepting the fact that there is validity in both these approaches, I want to approach Cole's utopian thoughts from a slightly different angle, from the utopian enterprise itself. A utopia is an effort to design suitable institutions to surround certain principles which describe the good life. The impulse to visualize one's principles, to make a model from them, seems to fulfil two different motives which rarely occur in their pure forms. The first is to project a sort of fantasy around principles which one does not believe will be realized; the Marxist criticism of utopias treats all utopias as fantasies. Such a utopia placates the utopian's idealism by insisting upon the gap between the ideal and reality. The classical utopias, such as those of More and Campanella, are like this. More separated his Utopia spacially from England, and gave it the ironic name meaning 'no-place'. Such a utopia is coloured with resignation – it is reasonable, but the world is mad.

Cole's utopia was much closer to the other sort. He believed that his principles could be realized, and that one could foresee the institutions that would embody them. He was healthily sceptical about the institutions he envisaged coming to exist in the exact manner he

[1] G. D. H. Cole, *The Next Ten Years in British Social and Economic Policy* (London, Macmillan, 1929), pp. 16, 21.

described,[1] but he still believed in the utopian enterprise. It was a semi-practical working model. Cole justified his utopian speculations by saying, 'When [The Guild Socialists] sketch the future, or become "Utopian", they do so only because they believe that, in order to work well in the present, it is necessary to have the greatest possible knowledge of the end to which the immediate work is directed.'[2] Cole's vision of Guild Society was not free speculation about an ideal separated from this world. It was a projection of what this world might become, guided both by the ideals of freedom, democracy and fellowship, and by tendencies at work in the contemporary world.

In other words, Cole could engage in utopian speculations only when both the 'Bolshevik soul' and the 'Fabian muzzle' were brought together on a picture of the future. Several pre-requisites were necessary before these two aspects of his personality could mesh in creating a utopia. The first pre-requisite was Cole's strong belief in freedom, democracy, and fellowship. These values made a new society necessary, and provided a basic feeling of what a good society would be like. Secondly, there was Cole's firm belief that the social environment could either permit or destroy human welfare.

For human well-being the supreme requirement is a social environment into which the individual can enter so as to find in it encouragement for his good, and discouragement for his bad, impulses and qualities. Robert Owen was right when he made this factor of moral environment the key to the human problem. Given a good enough social framework, the increase of knowledge can help men to raise their material standard of living; with a bad framework, it will chiefly add to their capacity for evil.

If the environment was so important, the conclusion was obvious: 'It follows that man's greatest task is the making of good societies.'[3] Since capitalist society was not a particularly good society, appealing to the wrong motives and destroying individual talents and creativity, it had to be replaced. If its replacement were inevitable, then there were no reasons for utopianizing; history would do the job. But Cole was no fatalist; he believed that men had to rebuild society according

[1] G. D. H. Cole, *Self-Government in Industry* (London, G. Bell & Sons, 1917), pp. 252, 257.
[2] G. D. H. Cole, 'The Meaning of Guild Socialism', *The Theosophist* (1921), 231.
[3] G. D. H. Cole, 'What I Believe', in 'Manuscripts and Proofs', Box 8, Cole Papers, Nuffield College, p. 123.

to plans which satisfied their basic needs. Finally, for Cole to make such a plan, the ideals he envisaged had to flow parallel to events and tendencies in the world. He had to find a vehicle for his utopian speculations, a prominent social force whose development indicated that it could reasonably lead to a society which would embody his fundamental principles. In 1919, in particular, Cole could feel that the 'immediate work' of the Labour movement was directed towards his ends; his utopia was in part a prediction or prophecy of what could happen.

The Guild Socialist believes what he believes, not so much as the result of a process of absolute reasoning, as because, if his fundamental assumptions are granted, the Guild Socialist solution of the social problem seems to him to spring simply and naturally out of the form in which that problem presents itself to-day. He claims, not to be imagining a Utopia in the clouds, but to be giving form and direction to certain quite definite tendencies which are now at work in Society, and to be anticipating the most natural developments of already existing institutions and social forces.[1]

Events did seem to allow radical change in the direction Cole wanted. The war had exposed 'the waste and the weakness, the loss of liberty and self-government, the sectionalism and the self-seeking which capitalism involves.'[2] Cole and his friends felt that the vehicle for social transformation lay at hand, partly as a result of the war. The war had helped create a militant industrial movement centring around the shop stewards, who seemed ready to reject both capitalism and bureaucratic solutions to the problems capitalism left behind.

The growth of radical workers' movements encouraged Cole, for his sympathies naturally lay with them, and their energies seemed directed towards the principles in which he believed. By extrapolating from various workers' demands, and combining them with ideas developed by S. G. Hobson and others, it became possible for him to write in a utopian manner. Utopia was practical; it made clear what the workers unwittingly strove for.[3] He could be a utopian and an intellectual observer at once; his practical and idealistic tendencies fused in the effort. This was especially true as the creation of a utopia was only part

[1] G. D. H. Cole, *Guild Socialism Re-stated* (London, Leonard Parsons, 1920), p. 11.
[2] *Self-Government in Industry*, p. 7; G. D. H. Cole, *Labour in War-Time* (London, G. Bell & Sons, 1915).
[3] *Guild Socialism Re-stated*, p. 11.

of the task he took upon himself. Simultaneously he thought about the transition to a Guild society, and to strengthen the forces of Labour, worked for the unions and for the Labour Party.

The genesis of Cole's utopian speculations lies in his principles. It is they which make the construction radically different from the existing society, giving it the apocalyptic quality which is such an important part of the utopian's mental commitment to his creation. Guild Socialism allowed Cole to develop his basic beliefs in individuality, freedom, fellowship, and democracy into concrete social forms. His ideals were the rationale for his utopia; their pre-eminence justified the effort.

As always, Cole insisted that the individual be recognized as an independent moral subject, and not be debased to the level of a hand or a tool. '[My] dominant idea is that the individual worker must be regarded not simply as a "hand", a decreasingly important adjunct to the industrial machine, but as a man among men, with rights and responsibilities, with a human soul and desire for self-expression, self-government, and personal freedom.'[1]

In making the recognition of individuality concrete and practical, Cole stated the case for freedom more directly and more extensively than he was ever able to do in later years. The following passage, more than any other, shows the emotional and intellectual significance which freedom had for him during his Guild Socialist period:

What, I want to ask, is the fundamental evil in our modern Society which we should set out to abolish?

There are two possible answers to that question, and I am sure that very many well-meaning people would make the wrong one. They would answer POVERTY, when they ought to answer SLAVERY. Face to face every day with the shameful contrasts of riches and destitution, high dividends and low wages, and painfully conscious of the futility of trying to adjust the balance by means of charity, private or public, they would answer unhesitatingly that they stand for the ABOLITION OF POVERTY.

Well and good! On that issue every Socialist is with them. But their answer to my question is none the less wrong.

Poverty is the symptom: slavery the disease. The extremes of riches and destitution follow inevitably upon the extremes of license and bondage. The many are not enslaved because they are poor, they are poor because they are enslaved. Yet Socialists have all too often fixed their eyes upon the material

---

[1] *Self-Government in Industry*, p. 5.

misery of the poor without realizing that it rests upon the spiritual degradation of the slave.[1]

Slavery was the enemy; and by slavery Cole meant any practice which made a man's life subject to the wills of leaders, bosses or managers who were not directly responsible to him. Freedom was a condition of self-determination which applied to all phases of life, rather than being restricted to politics. As a Guild Socialist, Cole's practical demand was for self-government in industry, the control of industry by the workers themselves. This freedom was both end and means; men would obtain a free society by becoming self-governing in their work.

This emphasis on self-government meant that democracy was a major aspect of freedom. Cole argued that it was inconsistent to admit democracy in politics and deny it in the rest of life.

We have never believed in democracy; for, if we had, we should have tried to apply it, not to politics alone, but to every aspect of human life. We should not have been democrats in politics and autocrats in industry; we should have stood for self-government all round.[2]

Democracy meant much more to Cole than it tended to mean later in the twentieth century. It was more than a political principle; it was a moral relationship among men. Democracy entailed respect for each individual as a moral subject, and sought to express each person's will and creativity in as many activities as possible.

One of the largest obstacles to democracy in the economic system was the debilitating inferiority conveyed in a wage relationship. Each Guildsman should be entitled to

1. Recognition and payment as a human being, and not merely as the mortal tenement of so much labour power for which an effective demand exists.
2. Consequently, payment in employment and in unemployment, in sickness and in health alike . . .[3]

Cole would have liked to assert the principle of equality of incomes, to express the equality of unmeasurable individuals; but he grew 'doubtful whether this method would be practical, at any rate in the

[1] Ibid., pp. 110–11.
[2] Ibid., p. 230.
[3] *Self-Government in Industry*, p. 155.

earlier stages'.[1] He insisted, however, that whatever distinctions in pay were allowed to remain would have to be so small as not to create class divisions. He would not have tolerated the gulfs still present in society, where one man may receive a hundred times as much as another. Rather than increase the pay of workers performing disagreeable chores, he proposed that they work shorter hours.[2]

This substantial equality was the necessary counterpart to designing a society in which everyone would play a part in making decisions. Without classes, the conflict of interests applying to a particular issue would be less bitter. Those who finally made decisions must be kept from becoming economically separate and capable of intimidating those who disagreed. One had to feel free before one would try to participate in self-government. Cole demanded mutually reinforcing changes in institutions and in people's attitudes – the feeling of freedom and the institutions which would allow self-government.

To root his principles in institutions, Cole drew upon various democratic constitutional techniques. The most important was the idea of separating powers and institutions according to their functions. This is not the familiar idea of separating powers according to the stages in the process of creating and enforcing a law. Cole and other theorists of the period around the First World War sought to make their separations on content lines.[3] A division between legislation and administration was clumsy, and did not significantly increase the individual's freedom; such a vertical separation of powers was vanishing even in America. Cole held that a different, horizontal sort of division had to be created, so that the individual's will on a specific subject could be represented more exactly.

Cole's use of the idea of function grew steadily more complex. His early Guild Socialist writings, those up to 1916 or 1917, placed a fair amount of stress upon a simple separation of the economic and political aspects of a Guild society. The separation between economic and political areas of society was a preliminary to the use of the principle

[1] *Guild Socialism Re-stated*, pp. 71–2.
[2] Ibid., p. 76.
[3] 'The Nature of the State', in *Self-Government in Industry*. See also Bertrand Russell, *Roads to Freedom: Socialism, Anarchism, and Syndicalism*, 3rd ed. (London, Allen & Unwin, 1920); Sidney and Beatrice Webb, *A Constitution for the Socialist Commonwealth of Great Britain* (London, 1920).

of function to fragment power more carefully within each area; Cole gradually grew more involved in separating functions from each other and in combining the ways in which a person should be involved in decision-making. Ultimately, as we shall see, the detailed application of function broke down the broad distinctions which Cole had sought to establish, making the whole enterprise more pedantic 'and less successful in serving the individual.

Cole defined a function as the purpose individuals seek in organizing.

We have seen that men make, and enter into, associations for the purpose of establishing common wants, that is, in terms of action, for the execution of common purposes. Every such purpose or group of purposes is the basis of the *function* of the association which has been called into being for its fulfilment.[1]

This definition clearly subordinated the institution and its function to the individual, rather than defining a function as an individual's duty. It is this difference in emphasis which clearly separates Guild Socialism from Fascism, which applied the principle of function in the opposite direction. As Cole defined it, function was largely a descriptive term; but Cole found in function a way of crossing the line between facts and values which is enshrined in G. E. Moore's description of the 'naturalistic fallacy'. The concept of function could yield two important kinds of judgments. First, an institution could be criticized for the way in which it did not fulfil the purposes for which individuals joined it. Secondly, and more importantly, various social purposes could be compared with each other and associations embodying them could be assigned areas of operation. Function thus became a way of analysing a whole society.

Function, we have seen, emerges when, and only when, an association is regarded, not in isolation, but in relation to other associations and to individuals, that is, to some extent in relation to a system of associations, a Society, and a system of associations and individuals, a community. Such a system evidently implies a more or less clear demarcation of spheres as between the various functional associations, in order that each may make its proper contribution to the whole without interfering with the others.[2]

One could not describe the relationship of functional associations to

---

[1] G. D. H. Cole, *Social Theory* (London, Methuen, 1920), p. 49.
[2] Ibid., p. 55.

the whole society by facts alone. The community's interest must be consulted. Here, Cole recognized, 'We have introduced a consideration of value which compels us to scrutinize the purposes of each particular association in the light of its communal value in and for the whole'.[1] It was only on these grounds that one could say that the object of a particular association, say a council of profiteers, was not a proper function. 'We cannot accept the objects of each association just as its members have made them, as making for a coherent society and a development of the sense of community.' But this recognition that an existing social purpose could be invalid did not justify discarding an empirical approach to the problem. The empirical approach was the strongest safeguard against an unduly subjective analysis of functions. 'If men have formed an association for one purpose, we cannot properly tell them that its function is to do something quite different which has never entered their heads.'[2] As he used the principle of function, Cole sought to start from facts about the existing institutional structure of society to arrive at judgments about an ideal structure.

In *Social Theory* he proposed 'to enumerate and classify the main forms of association – those which possess the greatest degree of social content, and to discuss briefly these dominant social motives which are constantly appearing in many diverse forms of associations'.[3] From such a study, one could conclude what were the essential purposes men sought in associations, although Cole recognized that his conclusions would not convince everyone. He devised a loose test: 'The key to essentiality is thus the performance of some function which is vital to the coherent working of Society, and without which Society would be lopsided or incomplete.' On these grounds, Cole declared that three general areas of association were most essential, 'political, vocational and appetitive association'.

Each of these must, I think, be regarded as essential. Each deals with a vital aspect of Social organization, with an 'interest' vital to the mass of members of the community, and each is based upon a deep-rooted and vital instinct of association. It is mainly on the right relationship of these three forms of association that the coherent organization of Society depends.[4]

[1] Ibid., p. 51.
[2] Ibid., pp. 53–4.
[3] Ibid., p. 63.
[4] Ibid., pp. 75–6.

Cole felt that other areas of association – social, propagandistic, provident, philanthropic, and religious – were less essential. Some of them would not be needed in an ideal society, while others – religious and social associations – he wanted to exempt from control by other bodies.

Having proceeded this far with the principle of function, Cole still had a major obstacle to surmount. 'Even if we hold that a particular form of association is essential, this is not by itself enough to establish the essentiality of any single association belonging to that class.' Here an irreducible vagueness entered his thinking, as long as it stayed on a theoretical level. Cole did not really solve the problem of defining how an association could be proved essential. His answer was reasonable, to return to empiricism. He sought out the specific inter-connections between functions in each area. One could separate one vocation from another in most cases, and the same went for the consumption of various kinds of goods. Cole felt that these industries would require separate organizations: mining, transport (or railways and road transport separately), iron and steel, cotton, agriculture, engineering and shipbuilding, building, and distribution. He had much more difficulty applying the concept of function to service industries, although the effort to organize basic services functionally does dominate much of *Guild Socialism Re-Stated*. One could also observe where demarcation problems between existing organizations were especially acute, and work to achieve a decent separation. Thus, although the concept of function had definite limits, it could help Cole evaluate human activities, and it forced his thinking into a healthy contact with social reality.

The principle of function enabled Cole to point to the social areas of life which the individual had to control in order to be truly self-governing. The individual had to join with his fellow workers to control the way in which their labour was organized. He had to control political decisions, that is, the solution of problems which arose directly from his life in a community. And he had to have a voice in the distribution of goods in society. Cole insisted that the only way in which the individual could control these areas of life was to separate them sharply from each other.

The basic division fell between man as producer and man as consumer. In each capacity an individual had interests in the economy:

Industry, in the widest sense, is a matter of both production and use. The product has to be produced, and it has to be determined who shall have the right to consume it. On the one hand, the decision of the character and use of the product is clearly a matter primarily for the user: on the other, the conditions under which work is carried on so vitally and directly concern the various sections of organized producers that they cannot afford to let the control of those conditions remain in the hands of outsiders.[1]

Once again, examining the implications of functional analysis led him to a traditional democratic technique, in a way that made that technique more meaningful. This duality of interests demanded a balance between them, since the supremacy of one or the other would be the tyranny of one point of view. Cole had libertarian reasons for establishing such a balance of powers. He sought to create a situation making 'the individual the link between [Society's] autonomous but interdependent parts'. On the one hand, the separation and balance of powers was designed to cut down the danger from an 'omnicompetent State'; and Cole used the principle of function to withdraw various activities from the state's control. He especially wanted to remove the state from the actual process of production; in the last stage of his Guild utopia he dropped the word 'State' altogether. On the other hand, Cole felt that the preservation of individual autonomy entailed forbidding such a concentration of powers anywhere. 'If the individual is not to be a mere pygmy in the hands of a colossal social organism, there must be such a division of social powers as will preserve individual freedom by balancing one social organism so nicely against another that the individual may still count.'[2] Such a division would enable the individual to rule, through representatives who could come close to representing his will in relation to particular purposes, while safeguarding him from tyranny by an omnipotent body. And a balance between social powers could also serve Cole's liberal belief in the sphere of private personal liberties.

Such a separation of powers and functions, however, could not alone lead to self-government. It might simply produce stagnation or a perpetual battle between various functional associations, each capable of blocking others. But a self-governing society had to satisfy basic needs. It had to satisfy them efficiently, without wasting energy and resources

[1] *Self-Government in Industry*, pp. 106–7.
[2] Ibid., pp. 91–2.

and without frustrating the workers' sense of community. Cole came gradually to see that efficiency required central planning of the nation's resources. He explored the implications of planning more thoroughly in the 1930s, but even in his Guild Socialist books he often spoke of coordinating supply and demand.

The need for efficiency and planning created difficulties for Cole's wish to provide self-expression in work and the full expression of all relevant interests. It is another appearance of the tension between his 'Bolshevik soul' and 'Fabian muzzle'. He tried to minimize it by arguing that bureaucracy was not the only form efficiency could take. Workers freed from their servitude to profits and to routines imposed upon them would be much more efficient.

... the statutes must try to combine freedom with efficiency – not that capitalistic efficiency which turns man into a machine and secures a dead level of mediocrity by the destruction of all native genius; but an efficiency based throughout on the development of individual initiative, emphasizing valuable differences ...[1]

This definitional answer to the problem of reconciling liberty and efficiency could not be completely satisfying. Cole felt, at least for a time, that the formula of 'decentralization, which differentiates without disintegration'[2] would get around the dilemma. Decentralization is an inherently messy concept, but it became more plausible when Cole worked it out in terms of functional divisions. The upper levels of Guild organization, for example, would care for financial relations, while the factory and workshop concerned themselves with the physical techniques of production. By 1920, Cole had come to see that one could not divide techniques of production neatly from their costs.

Further concessions to the need for efficiency appear in Cole's elaborate efforts to describe techniques for choosing leaders and officials. He emphasized direct democratic elections at the expense of voting by widespread publics.

At every stage ... wherever a body of men has to work under the supervision of a leader or officer, it must have the choice of that officer. And, in the same way, every committee must be appointed directly by those over whose work

[1] Ibid., p. 252.
[2] Ibid., p. 246.

it is to preside ... this is the general principle on which Guild democracy must rest.[1]

He interpreted this literally; where an officer presided over a committee, the committee should choose him, and the rest of the workers should have only an indirect part in his election and recall. Cole felt that direct elections only worked well when the electors had personal knowledge of their candidates' ability in the activities that they would control. In another concession to efficiency, Cole decided that experts were not to be elected, but were to be chosen by committees, after passing some sort of examination. 'There is no need for a more directly democratic method, because the function of this type of expert is in the main advisory, and he does not come into direct relations with or control any body of workers.'[2]

But while all of this indirect procedure can be justified by Cole's conception of democracy, it reains a compromise, as the following quotation graphically reveals:

I would ask whether the system of organization ... does not offer a reasor- able prospect of combining with the freedom Guildsmen desire the safe- guards Capitalism has taught Collectivists to regard as necessary. I had almost said 'necessary evils'; but I fear that many a Collectivist no longer regards such a system of safeguards as an evil.[3]

Personally, he hoped that as much as possible of this representative system could be dispensed with. 'Given free choice of leaders and free criticism of them when chosen, a good deal of the mere machinery of democracy might remain normally in the background.'[4] Even while Cole was constructing an elaborate model of a better society, he remembered that a healthy society would have to function with the minimum of conscious political control, and allow plenty of room for negative freedoms.

We are now able to describe in a little detail the institutional forms with which Cole tried to surround these constitutional principles, in turn derived from his basic beliefs in the individual and fellowship. Broadly, we may say that there were two stages in Cole's experimenta-

[1] Ibid., p. 255.
[2] Ibid., p. 267.
[3] Ibid., pp. 256–7.
[4] *Guild Socialism Re-stated*, p. 58.

tion with Guild institutions. The first task was to develop the theory of the Guild itself from S. G. Hobson's articles and from the preliminary exploration the Cole group codified in the Storrington Document. This step dominates the articles Cole collected into *Self-Government in Industry* in 1917. Here, his emphasis fell on the organization of production itself, and on the answers to objections concerning the use of machinery and the degree of freedom possible within the Guild. Cole wrote from a position still influenced by Syndicalism, concentrating on the part of the Guild society closest to the feelings of the workers. The representation of the consumer, an essential part of Guild theory, was covered vaguely, and largely left to the state. The second stage saw Cole's more original contributions to Guild Socialism. In his later Guild Socialist writings, Cole turned to the consumer and differentiated his needs from politics. He then pushed on to an elaborate remodelling of society around the concept of function, culminating in the theory of the Guild Commune. This theory is Cole's most utopian construction, but it was embedded in a practical framework. *Guild Socialism Re-stated* developed the Guild Commune, while *Chaos and Order in Industry* examined the tactics necessary in each industry, and *Social Theory* probed the philosophical bases of Guild institutions. After 1923 he grew tired of the elaborate structure of *Guild Socialism Re-stated* and treated the principles discussed in *Self-Government in Industry* as the core of the 'Guild Idea'.

The basic concept, the Guild, was quite simple. 'A National Guild would be an association of all the workers by hand and brain concerned in the carrying on of a particular industry or service, and its function would be actually to carry on that industry or service on behalf of the whole community.'[1] Thus it was a literal substitution of communal interests and workers' organizations for profit and capitalism. When Cole and others said that the Guild would include 'all the workers by hand and brain', they meant this literally. Skilled and semi-skilled workers, clerical workers, foremen, and managers would all belong to the Guild.[2] The concept of a Guild applied most clearly to developed

---

[1] Ibid., p. 46.

[2] Ibid., p. 47. Cole, I feel, did not envisage a Guild society with a high percentage of unskilled labourers. Such a society would have been inconsistent with his belief in creative work.

producing industries and to the railways. Major Guilds would include mining, iron and steel, cotton, agriculture, engineering and shipbuilding, building, transportation, and distribution. Each industry would be self governing; no one could become an official who was not a member of the Guild, and all officials would be chosen by the men under them. The Guild would be a self-contained industry organized for the production of goods rather than of profit.

Cole desired a sort of 'Guild *laisser-faire*', in which decisions would be made by the people who had to work by them. The health of the whole Guild system depended upon the workshop. Only people who had control over their conditions of labour would be able to act freely in the larger society. Workshop control meant 'an entire change in the form of factory discipline and the arrangement of the work of the shop largely not under orders from above but by collective arrangement among the workers themselves'.[1] The workers should elect their own foremen, and settle disputes over discipline and job assignments through workshop committees. On a slightly more complex level, Cole treated the factory as the appropriate unit to decide questions of methods of production. Under Guild conditions, Cole hoped for a revival of the care and individuality of craftsmanship. Self-governing craftsmen could reduce machinery to its proper place, eliminate dirty and repetitive work, and end slipshod methods of machine production. Cole hoped for a fair degree of competition between individual factories; but they should compete in quality rather than in price.

The local branches of each Guild will . . . be free to adopt and apply new inventions, to specialize on certain products, and in general to adapt production to its own ideas and local needs. This freedom will however be subject to the observance of the regulations laid down by the national Guild authority and to the national fixation of general conditions, e.g. hours and factory amenities, etc.[2]

Thus, despite his effort to strengthen participation in decision making on the most-personal levels, a second aspect of this 'Guild *laisser-faire*' threatened to cancel-out workshop autonomy. Cole shifted a formidable list of functions to the Guild, away from direct surveillance by the political apparatus of society. National Guilds would establish

[1] G. D. H. Cole, 'Workers' Control', *Railway Service Journal* (April 1934).
[2] The Storrington Document.

general regulations affecting the organization and methods of production. They would obtain raw materials and market the largest share of finished goods. '. . . they would act on behalf of the Guild in its relations both with other Guilds, and with other forms of organization, such as consumers' bodies, within the community, or with bodies abroad.'[1] The central function left to the national Guilds was the coordination of output to make the supply of particular goods coincide with demand. The coordination of supply and demand entailed planning the quantities of commodities to be produced and setting the prices to be charged. In both cases the Guild would have to consult with the representatives of consumer interests; and the decisions reached would limit the decisions workshops and factories could reach on work rules and methods of production.

Although Cole and the Guildsmen had attempted to give as many functions as possible to the factory and the workshop, the Guilds' national administrations would have been more powerful than he would have liked. Cole counted on the workers' willingness to protect workshop self-government. The rest of the task of securing workers' control would have to be accomplished by constructing an elaborate electoral system to achieve the maximum possible representation for various interests within the Guild. Cole adapted his model of the Guilds' administrations from those prevalent among trade unions. A National Delegate Meeting would be 'the ultimate governing body . . . serving both as a final appeal court and as the initiator of the general lines of Guild policy'. The delegates should be chosen 'by general ballot of the members of each craft in each district'.[2] Each Guild member would vote twice for members of the National Executive; he would have a district representative and a craft representative. Proposed policies would thus have to satisfy both regional and craft interests. The third element in the National Guild administration, the General Secretary, was clearly intended to be subordinate to the National Executive. Cole attempted to secure this subordination by having the Executive choose the General Secretary and by giving the Delegate Meeting the power to veto his proposals. However, the presence of similar powers in many trade union constitutions has

[1] *Guild Socialism Re-stated*, p. 60.
[2] *Self-Government in Industry*, p. 260.

not prevented General Secretaries from becoming dominant figures.

Cole's most significant deviations from trade union practice came from his firm conviction that there was such a thing as a craft interest which deserved expression, a sort of general will pertaining to an occupational grouping. Cole felt that this general will would be adequately expressed by the Guilds. The Guild, which would grow out of the union, would replace it, by providing for direct self-government and by reducing the importance of wage disputes. 'The employers' association and the Trade Union would alike be out of place as primarily offensive and defensive forms of organization, and the main types of association would find their motives not in defence or offence, but in social service.'[1] Many, however, have protested that this would not mean real industrial democracy, since it would mean the subordination of dissenting groups and interests. They have pointed out that the protection of a union disappears when that union becomes management as well.[2] Cole sought to forestall the objection by representing special interests separately.

The final body on the industrial side of Guild society, both in the 1917 model and in the 1920 model, was to be a Guild Congress. In the Storrington Document, the founders of the N.G.L. had specified that 'The Guild Congress will be the ultimately sovereign authority in all matters affecting the Guilds as a whole, and will decide such differences as may arise in the relations of Guild to Guild'. Cole soon came to quarrel with the whole notion of sovereignty, and undoubtedly intended to hold the sphere of competence of the Guild Congress to a minimum. It is interesting to note that he did not bother to elaborate on the details of its election. Being composed of an Annual Meeting and an Executive Committee on which each Guild would be represented, it would resemble the T.U.C.

The prime function of the Guild Congress was to represent the Guilds collectively on problems arising out of their relationships with the rest of the community. The need for this kind of representation was inherent in the Guild Socialists' conception of society. They

---

[1] *Social Theory*, p. 155.
[2] See Hugh Clegg, *Industrial Democracy and Nationalization* (Oxford, Basil Blackwell, 1955), p. 131.

insisted that consumers could not be ignored, even if they were the same people as producers; consumers had rights which involved a share in the control of industry. If consumers had a distinct interest in the working of industry, then its operation could not be left totally to the workers as the Syndicalists had urged. The Guildsmen therefore set out to create a system of joint control which would embody the greater part of the Syndicalists' claims. The workers had to be free to organize production itself; the consumers' interest concerned the use of what was produced. In *Self-Government in Industry*, Cole wrote that 'the consumers ought to control the division of the national product, or the division of income in the community . . .'[1] The discussion of this right led Cole into what is essentially a rejection of the idea that society might be functionally divided into consumers and producers, although its real implications only emerged with the theory of the Guild Commune.

In the Storrington Document and in *Self-Government in Industry*, Cole assigned the task of representing consumers to the State. He argued that 'the State only represents the individual in his particular aspect of "neighbour", "user" and "enjoyer".'[2] He was still resisting S. G. Hobson's argument that the state represented the individual as citizen,[3] because he felt it opened the way to state sovereignty. By 'the State', Cole meant something like the existing political organization, short of its control of the productive side of industry and of its sovereignty on matters like taxation, and restricted to representing people as inhabitants of a particular area with common needs.[4] Thus expressed, the needs represented by the state could not be allowed to overshadow self-government in work. 'The partnership, to be worth anything, must be a partnership of equals, not the revocable concession of a benignant and superior State, and, to make it real, the Guilds must be in a position to bargain on equal terms with the State . . . The Guild must reserve the right and the economic resource to withdraw

---

[1] *Self-Government in Industry*, p. 106.

[2] Ibid., p. 79.

[3] S. G. Hobson, *National Guilds: An Inquiry into the Wage System and the Way Out*, 3rd ed. (London, G. Bell & Sons, 1919), pp. 255–6.

[4] *Self-Government in Industry*, pp. 77, 81. This geographical or territorial definition of the state was an important assumption; it recurred in his emphasis on regionalism and decentralisation, and also helped limit claims to sovereignty on the part of political bodies.

its labour; the State must rely, to check unjust demands, on its equal voice in the decision of points of difference, and on the organized opinion of the community as a whole.'[1]

Cole thus turned to collective bargaining for his model of democratic decision-making. Nor would negotiations be restricted to the state and the Guilds Congress; Guilds should negotiate on national and district levels with the state, with local governments, and with *ad hoc* bodies. Cole does not seem to fear that these negotiations would be too remote from the workers, or that their importance would erode local participation in Guild decisions. He hoped that the general atmosphere of equality in a Guild society would reduce the chance of deadlock between a Guild and the state. More significantly, he spelled out concepts to be used in bargaining that could reduce the area of sheer force.

The essential problems which would test such a system were taxes and prices. In each of these cases collective bargaining was bound to be long and difficult. In the case of prices, the first step would be to calculate a 'natural price' which was 'to be determined by the cost of raw material plus the income of the Guildsmen reckoned on a basis approximating more or less nearly to a common time-standard of value.' Under optimum Guild conditions, it would not be at all difficult to calculate a 'natural price', because all the members of the Guilds would be receiving the same pay. But this 'natural price' would not necessarily be the actual selling-price of the goods produced. Cole, like many socialists, entertained the idea of providing free transportation, health, bread, milk, and other services. '. . . it is enough to say that Society will probably give free all things which all men need in fairly equal measure, and cheap those things which it wishes, for one reason or another, to see more widely used.'[2] This passage implies the widespread substitution of a 'just price' for a 'natural price',[3] and would definitely complicate the negotiations between the community and the Guilds. For, if some goods and services were to be provided below cost, others

[1] Ibid., pp. 109–10.
[2] Ibid., pp. 285–6.
[3] Cole's conception, which we have called a 'just price', goes farther than more recent writers believe the medieval conception of a 'just price' went. Raymond de Roover, 'The Concept of the Just Price', *Journal of Economic History*, XVIII, No. 4 (December 1958), 418–34, argues that the just price was most commonly the market price.

presumably would have to be sold for more than cost, in order to equate the supply of goods as a whole with monetary demand. But if one Guild were producing for sale below cost, while others were selling at cost or perhaps even at a specified price above cost, some means had to be provided to restore equality of incomes between the members of different Guilds. It would be a violation of Guild principles to allow one Guild to profit from the community's needs and make its members richer, especially if its profits came from making a less essential product than those sold below cost. To transfer the necessary income, S. G. Hobson had proposed using taxation, or, as Guildsmen often put it, 'a substitute for economic rent'. The state, as the representative of the consumers charged with providing for certain essential services, would draw up its budgets and demand the total needed from the Guilds, not from individual tax payers. The state and the Guild Congress would decide jointly how much was to be demanded from each Guild. The amount of quasi-rent taken from each Guild would have to be calculated to leave individual Guild members' pay in balance. Cole very likely underestimated the technical problems of forecasting these calculations would set. Accepting the fact that Cole felt this system of taxation was workable, he argued that it would effectively protect the community against exploitation. Since 'economic quasi-rent' would be determined from a Guild's total sales, minus the amount to be set aside for pay, a price increase would show up in the amount left after deducting pay and material costs, and would be taxed.[1] Cole did not assert that the whole of the price rise would be taxed away, however. Apparently all Guilds would contribute the same percentage of their surpluses – and so one Guild might still gain by raising its prices more rapidly than others.

Such a system of Guild *laissez-faire*, with the tax structure struggling to offset price rises, does not look very satisfactory. Cole tended more and more to come to an institutional solution which would not let prices get out of control. Hence the solution of assigning both prices and taxes to the same authority, a joint body representative of the Guilds and the state. This became the Guild Commune. We have already seen some of the preoccupations which, by 1920, led Cole to reshape his utopian speculations. Already he had come to the con-

[1] *Self-Government in Industry*, pp. 283–4.

clusion that the interests of producer and consumer could only be reconciled in a joint body on which each had ample representation. He gradually realized that he had assigned financial functions of overwhelming importance to this joint body. Some questions were too detailed and demanded too much planning to be handled by anyone other than the functional representatives of the whole community. Thus the community came to dominate both producers and consumers, who in earlier models had been left to negotiate directly with each other.

Other pressures led towards the Guild Commune. Early Guild theory had focussed upon the producers; now Cole moved on to reevaluate the nature of consumption. S. G. Hobson later saw this as the introduction of a Fabian element, distorting the purity of early Guild Socialism.[1] Other members of the N.G.L. helped call his attention to the needs of the consumers. Leonard Woolf argued vigorously that the Co-operative movement should organize the distribution of goods,[2] and Cole yielded much to his argument. Sidney Herbert introduced the question of *ad hoc* representation for consumers.[3] Finally, the Russian Revolution began to have a theoretical impact upon him. The Russians revived the anarcho-syndicalist definition of the state as the holder of coercive power for class purposes, and asserted that the bourgeois state had to be destroyed. This argument fitted in well with Cole's pluralistic distrust of the sovereign state; Cole employed a quasi-Soviet vocabulary in describing the substitute for a sovereign state he evolved in *Guild Socialism Re-stated*.

In his early Guild Socialist writings, Cole had basically accepted the Webbian solution: All consumption was to be represented through the state. Now, he rejected the state's claims to represent the consumer. He accepted Leonard Woolf's argument that 'the representation of the consumer cannot properly, in a democratic society, be entrusted to a "political" body'. 'The representation of the consumer,' Cole continued, 'whether generally or in relation to any particular kind of

[1] S. G. Hobson, *Pilgrim to the Left: Memoirs of a Modern Revolutionist* (London, Edwin Arnold, 1938), pp. 187–8.
[2] Leonard Woolf, *Cooperation and the Future of Industry* (London, Allen & Unwin, 1918).
[3] See *The Guildsman*, No. 27 (February 1919), p. 8; Cole's comments, *The Guildsman*, No. 28 (March 1919), pp. 3–4.

consumption, must be specific, functional, *ad hoc* representation.'[1] Cole immediately divided consumption into two main sections. The first was personal consumption, including routine household shopping. These goods catered for individual taste; and Cole decided that the Co-operative Societies were the proper agency for organizing such consumer goods. The other category contained undifferentiated mass goods such as water and electricity. In many cases they were natural monopolies. For these goods, the Co-operative Societies were not the proper agency; here the collectivists were nearly right, but Cole could no longer give control over 'collective consumption' to the state. Rather, he decided that a section of the existing municipal government should be detached and assigned the function of representing the consumer in the production and distribution of these goods. This agency he called the 'Collective Utilities Council'.

These two types of consumption were both 'economic'; but a third type required yet another independent organization. Public functions such as education, public health, and civic amenities were not industries, but they were important activities requiring consumer representation. For these services Cole demanded the formation of Cultural Councils and Health Councils, which would take over and expand the civic services which local authorities had managed. To avoid the multiplication of *ad hoc* authorities, the Cultural Councils would be expanded to include music, drama, and the arts, as well as education. Cole had not much patience with a narrow concept of education.

Each of these Councils and Societies, representing various kinds of final consumption in Guild Society, would negotiate with the Guilds engaged in making particular goods or performing the services concerned. A quotation discussing the functions of Cultural Councils is illuminating:

As in the case of the economic relationships described in the last chapter, it would be essentially, not an antagonistic, but a cooperative and complementary relationship. The Councils would exist to make articulate the civic point of view, the vital spiritual and physical demands of the people, and to cooperate with the various Guilds which would have entrusted to them the task of supplying these demands. There are spiritual and physical as well as

[1] *Guild Socialism Re-stated*, p. 85.

economic demands, and in these spheres articulate demand must meet and cooperate with organized supply.[1]

Virtually every Guild and every Council would have contacts with all the others; the attractive simplicity of the early Guild Socialist structure was gone. The problem of designing such a differentiated system of functions was that it demanded more conscious cohesive action. Half-way through *Guild Socialism Re-stated*, Cole admitted that 'what we have not yet done is to give any idea of the working of all the groups as parts of a single system, that is to say, of the communal, as distinct from the functional, organization and working of Guild society.'[2]

In order to make Guild society run harmoniously and respect the needs of the community as a whole, Cole felt impelled to introduce an expanded joint body on which all the particular functional points of view would be represented. This he called the Commune. In a sense, the Commune took the place of the political apparatus of existing society which Cole had sought to destroy by the fragmentation of consumers' interests into the Co-operatives, the Collective Utilities Councils, and the Cultural and Health Councils. But Cole chose not to call it the state. For some time he had been combating the concept of a sovereign state, and the Commune was designed to be his way around the whole problem of sovereignty. He sought coordination without compulsion. Cole argued that the new body would not be like the existing state, which would have been replaced by functional organizations.

... it is, of course, perfectly clear that the functional democracy which we have been expounding requires and must have a clearly recognized coordinating agency, and there would be no objection to calling this agency 'the State', if the name did not immediately suggest two entirely misleading ideas. The first is that this new body will be historically continuous with the present political machinery of Society: the second is that it will, to a great extent, reproduce its structure, especially in being based on direct, non-functional election. The coordinating body which is required cannot be, in any real sense, historically continuous with the present State, and it must not reproduce in any important respect the structure of the present State. That it will not inherit most of its functions we have seen already.[3]

[1] Ibid., p. 109.
[2] Ibid., p. 91.
[3] Ibid., p. 121.

Among the undesirable traits of the modern state was its concentration upon coercion. Coercion should be replaced by coordination; the only form of coordination that would not be coercive would be self-coordination by functional groups acting together. Here again, by viewing group interests as particular general wills, he settled for a system of indirect representation as far as the individual was concerned. The Commune, at each of its levels, was likely to include at least the representatives of the following groups:

1. The industrial Guilds, represented either individually or through the Guild Council;
2. a Co-operative Council;
3. a Collective Utilities Council;
4. a Cultural Council; and
5. a Health Council.

This variety of representation would be needed in a local commune; there was also to be communal organization on the regional and on the national levels. Naturally, Cole hoped for the greatest possible decentralization, including the revival of the ward as a political unit; but the Communal structure inevitably raised serious fears of overcentralization and bureaucracy. He attempted to allay these fears, in himself and others, by what we might call pious hopes:

... by far the greatest part of the work of the community would be carried on and administered locally or regionally, and the central work would be divided, according to function, among a coniderable number of distinct organizations. There would therefore be neither need nor opportunity for a centre round which a vast aggregation of bureaucratic and coercive machinery would grow up ...[1]

When we look at the functions which Cole allotted to this Communal organization, we will be inclined to doubt the efficacy of such a wish. Cole had never counted coordination as a function,[2] and this undoubtedly allowed him to be more sanguine. But 'coordination' in 1920 was a much more involved matter than the 'coordination of supply and

[1] Ibid., p. 136.
[2] *Social Theory*, p. 134. In other parts of this book, e.g., p. 101, Cole did refer to co-ordination as a function; but I feel that I am correct in saying that it was not a function in the same sense as production or distribution, and that Cole did not feel that it carried the same sort of coercive power.

demand' which he had concentrated on in 1915. The Commune would have the last word on:

(a) financial problems, especially the allocation of national 'resources, provision of capital, and, to a certain extent, regulation of incomes and prices;
(b) differences arising between functional bodies on questions of policy;
(c) constitutional questions of demarcation between functional bodies;
(d) questions not falling within the sphere of any functional authorities, including general questions of external relations;
(e) coercive functions.[1]

The allocation of these functions to the Commune tended to make the national Commune a sovereign body, something which Cole earnestly wanted to avoid. The basic question would be whether the local bodies could protect their decentralized functions from inroads caused by the increased financial powers in the hands of the national Commune. In 1917, Cole had kept pay out of the joint body's hands by trying hard to make incomes equal; now the Commune was to have the last word on incomes. The most important of the new powers, however, was the allocation of national resources. Earlier, Cole had come closer to a traditional utopian assumption, that the nation's resources would be abundant enough to avoid the need for conscious planning by a central authority. The Guild Commune replaced this earlier Guild *laissez-faire* with national planning. This sort of planning was to be the most significant new idea in western socialism in the inter-war period; it involved more bureaucratic control than the Guildsmen would have liked.

The impact which planning had on the cherished principle of a balance between consumer and producer is easy to trace. It diminished the independence of the Guild. For example, one of Cole's strongest arguments, held in common with other pluralists, was that all sorts of bodies developed their own legislation. He had sought to extend this to the Guilds. The courts, as described in *Self-Government in Industry*, would apply Guild and state law equally. Now, however, he found himself qualifying the sense in which Guild rules would be law. They would be like by-laws, operating 'only within the powers conferred by the communal constitution'. 'Any law of a functional body involving coercion should, I think, only become enforceable in the communal

[1] *Guild Socialism Re-stated*, pp. 139–40.

courts after ratification by the Commune, except in so far as the coercive power was definitely assigned to the functional body under a constitutional law of the Commune.'[1] He furthermore felt that the National Commune should have the power to declare in any disputed case which interpretation of the law was binding.

The Guild Commune was thus a less visionary, more orderly construction. It put less of its stress on 'self-government in industry' and the release of the craftsman, more on communal motives. It was a more practical pattern, because it recognized economic problems connected with the provision of capital and the allocation of resources which the earlier works had ignored. By the same token, it was more collectivist, and the sense of openness and freedom which pervades *Self-Government in Industry* or *The Meaning of Industrial Freedom* is partially lost. Cole tried to restore this feeling by opening up other freedoms, especially for people other than the manual workers, but these new freedoms do not succeed. Instead they blur the outlines of Guild Society to allow previously banned forms of activity, especially small business. In being more practicable, the Guild Commune loses the sort of socialist utopianism which made it an entirely new world; it becomes a retouched, somewhat equalized Great Britain. Cole could no longer defend it as the best possible society; he was reduced simply to arguing that it was much better than capitalist Britain.

I am conscious also that the impression conveyed by this book . . . may be that of a terrible and bewildering complexity of social organization in which the individual will be lost. I ask any one who is inclined to hold that view to devote a brief period to studying the social organization of to-day, not merely in its parliamentary and political forms, but with all its complexity of capitalism, labor, professional, cultural, and other forms of association. Let him then ask himself which is the more complicated, and whether it is not the case that the conditions of to-day result everywhere in a medley of conflicting and warring associations formed, for the most part, in order not to fulfil a social function, but to get the best one of another. He will find the structure which I have described both far less complicated and far better adapted to its purpose than the structure of existing capitalist Society.[2]

By the time Cole wrote this, the process of building a utopia had nearly destroyed the idealism which was its source.

[1] Ibid., pp. 150–1.
[2] Ibid., pp. 159–60.

CHAPTER 3

THE FLOWERING AND DISINTEGRATION OF GUILD SOCIALISM

While evolving such a precise picture of the principles and institutions which should form a Guild Society, Cole had to face the problem of achieving it. Cole did not think out his utopia first and then ask how to get there; the two processes were simultaneous. The techniques of getting to a Guild Society left a profound impact on what that society would be. The whole construction of his utopia depended on the fact that the Guilds could grow out of Trade Unionism. But the utopia came first logically; its principles were established first in Cole's mind. Cole knew two worlds, the existing world and the world of socialism, even when he had not yet constructed an institutional model of socialism. He thought of the process of moving from the one to the other as a transition in which there were fewer principles guiding his thought. He was more prepared to be pragmatic about politics on the path to the Guilds.

This did not demote the transitional steps to a lower rank; in fact, it made Cole spend more time thinking about them. As he said, 'It is of no use to cry "Control", without formulating as clearly as possible the next steps that have to be taken in the direction of control.'[1] These steps greatly depended on the state of the Labour movement. They were extrapolations of the most energetic parts of the movement. Cole's major solution to the problem of transition was the idea of encroaching control, which relied upon the militancy shown by the shop stewards and other workshop organizations towards the end of the First World War. The idea of encroaching control faded as these organizations ran into greater difficulties after the war; Cole went on to consider the uses of political and revolutionary action. Finally, after the failure of the Miners' Bill, Cole found the formation of working Guilds the only hope of obtaining Guild Socialism.

During the early and middle years of the war, Cole was not able to

[1] G. D. H. Cole, *Self-Government in Industry* (London, G. Bell & Sons, 1917), pp. 21–2.

find an adequate vehicle for the transition to Guild Socialism. As the war dragged on, and as sections of the working classes showed increased distaste for it, the end of this period of forced waiting came into sight. In the summer of 1917, Cole published his first book on the ideas of Guild Socialism, *Self-Government in Industry*. The Preface reveals how the war had held back his reassessment of the aims and policies of the Guild movement. 'This book was originally planned in 1913, as a sequel to my "World of Labour",' he wrote. 'I threw it aside on the outbreak of war; but during the past year I have thoroughly revised it, and added so much new matter as to make it practically a different book.'[1]

The publication of *Self-Government in Industry* is symbolic, for it indicates that Cole was beginning to emerge from the war-induced position of defence. The curve of Labour's militancy, and thus of Cole's, was beginning to rise again. A magnificent example of this – and of its limitations – occurred when the *Herald* arranged to hold a pro-Russian rally at the Albert Hall in 1918. The management found a pretext for denying the use of the hall, so the electricians pulled the fuses and left the management with no choice but to allow the rally to take place.[2] Labour militants were willing to interpret such a token resistance as the sign of a new spirit. S. G. Hobson wrote in his autobiography: 'In this hectic atmosphere thousands of wage-earners had a new vision. They were not thinking of the cut of their clothes or the shape of their boots; they were dreaming of a new spirit, perhaps even a new regime, in the workshop.'[3]

In this somewhat unreal atmosphere, the individuals and groups with ideas of a new society thrived, and the workers seemed to go along with them. Militants and intellectuals influenced each other as they experienced, for a short time, substantial agreement on goals and short-run policies. The shop stewards had tapped a pool of energy, which might lead to a reorganization of the forces of Labour around the workshop and the creation of an 'industrial army'. The big unions, as they prepared their demands, added workers' control to their

[1] *Self-Government in Industry*, p. vii.
[2] George Lansbury, *The Miracle of Fleet Street: The Story of the Daily Herald* (London, Labour Publishing Co., 1925), pp. 60–4.
[3] S. G. Hobson, *Pilgrim to the Left: Memoirs of a Modern Revolutionist* (London, Edward Arnold & Co., 1938), p. 193.

nationalization schemes. The N.G.L. and L.R.D. found themselves called upon for facts and advice. These were all signs that could feed a basic confidence. In such an atmosphere, utopianizing became practical politics.

This atmosphere of Reconstruction was the last burst of the optimistic mood of 1914. It sprang up again, all the stronger for the years of tension which had intervened. Intellectuals and cranks of all sorts raced to offer schemes for a new England. The advocates of nationalization, profit-sharing, and co-partnership reappeared. The most prominent of the new proposals, other than the Guild Socialist, was that of the Whitley Councils, which also claimed to satisfy the workers' demand for control of industry. These rival schemes helped force Cole into the arena, to combat an inadequate measure of workers' control with the real thing. But his entry with plans based on Guild Socialism was not simply opposition to the facile schemes and slogan-stealing of others; it was a genuine attempt to seize upon a real opportunity.

The reformers could hardly have had an inkling of the disasters ahead that would make mincemeat of their hopes. Not even the most jaundiced could have foreseen the massive unemployment of the 1920s and 1930s. Even when the Socialists wrote that capitalism had demonstrated its incompetence during the war and would collapse, they saw this impending collapse as an opportunity, not as chaos. The capitalist superstructure would disintegrate, and Socialists would then build their new society. Cole himself believed in 'the general adaptability of the economic system'.[1]

The optimism of Reconstruction also depended on estimates of the popular desire for a new society. S. G. Hobson exemplified one extreme: 'Will young men, who now understand the rifle, the barricade, the wild whirling joy of a dash against the enemy with death as possible guerdon, contentedly lapse into wage-servitude?'[2] Cole, much calmer and less romantic, still accepted a mild form of the same assumption:

Mr Sidney Webb ... said, apparently with satisfaction, that the workers would return from military service in a more disciplined frame of mind, and that one effect of the war would be to crush the spirit of revolt ... It seems at least as probable that those who return from a life spent in the open air will

[1] G. D. H. Cole, *Labour in War-Time* (London, G. Bell & Sons, 1915), p. 277–8.
[2] 'Guild Principles and the War', *New Age*, vol. XVI (19 November 1914), 67.

be far more intolerant of the routine and the petty oppressions of the work-shop, and far readier for some sort of revolt against it. Here is at least a hope that the coming of peace will herald the coming of a more militant Trade Unionism.[1]

Clearly Cole's assessment of Labour's opportunities was more cautious. His works were full of attempts to predict the forces which could be used against a reconstruction of society; he constantly sought to anticipate the ways in which Labour could be led astray. But these cautions and predictions were pessimistic according to Sorel's use of the word, not in the commonly accepted sense. Cole made them in order to increase the workers' chances of reconstructing society, not to dissuade anyone from making the attempt.

The two revolutions of 1917 in Russia came at the right psychological moment to feed these hopes. The first revolution stimulated the general desire for peace and regeneration; the second revolution drew a more directly socialist response. 'At once, the world was confronted with a new situation. In one Commonwealth – and that until recently the most reactionary of all – the working class was in power, and the "rights of property" were overthrown.'[2] The early libertarian and socialist tones of the Russian Revolution made a profound impact on Cole. Whatever else happened, however much Cole disagreed with Russian internal and foreign policy, he never lost the conviction that the Russians had brought about the first revolution against capitalism. In his *History of Socialist Thought*, he perceptively noted that 'there was ... among Socialists in the advanced capitalist countries, a certain sense of guilt because the Russians, who were deemed so backward, *had* overthrown both Czarism and capitalism and had put a kind of Socialism in their place ...'.[3] This feeling of guilt, and other feelings which went along with it, gave the Soviet Union a claim for respect and support which was reinforced by the allied attempts to aid counter-revolutionary movements in Russia and in Poland. In 1920, when he was already beginning to come under Communist attack, Cole main-

---

[1] *Labour in War-Time*, p. 289.
[2] G. D. H. Cole, *Labour in the Commonwealth: A Book for the Younger Generation* (n.p., n.d.), pp. 51–2. A review by Robin Page Arnot, *The Guildsman*, No. 31 (June 1919), p. 9, gives the publisher as Headley Bros., probably of London; the date of publication is probably early 1919.
[3] IV: *Communism and Social Democracy*, i. 4.

tained that 'It seems to us to be the bounden duty of every Guildsman to support a Socialist revolution against capitalism, in this country or in any other, however he may dislike, or even disapprove of, the methods which it employs.'[1]

From 1917 down to the middle of 1919, Cole's basic attitude was one of benevolent curiosity. It was hard to get information about Russia that could be relied upon, but Cole, using the pseudonym, 'Hussein', devotedly reported in *The Guildsman* on all the books that appeared. Every little scrap of news could be used to buoy up militant spirits. The burning question, to Cole, was whether the Russian showed signs of progress towards a Guild system. He liked the increased power that unions and co-operatives seemed to have in Russia after the second revolution. Soviet practice seemed to enshrine Guild principles of workers' control and decentralization. Margaret Cole reported for *The Guildsman* on a lecture Cole delivered to the London group of the N.G.L.:

He did not actually advocate swallowing the Soviet system whole, explaining that it expressed a need rather than a theory . . . but suggested that the most interesting fact was the tendency to divide, to set up workshop committees for the controlling of industry, leaving the rest to the local Soviet, linked up federally in a Central Soviet, and a National Congress of Soviets. These two facts – the separate representation of industry and politics, and the federal organization of the State – are what commend the Soviet system to Cole's mind.[2]

These hopeful signs led Cole to conclude, 'I believe that the natural evolution of the Soviet system, in time of peace, will be towards a solution on Guild lines'.[2] Thus the Russian revolution reinforced his militancy; it was not until the middle of 1919 that Russian developments clearly diverged from Guild lines, and began to pose problems for Guild Socialism.

From the very beginning, Guild Socialism had been a reaction against nationalization, the dominant Labour policy for the transition

[1] 'CC', 'Notes of the Month', *The Guildsman*, No. 38 (February 1920), p. 2. 'CC' indicates that the Coles wrote these notes; I am assuming that anything published under their initials would reflect G. D. H. Cole's point of view, although Margaret Cole may well have written the passage quoted.

[2] M.I.C., 'Guildsmen and the State', *The Guildsman*, No. 30 (May 1919), p. 8.

[3] G. D. H. Cole, 'Guilds at Home and Abroad', *The Guildsman*, No. 34 (October 1919), p. 10.

to Socialism. Nationalization meant reliance upon politics and Parliamentary organization; Hobson and Orage reversed this Fabian emphasis upon politics. 'E.P.P.P.P.', or 'Economic power precedes political power',[1] was their slogan. Cole agreed with them. The essential problem was to introduce democracy into the distribution and exercise of economic power. Consequently, the workers had to increase their economic power and extend it to cover new areas. The Trade Unions, as the economic voice of the workers, were necessarily the vehicle for attaining Guild Socialism; Cole had decided this by the time he published *The World of Labour*. Here was the prime form of working-class organization, already showing signs of wishing to remake society. Cole gained hope from a decade of militant outbursts, from the pre-war strikes, Industrial Unionists and Syndicalists, through the shop stewards' movement to the miners and railway workers in 1920. He felt that his speculations made conscious and articulate the real demand present in the workers' actions. The realization of Guild Socialism, he wrote in 1920,

... is made necessary and possible by the emergence and power of Trade Unionism, and Trade Unionism is the principal instrument by means of which it must be brought about. The growing strength of Trade Unionism is beginning to make impossible the continuance of industry under the old conditions; there is no remedy but in making Trade Unionism itself the nucleus of a new industrial order. Our problem, then, is that of turning Trade Unions into National Guilds.[2]

Cole and his friends in the N.G.L. and L.R.D. understood the unions much better than did Hobson, Orage, and Penty. Consequently, they were prepared to take over the task of developing Guild theory and strategy. Theories about the Guilds were, in one sense, a mammoth projection of tendencies already at work. The unions had to become the basis of the Guilds, changing from instruments of protection into instruments of self-government. The strategy of Guild Socialism depended even more closely upon the direction taken by trade unionism. Several forces, especially Industrial Unionism, the amalgamation movement, and the shop stewards, all had much to offer, but their

[1] See S. G. Hobson, *National Guilds: An Inquiry into the Wage System and the Way Out*, 3rd ed. (London, G. Bell & Sons, 1919), p. 16.
[2] G. D. H. Cole, *Chaos and Order in Industry* (London, Methuen, 1920), p. 45.

popularity fluctuated considerably. Cole and his friends had to keep abreast of the latest developments, to side with the forces that offered most for Guild Socialism.

Primarily Cole sought changes in trade unionism that would increase democracy, both within the unions and in relation to employers. This was both the means and a goal, on many levels. It was the purpose of Guild organization, as well as being good in itself for industry as it existed. But Cole also felt deeply that greater internal democracy would increase the militancy of the Labour movement as a whole.

It is important to notice that to Cole Guild Socialist policy, trade union structure, and the attitude of the workers were inseparable. From the very beginning of his Guild writings, Cole offered the unions the crystallization of an attitude – the urge for self-government or workers' control. That is, his policy was simply the progressive realization of its motivating impulse. Policy and union structure had to meet the basic requirements of giving the workers a taste for control and of educating them in the arts of self-government – and the only way to do it was to give the workers increasing amounts of control. To this basic policy Cole gave the name 'encroaching control'. In *Chaos and Order in Industry*, Cole gave a useful brief definition of encroaching control: 'In general terms, it may be defined as a policy of transferring from the employer or his representatives to the organized workers through their Trade Unions and workshop organizations as many as possible of the functions at present controlled by capitalism in the sphere of production.'[1] Elsewhere, Cole made it quite clear that this meant the total transfer of all suitable functions, for he was faced with slogan-stealing competitors such as the Whitley Councils and various forms of 'co-partnership'.

It is not the same as 'joint control', with which it is sometimes confused; for 'joint control' aims at the cooperative exercise of certain functions by employers and employed, whereas 'encroaching control' aims at taking certain powers right out of the employers' hands, and transferring them completely to the organized workers. A quite simple instance will plainly illustrate this fundamental difference. 'Joint control' involves joint works committees, on which employer and employed work together; 'encroaching control' involves Trade Union shop stewards' committees, which the employer has to

[1] *Chaos and Order*, p. 117.

recognise, but to which neither he nor any representative of his interests is admitted.[1]

Thus Cole wanted to establish a stringent set of requirements for encroaching control, to prevent the workers from being led into bargaining machinery that would tie them closer to the capitalist system. '... the maintenance of the strength and independence of Trade Unionism must be in all things the first consideration; and no immediate step that seems a gain, however great, must be taken if it involves, even in the slightest degree, a sacrifice of Trade Union independence or strength'.[2] Labour must not undertake to guarantee profits or to make its pay depend upon profits, and it must reserve the right to terminate any agreements whenever feasible.

But Cole's own urge to be practical often forced him to transgress this rule. Neither management nor the Unions could commit themselves to such uncompromising positions. And Cole was ready to accept many forms of collective bargaining as first steps towards encroaching control. In general, he argued that whatever machinery existed should be used. In the Storrington Document, the founders of the N.G.L. asserted that

> ... the Trade Unions must secure machinery for the exercise of ... continuous interference. Such machinery will in many cases develop out of the existing machinery of arbitration. Conciliation and Arbitration Boards, which have so far served to tie down the workers and to impose upon them the final verdict of a supposedly 'impartial' authority, must be changed into Negotiation Boards, free from all restrictive agreements and recourse to external authority. The object of this negotiation will be not merely to deal with questions of wages, conditions and discipline, but also to assume an ever-increasing control of management.

What mattered was not the machinery, but the spirit in which it was used. If it were used in the spirit of class warfare without binding the workers to the existing modes of production and exploitation, virtually any tactic was acceptable.

Encroaching control operated on a basic principle: If a function were removed from the hands of the employers, it would weaken their

---

[1] *Guild Socialism Re-stated*, pp. 196–7.
[2] *Self-Government in Industry*, p. 328. See also G. D. H. Cole, *The World of Labour* (London, G. Bell & Sons, 1913), pp. 285–9, 318–19.

general position, make it more difficult for them to exploit their workers, and perhaps reduce them to impotence.

A class that becomes atrophied is doomed to decay. The power of any class in any stage of human society rests ultimately upon the performance of functions. These functions may be socially useful or anti-social: an anti-social function may be just as good an instrument of survival as a social function. But as soon as a class is left without functions the decay of its power and prestige can be only a matter of time . . . we, in our day and generation, shall succeed in overthrowing industrial capitalism only if we first make it socially functionless.[1]

We can see the fragility of this basic principle, but for a time Cole could not. He came at it from the other side, seeking a plausible way to socialism. In the concept of encroaching control Cole felt that he had found a formula which made intelligible what the unions had been doing. Assuming that the function of Trade Unionism was to conduct class-struggle and that enough of the workers could be brought to fight for control, encroaching control became reasonable. It filled his intellectual needs; developing from their present activities, it directly linked the unions to the Guild future. Logically, it was thus more likely to bring about its aim than direct revolution.

This transference is, indeed, a logical development of Trade Union activity as it has existed in the past. The aim of the Trade Unions in the various trades and industries has been so as to organize the workers as to control the supply of labour, and by means of this control to prescribe conditions with which the employer must comply in order to get labour to work for him.[2]

Encroaching control was merely a matter of extending and making positive an existing encroachment upon the jealously-guarded pre-rogatives of management.

The place to begin, Cole felt, was with the workshop. In the work-shop the workers faced the power of capitalism directly; there they learned to desire control. There also individual workers could directly attack in a democratic fashion. The workers could concentrate their power on taking over specific functions, which Cole considered the outposts of capitalism. Questions concerning the manning of machines, the tempo of work, and the introduction of new processes were among

[1] *Self-Government in Industry*, p. 173.
[2] *Chaos and Order in Industry*, p. 117.

these 'outposts'. The main function of management which had to be threatened was discipline. The unions had to establish control over discipline.

by taking from the employer and transferring to themselves the right to appoint workshop supervisors, foremen, and the like, and so making the discipline of the shop a matter, no longer of imposition from without, but of self regulation by the group as a whole.[1]

The most complete form of encroachment upon discipline in the workshop that Cole could imagine was the 'collective contract'. The collective contract would make the local Union the effective operator of a factory or workshop. The Union would contract to perform the necessary labour,

. . . substituting as far as possible for the present individual relationship of the employer to each worker, whom he, through his representatives, hires, fires, and remunerates individually, a collective relationship to the employer of all the workers in the shop, so that the necessary labour is in future supplied by the Union, and the workers substitute their own collective regulations for 'hiring and firing' for these of the employer, and, wherever possible, enter into a collective contract with him to cover the whole output of the shop, and themselves, according to their own Union regulations, apportion the work and share out the payment received.[2]

The concept of a collective contract has an interesting history. It was probably adapted from Labour customs;[3] Cole and his friends stated it vaguely in the Storrington Document, and it received further elaboration at the hands of John Paton, a young toolmaker from the Clyde who became Organizing Secretary of the N.G.L.

Neither this concept nor the broader idea of encroaching control obtained widespread application. One may feel that this was because the concepts themselves were so fragile. They demanded a careful, subtle dedication to bringing about revolution by conscious encroachments. These encroachments underestimated the intelligence of the employers, while posing heavy demands on the patience of the workers

[1] *Guild Socialism Re-stated*, pp. 198–9.
[2] *Guild Socialism Re-stated*, p. 199.
[3] One precedent known to Cole was the butty system in coal mining, in which a miner would contract to work a particular seam and then hire fellow-workers to help him. Collective contract differs from the butty system in being a union function, and in that the reward would be negotiated rather than set by competitive pressures. The ganger system of Coventry stands midway between the butty system and a collective contract.

who wanted self-government. The militant minority tended to tire of the deliberate, roundabout approach of the Guildsmen; the idea of direct revolution gained ground among the shop stewards, some of whom later participated in the formation of the British Communist Party.

But much of the failure of the concept of encroaching control lay not so much in the idea itself, as in the rapid change of conditions after the First World War. Encroaching control was an effort to describe the possible evolution of the Labour movement in a period of intense local effort, strong irritation with rising prices and infringements of working rules and high employment. These conditions prevailed at the end of the First World War, and, as long as they prevailed, the ideas of the Guildsmen made converts among some of the important union leaders of the younger generation – Frank Hodges, Robert Smillie, George Thomson of the Draughtsmen, George Hicks and Harold Clay.[1] But within three years, all three of these conditions had vanished, and the idea of encroaching control could not survive without them.

The final weakness of the idea of encroaching control was that it depended upon local action. During the First World War, this was not a weakness, for neither business nor the Government was prepared to crush a local union in a strategic position. However, in a society dominated by concentrated economic power, purely local action could in normal circumstances be easily overcome. Trade Unionism therefore had to develop national power to match the power of the employers. Cole realized this even before he developed his theories of encroaching control. In speculating about the kind of national power that Labour needed, Cole relied heavily upon ideas developed by the Industrial Unionists during the strike wave that preceded the First World War. These ideas had accompanying defects which bedevilled Cole. On the one hand, Industrial Unionism conflicted strongly with the realities of British unionism, which had grown up in a haphazard fashion. On the other hand, even if Industrial Unionism could be created, it would not necessarily lead to Guild Socialism. But it was a practical necessity.

[1] See articles by Frank Hodges and Robert Smillie in Arthur Gleason, *What the Workers Want* (New York, Harcourt Brace, 1920); Margaret Cole, *Growing Up Into Revolution* (London, Longmans Green, 1949), p. 70.

No other form of working-class organization could possibly provide enough force to fight capitalism. Craft unions had a dual weakness, of will-power and man-power. They were too much divided among themselves, and sought sectional interests rather than pursuing the class war. They refused to enrol unskilled workers and obtained higher wages than less favoured members of the working-class. On the other hand, 'Industrial Unionism ... alone is consistent with the class struggle; it alone is true to the principle of democracy and fraternity'.[1] Industrial unions organized all the workers in major industries, and met the employers head on. They could paralyse capitalism and take over responsibility for running industries.

Once he had decided that industrial unions were the proper mode of national organization, Cole was able to improve theories about the transition to Guild society. In the articles that first stated the Guild ideal S. G. Hobson had spoken vaguely of making unions 'black-leg proof' so that they could seize control. Cole had gained with his friends in the L.R.D. a knowledge of the unions that older Guildsmen could not match, and could specify the changes needed in various industries more precisely and realistically. He had an intimate knowledge of the actual jungle of tangled jurisdictions and rights in which Industrial Unionists and various unofficial amalgamation movements operated. Long after the end of Guild Socialism he continued to repeat his arguments for trade union reorganization.

It was not enough to build industrial unions to seize power. Unlike most Industrial Unionists, Cole argued that the form in which power was obtained was crucial, for it would determine the shape of society to come. If they were organized properly, industrial unions could grow directly into Guilds. However, many efforts to create industrial unions also contained defects that could impede the growth of self-government in industry. In particular, Cole wanted to oppose those forms of industrial unionism that would unite workers who would later have to be separated into different Guilds. Some, in their eagerness to match the power of the employer, wanted something closer to 'company unionism'. That is, they wanted an industrial union to include all the services or products manufactured by a particular company, so that hotels run by railway companies would be unionized by the N.U.R. instead of by

[1] *Self-Government in Industry*, p. 132.

the ancestor of a Distributive Guild or Collective Utilities Guild. The general labour unions created other demarcation difficulties for Cole. He argued that these unions should not attempt to organize their workers permanently, but should constitute a 'general clearing-house for labour', funnelling their members into true industrial unions as rapidly as possible. This idea, of course, was not likely to take root; the general unions, which were often quite militant, paid lip-service to Industrial Unionism, but generally meant by it that they were to become the 'One Big Union' beloved of Industrial Unionists.[1]

While Cole hoped to replace more than eleven hundred unions with some twenty industrial unions, he had to recognize that the craft principle had validity and should not simply be destroyed. Workers using a particular process and sharing certain skills had a genuine common interest, even though that interest would have to be subordinated to their class interest. Cole recommended the procedure which the N.U.R. had adopted, that of granting internal representation to crafts within a national union. We have already seen him use the same principle in describing forms of representation within Guilds.

Cole recognized that many problems in amalgamating unions could not receive simple logical answers. Officials and workers often had vested interests which could not be ignored. A union with stronger finances would not want to be saddled with members of a more militant union who might exhaust their strike fund or obtain more in benefits than they had contributed. Cole recommended that the pension funds of the existing unions be kept separate, while a new fund were established for the amalgamated union, but this did not completely solve the problem.

Cole felt that amalgamation offered an unparalleled chance to replace fossilized officials. At least one reader of the *Herald* felt that Cole was preaching disloyalty, but he was not. The Industrial Unionists were ready to create new, rival industrial unions to compete with existing unions; Cole, however, recognized the futility of going outside the

---

[1] G. D. H. Cole, 'The Problem of Trade Union Structure: V', *Herald* (10 March 1917); Cole and Mellor, 'The Hope for the Greater Unionism', *Daily Herald* (31 March 1914), p. 4; *Chaos and Order in Industry*, pp. 146–7.

existing union machinery. But he did feel that many union leaders had a proprietary feeling towards their members:

> 'I am a blessèd Glendoveer:
> 'Tis mine to speak, and yours to hear.'

There are Glendovers and to spare in the Labour movement, and the powers that be take great delight in calling them 'blessed'.[1]

In the interests of internal democracy and of the class struggle alike such leaders had to go; when it came to such a decision, Cole was ready to sacrifice the hard-won supremacies of leaders without meaning to incite disloyalty in the Labour movement. But inevitably the less militant among the officials would defend themselves with such charges.

Any effort to reorganize British Trade Unionism along industrial lines thus ran into problems that by themselves could have kept Cole busy for the rest of his life, with little prospect of success. Nor was Industrial Unionism the whole solution to the problem of creating a union structure that could wage class war. Even industrial unions would have to be coordinated into a single effective force. For two reasons, Cole found it hard to suggest a solution to this problem. He supposed that there would have to be some sort of 'general staff of Labour', but there were rival claimants to the position. At first, he tended to side with the General Federation of Trade Unions, but he later dropped it when it ran into difficulties. Neither the T.U.C. nor the joint committee formed by the T.U.C. with the reconstructed Labour Party satisfied him completely.[2] The more basic reason for his vagueness was that, while some sort of 'general staff' was necessary for short-term Labour policy, it would perhaps be an obstacle to the necessary decentralization of Guild Socialism. He argued that, in a Guild Society, there would be no reason for anyone to oppose decentralization; but we may feel that this was wishful thinking. The dilemma was central – for fighting purposes, Labour had to create 'One Big Union' or a reasonable substitute, but this would imperil the growth of workshop democracy necessary to prepare the workers to fight for Guild Socialism.

---

[1] *Self-Government in Industry*, p. 137.
[2] *The World of Labour*, pp. 243 ff.; Cole and Mellor, 'Open Letters to the Trade Union Movement: II', *Herald* (14 August 1915).

Furthermore, as Cole became aware of these theoretical and practical weaknesses in his reliance upon industrial unionism and encroaching control, he discovered a fundamental limitation upon their effectiveness. As he began to study those community needs which must be incorporated into the Guild Commune, he saw that strikes, collective contracts, and other industrial encroachments would not destroy the financial power of capitalism. Even if the employers could be forced to grant the management of the factories to the workers, Guild Socialism would be far away.

The democratic government of the factory by those engaged in it would be the plainest sign of a change in industry. But it would not by itself destroy the wage-system. The employer might hand the management of his factory over absolutely to the workers employed in it, or even to the Trade Union of their industry . . . And, having done all this, he might conceivably continue much where he is to-day – he might go on buying and selling commodities or stocks and shares, and he might still draw from the community his toll of rent, interest and profits. Having won the control of the factory, the workers would only have democratized the management; they would not have overthrown the wage-system, or socialized industry itself.[1]

Thus, Cole realized that he would have to devise a way of ousting the current possessors of industry, finance, and power not only from the direct control of production, but also from the control of capital and marketing which indirectly controlled the lives of the workers. As the urgency of this problem grew in his mind, Cole turned back towards traditional solutions. We have already noticed that he wanted the Co-operative movement to take over many distributive processes in the Guild Commune; the early co-operators had had similar hopes. But Cole felt that the co-operatives could not become the main means of gaining control of finance and marketing. He therefore wavered between the two classic answers to the problem – the collectivist use of political means, and the Syndicalist idea of a general strike, or some other means of direct, possibly violent, revolution.

In *The World of Labour*, Cole had rejected both revolution, whether by conspiracy or by the general strike, and Parliamentary politics. When he reconsidered them after the First World War, he did not discard his concept of encroaching control. He asserted that neither revolution nor political action could succeed unless encroaching control

[1] *Self-Government in Industry*, pp. 170–1.

had prepared the way, by giving the Labour movement more economic power and by inspiring the workers to desire democratic control of industry.[1] However, he did not really integrate his belief in encroaching control with either political action or revolution. Rather, he changed the direction from which he approached the problem. Encroaching control was logical when one worked backward from Guild Socialism towards current social organization. Contemporary developments in Russia and in England forced Cole to consider revolution and political action. He had to evaluate each proposal pragmatically, to see whether either revolution or Parliamentary action could lead to Guild Socialism, and whether either was attracting the support among Labour militants needed for success. Much would also depend on how the capitalists chose to protect their privileges. These questions came to a head in 1919 and 1920, when the Sankey Commission was discussing the nationalization of coal and when some of the shop stewards and other militants were considering forming a Communist Party. Cole debated them with his friends in the N.G.L. and the L.R.D.; their arguments helped shape the alternatives among which he had to choose.

Most of the Guildsmen's early work had dealt with the 'Guild Idea'; after the war, however, many felt that the movement would have to advance beyond propaganda and criticism. In 1919 the Guildsmen tried to make the League into an instrument for obtaining influence and acting 'practically'.

G. D. H. Cole outlined, on behalf of the Executive, a scheme for throwing the whole of our resources into an immediate campaign for greatly augmenting our funds and widening the range of our propaganda. In this venture we had been promised the help of Mr Clifford Allen. It was proposed to hire an office, and to engage two full-time paid officers – one for organizing and secretarial work, the other for clerical duties.[2]

In Cole's mind, practical action meant closer association with other sections of the Labour movement. His personal activities ranged throughout the whole movement; and he wanted to bring the League, as the propaganda body concerned with the way society should be reconstructed, into a similar connection with the rest of Labour. Cole

---

[1] *Guild Socialism Re-stated*, pp. 185–7.
[2] A.E.B., 'Guildsmen in Conference', *The Guildsman*, No. 32 (July–August 1919), pp. 9–11.

argued that the N.G.L. had to make clear its stance on the left wing of the Labour movement.

The need for working-class solidarity led Cole to support the policies pursued by other sections of the movement. In 1920, he argued that 'Labour is always right',[1] accepting the means to socialization that the workers seemed to want, and denying that the tension between his methods and those preferred elsewhere in the movement was irreconcilable. He took the N.G.L. into the agitation for the Miners' Bill, even though this meant accepting Parliamentary tactics. This stand threatened to alienate both the 'Right' of the N.G.L., which had little commitment to socialism, and the 'Left', which was considering more revolutionary tactics. His participation in the agitation for coal nationalization included several appearances as a Labour witness before the Sankey Commission. Cole argued that nationalization should be accompanied by local workers' control measures. Unfortunately, he mentioned in his testimony some Derbyshire pit committees, and was later unable to give more detailed evidence.[2] This failure damaged the case for workers' control, but to attribute any importance to this failure would be to ignore the Government's unwillingness to use the Sankey Commission's conclusions.

Such a policy meant that Cole had to temper his deep-seated antipathy to Parliamentary politics. He was incapable of playing the 'politique du pire', hoping for everyone else's plans to fail so that his own pet projects could be left with no opposition. Cole justified his renewed interest in politics in the terms of his early Guild Socialist utopia:

Is not our object to bring into being a system of democratic Guilds working in conjunction with a democratic State? Can we regard the structure and form of that State as irrelevant to the creation of National Guilds, or to the realization of Guild Socialism?[3]

This led him to an interesting reappraisal of the National Guilds League's emphasis on industrial action, which had been codified in 'encroaching control' and 'collective contract'. Orage had summed it

[1] CC, 'Notes of the Month', *The Guildsman*, no. 48 (December 1920), p. 2.
[2] See Cole's testimony, reprinted in Arthur Gleason, *What the Workers Want*, pp. 409 ff.
[3] G. D. H. Cole, 'Political Action and the N.G.L.', *The Guildsman*, No. 27 (February 1919), pp. 22–3.

up in the motto, 'Economic power precedes political power'. Before the war, Cole himself would have been moved to interpret this in a Syndicalist manner, insisting that politics were nearly worthless;[1] but by 1919 he had changed his mind. 'E.P.P.P.P.'

only meant that political action is secondary to industrial action, and does not at all absolve us from the necessity of making up our minds about its form and content . . . we must work at the reorganization, and also at the limitation in function and power, of the State from within by means of political action.[2]

In another two years, he would no longer even assert that 'political action is secondary to industrial action.'[3]

In other words, Cole retreated from his strong antipathy towards Fabianism. The Fabian side to his social philosophy became prominent once more as he turned his attention to the short-term needs of Labour. He accepted collectivist policies as a half-way house to Guild Socialism. The crucial case was nationalization, which the miners and the railwaymen saw as their next step. Cole accepted this, and sought to draw solace from it. He argued that nationalization could provide Guild Socialists with several advantages:

. . . it makes the adoption of a reasonable form of control possible in the nationalized industry, and . . . by reducing the capitalist to a more obviously functionless bond-holder or rentier, it makes far easier the subsequent annihilation of his claim, which ceases to have even the apparent relation to social service arrogated at present.[4]

He contended forcefully that a centralized, nationalized industry created the kind of environment in which the workers would realize the importance of their controlling production. Bureaucratic control would awaken their desire for freedom. It would drive them into constant encroachments on 'the prerogatives of management' in order to remove minor grievances.

---

[1] *The World of Labour*, p. 400; but he carefully said that political action would have long-range uses when Labour's impotence had been overcome by industrial means.

[2] G. D. H. Cole, 'Political Action and the N.G.L.', *The Guildsman*, No. 27 (February 1919), pp. 2–3.

[3] See CC, 'Notes of the Month', *The Guild Socialist*, No. 57 (September 1921), p. 2. The name of *The Guildsman* was changed to *The Guild Socialist* in July 1921 when it was discovered that a Church journal had the same name. Issues of the journal under its two names bore consecutive numbers.

[4] *Guild Socialism Re-stated*, p. 206.

Cole still had his doubts concerning nationalized industries and other forms of state control, but he was willing to run the risk rather than allow capitalism to regain unquestioned ownership of the means of production. A resolution he proposed to the 1919 Annual Conference of the N.G.L. reveals his ambivalence concerning the short-term uses of state action. While he proposed 'the nationalization of industry over the widest possible area', because the trade unions could not take over the trading and financial functions of capitalism, he did not desire a fully nationalized economy. In industries which were not nationalized, he recommended 'as a temporary measure the continuance and extension after the war of the method of State control through representative bodies which is now in force in several industries'. Such a mild policy raised the spectre of co-opting the workers into 'immoral profiteering conspiracies'. Cole warded off the spectre with a reference to 'equal Labour representation and full publicity of proceedings'. 'Full publicity of proceedings' clearly raises echoes of the Webbs' famous slogan, 'measurement and publicity'. Representative bodies would be both a protection against an offensive by the employers, and the first step towards full workers' control. In the meantime, the state should be kept out of the workshop. Given these safeguards, state control and nationalization were safe enough to be of use to the workers.[1] Cole argued that contemporary needs and the progress of the Guild movement had made the common pre-war talk of the 'Servile State' out of date.

Nationalization had fundamental defects that had made Cole reject it as a means of obtaining Socialism before the First World War. The need to reconsider it did not remove his objections, although it offset them to some extent. Nationalization by purchase of basic industries would hardly change the basic structure of society. In a brilliant passage, Cole had inverted one of the basic Fabian metaphors:

'Municipal debt is only municipal capital.' How easily, in their anxiety to find an answer to Moderates grousing at the growth of municipal indebtedness, Socialists swallowed that plausible debating answer of Mr Shaw's. A municipality desires to own its tramways – it therefore buys out the existing company. It then owns its trams; but in acquiring them it has run up a debt. But, we are told, just as the indebtedness of any company is its capital, so

---

[1] 'N.G.L.: Third Annual Conference', *The Guildsman*, No. 20 (July 1918), pp. 9–10.

municipal debt is municipal capital. True; and, by a parity of reasoning, Municipal Socialism is Municipal Capitalism, and nothing else. Just as the company pays interest to its shareholders, the municipality continues to pay interest to private capitalists. It merely guarantees their dividends, which were before more or less precarious.[1]

Nationalization would probably substitute one property right for another, perpetuating the ruling class in a stronger position. The traditional answer to this criticism was that the Government could then tax this property right away from its possessors. However, we may feel that for the Government to be able to do this, it would need truly overwhelming strength and resolution. The proponents of nationalization expected the Government to gain this strength from having the physical control over production, if it did not already have it.

But if nationalization were to have these overtones of expropriation, Cole still doubted that it would occur. The financial power of the capitalist class was the major stumbling-block, as it had been for the theory of encroaching control.

The assumption of the financial functions of Capitalism by the State, even in the interests of the capitalist classes, would, indeed, do more than anything else to atrophy the capitalists; but for that very reason it can happen only through an egregious capitalist blunder. I should welcome the nationalization of banking and finance; but I do not expect them to happen . . . We cannot . . . afford to count on capitalist blunders . . .[2]

Thus, as Cole thought about ways of getting around the financial power of capitalism he began to work himself into a position from which he could see no really efficacious way of obtaining Guild Socialism. In such a mood, he was prepared to reconsider the idea of revolution.

Cole had always used the word 'revolution' in the intellectual Socialist manner, to refer to any sweeping change in the shape of society. He admitted that a revolution probably involved using some force, but argued that it didn't automatically mean civil war. Some sort of revolution would possibly accompany major changes, since the possessors of economic power might resort to violence to protect their

---

[1] *Self-Government in Industry*, p. 195.
[2] *Self-Government in Industry*, pp. 189–90.

interests. But this had been a rather academic speculation. By the beginning of 1920, however, the success of the Russian Revolution forced the ambiguities of 'revolution' on Cole's attention, driving him gradually to elaborate his views on the uses of force in society, the forcible changing of society, and the dictatorship of the proletariat. And, for the first time, these questions appeared within the movements to which Cole belonged as practical problems the answers to which would affect his actions. Until several months after the war, the Russian Revolution had remained purely a subject for external speculation. Then it rapidly divided various national Socialist movements, as some Socialists decided that the same processes must be followed in their own countries.

Cole could not ignore the possibility of a revolution; it was at least an open question to him. As late as September 1920, he would not have been surprised by direct action used on behalf of the miners and the Russians in Poland, which would have created a potentially revolutionary situation. And revolution had a sort of attraction to him. If revolution were possible, and if he would embrace it, it offered a shorter route to Guild Socialism. Reckitt wrote that

The Russian Revolution posed not only an intellectual but an emotional problem for Cole. Despite his somewhat remote, even chilly manner, Cole was at heart a romantic and warm-blooded Socialist, and 'revolution' had for him the attraction which it often has for the academic left-winger. 'All things that once were great out of destruction grew' was an apothegm which he was fond of quoting.[1]

Many of his closest friends were swayed by the idea of revolution, and it is natural that he gave it more attention for this reason. There was another reason, a personal one perhaps, for not ignoring revolution: One had to face facts without cowardice. Cole said in a lecture, 'The advocate of an evolutionary policy must . . . see that he did not lie under the suspicion of funking revolution or placing himself in opposition to it in principle'.[2]

The debate over revolution seems academic now, but it had an important impact upon his career. It signalled the end of one of his

---

[1] Maurice B. Reckitt, 'G. D. H. Cole, the L.R.D. and the N.G.L.', unpublished manuscript.
[2] 'Prospects of Guild Socialism', *The Guildsman*, No. 49 (January 1921), p. 9.

major periods of development. For several years, Cole had been growing mentally as part of a group working out the implications of a major idea. The fight over revolution disrupted the National Guilds League, destroying the fellowship which he prized so highly. It dealt Guild Socialism a crippling blow which contributed to its decline. At the same time, it saw the beginning of Cole's dissatisfaction with Guild Socialism, which grew until he was forced to rethink his position completely. Finally, the debate over revolution revealed Cole moving towards the tolerance and maturity of his later work for the Labour movement. In the debate, he tried to reach a solution that would be practical and might allow both the warring factions to continue to work for Guild Socialism.

Within the National Guilds League, all sorts of friendly divisions had developed before this occurred. Cole described them in 1919:

Like most young and growing ideas, it [Guild Socialism] attracts persons of very different temperament, training and interest – the worker, upon whom experience of the factory system has forced the consciousness of the need for industrial democracy – the professional, finding his desire to do good thwarted by the profiteering motives of capitalism – the theorist, finding in Guild Socialism a possible reconciliation of conflicting aims of which men are conscious in Society.[1]

There were bound to be tensions in a society which included ex-collectivists and ex-Syndicalists, pragmatists and idealistic theorists, shop stewards, middle-class intellectuals with religious or medievalist motives, and active socialists. Some members were much closer to Hobson's original idea of 'National Guilds' with a sovereign state than to Cole's developing Guild Commune speculations. By themselves, these divisions of opinion were not irreconcilable. None ranged over the whole area of Guild theory and practice, and general agreement was usually reached on short-run policy. The general atmosphere was, in Hobson's phrase, one of 'genial heresy-hunting' rather than war *a l'outrance*. In the 1917 Conference, for example, a strong debate over 'memorandum A' and 'memorandum B', two policy statements, had ended in an agreement to restudy the whole question. Neither side won; no one was willing to push the issue so far. But with the growing willingness of some Guildsmen to copy the Bolsheviks, the atmosphere

CC, 'Notes of the Month', *The Guildsman*, No. 33 (September 1919), p. 1.

was transformed. In 1920, for the first time, a really irreconcilable split developed. It crystallized around the issue of the Russian Revolution and the dictatorship of the proletariat.

The 'Right Wing' became noticeable as the end of the war brought the need for practical action. The label is not entirely accurate; in fact, A. E. Baker very cogently argued that the Right was really the Left, since it was more democratic and libertarian.[1] But the Guildsmen most influenced by the Soviets finally succeeded in labelling the group led by Maurice Reckitt, A. J. Penty, A. E. Baker, and Mrs Townshend as the Right. This group considered the Guilds a utopian ideal, which the N.G.L. had the duty to disseminate. They preferred Hobson's early picture of National Guilds, in which the state was a constituent element representing all the people as citizens, to Cole's later Guild Commune. Maurice Reckitt reaffirmed this in *The Guildsman*. 'I will not surrender a moral and positive ideal of the State in exchange either for a coercive mechanism or for a nebulous complex of "functional associations" which can be conveniently harmonised with the fashionable vocabulary of sovietism.'[2] For them, National Guilds were a non-partisan alternative to socialism, which they felt was outmoded. They were thus sceptical of Cole's efforts to move the N.G.L. closer to the Labour movement.

The Right remained true to the liberal values of Guild Socialism. They especially disliked the idea of the dictatorship of the proletariat, which threatened traditional negative liberties. Rowland Kenney argued that he would only accept a change in society brought about by rationally convincing a majority.[3] As tempers grew more frayed, this ideological purity looked like cowardice to some. Cole rather unfairly charged, in the discussion of the Soviet Resolution, that 'our right wing, in a panic lest something may really be going to happen, is trekking at its best speed for the land of spiritual values, in which gross material things may be forgotten'.[4] Cole's cruel reaction at this point probably owed something to the need to combat the appeal the Right

---

[1] 'The Leftward Way', *The Guildsman*, No. 41 (May 1920), p. 4.
[2] Maurice B. Reckitt, 'Guildsmen at the Cross Roads', *The Guildsman*, No. 41 (May 1920), pp. 4–5.
[3] 'Our Faction Fight', *The Guildsman*, No. 45 (September 1920), p. 4.
[4] G. D. H. Cole, 'Guilds at Home and Abroad', *The Guildsman*, No. 48 (December 1920), p. 10.

could make to his idealistic side. But he was uncomfortably aware of the weakness of fastidiousness in politics, and felt Guild Socialism had to adapt in order to grow.

The members of the Right did not ignore the inadequacy of encroaching control and political action, but they sought to avoid revolution by seizing upon the credit proposals expounded by Major Douglas and Orage in the *New Age* from 1919 on. Their acceptance of Social Credit was not fortuitous; as far back as 1917 members of the Right had considered finance the weak spot in Guild proposals for taking over society by industrial action. A system of national dividends eventually come to look to the Right like a way around this dilemma, gaining equality of incomes without the use of force and neutralizing the power of finance over industry. This would allow them to substitute an 'automatic' financial device for more drastic policies, accepting property but removing exploitation based on inequalities in property.[1] Cole considered the Douglas scheme in several articles in *The Guildsman*. He felt that Douglas' argument designed to prove the inevitable shortage of purchasing power was foolish, and that the Douglasites would not be able to destroy the financier with their little weapon. More fundamentally, Douglas accepted profits and interest, which were 'usury'.[2] In the 1930s, Cole returned to give Douglas a closer look, when he became more interested in the currency reformers; in 1920, however, this was enough to make Cole suspicious. The Right could not offer an alternative that met the live issues of the day, Cole felt; Major Douglas and the 'Guild Idea' were not enough.

Thus, by the beginning of 1920, the Right had rallied around a number of points that conflicted with the directions pursued by a majority of active Guildsmen. The dominant group in the N.G.L. had usually been a 'Centre-Left' collection comprising Cole, Mellor, Page Arnot, W. Norman Ewer, and many of the other prominent Guildsmen. In the Annual Conference of May 1920, this 'Centre-Left' group sponsored a 'Soviet Resolution' which offended the members of the Right. 'Cole, Mellor and Page Arnot were compared to Robespierre,

---

[1] C. E. Bechhofer and Maurice B. Reckitt, *The Meaning of National Guilds*, 2nd ed. (London, Cecil Palmer & Hayward, 1920), p. 262.

[2] G. D. H. Cole, 'Guilds at Home and Abroad', *The Guildsman*, No. 48 (December 1920), p. 10; S.C.L., 'The Annual Conference of 1920', *The Guildsman*, No. 42 (June 1920), pp. 5–6.

Danton and Marat.'[1] In the resolution, they declared their support for Soviet Russia against the attitudes that Churchill and others sought to export. In addition, they affirmed that similar methods might be necessary in Britain, and committed themselves to discuss this point with other organizations.[2]

Cole made it clear that he dissented from this last proposal. The price for his support had been a clause asserting that British socialism might not have to adopt Russian methods. However, many of those who had supported the Soviet Resolution were much less cautious. Among them were Arnot and Palme Dutt, who were founder-members of the British Communist Party; others went along for a brief flirtation with the Party. The far Left argued that the logical policy was to prepare to lead the revolution they felt was coming. Palme Dutt presented the stark outline of their case:

> What the communist insists on is that the transference of power must take place before the reconstruction can begin or the reconstruction will not be socialist. If the work of the social change is attempted and begun while the power is still in capitalist hands, then all the specific efforts made only work out in an entirely different direction.[3]

Thus the policies which Cole advocated as partial steps towards Guild Socialism had no real use. Dutt scathingly said that 'encroaching control' was a 'safe idea' – 'it neither controls nor encroaches'.[4] Ellen

[1] S.C.L., 'The Annual Conference of 1920', *The Guildsman*, No. 42 (June 1920), pp. 5–6.

[2] The Soviet Resolution

This Conference, holding that the firm establishment of Guild Socialism is impossible without the supersession of the administrative and coercive machinery of the Capitalist State by forms of organization created by, and directly expressing the will of the workers themselves, welcomes the Soviet system as a form of organization complying with this condition. It holds however that the exact form of organization required in any country cannot be determined in advance of the situation which calls it into being, and it therefore cannot affirm that the Soviet system is necessarily the best or the only form of revolutionary organization for this country. Affirming its solidarity with the Russian Soviet Republic, it holds that the methods of applying here the common principles on which this solidarity is based may differ as widely as the conditions differ from the methods adopted in Russia. It therefore decides to appoint a special committee of five members, with powers to consult other organizations which have affirmed their solidarity with the Russian Soviet Republic, for the purpose of formulating a programme of action.

(Text in 'National Guilds League – Various Papers', Cole Papers, Nuffield College.)

[3] Cited in Ellen Wilkinson, 'With the Revolutionaries', *The Guildsman*, No. 41 (May 1920), pp. 5–6.

[4] Palme Dutt, 'The Dictatorship of the Proletariat', *The Guildsman*, No. 34 (October 1919), pp. 4–5.

Wilkinson ridiculed the Building Guilds, another effort to prepare some of the institutions of the new society in the bowels of the old one:

Is the National Guilds League content to amuse itself with its box of bricks, or will it range itself with the revolutionaries throughout Europe who are working for an immediate revolution, offering the Guild theory as its contribution to the building of communist society after the transference of power has taken place?[1]

This policy entailed the acceptance of Lenin's definition of the dictatorship of the proletariat as action by enlightened minority on behalf of all the workers; it led logically to the formation of the British Communist Party.

It was at this point that the far Left parted company with Cole. In a Special Conference in December 1920, the issue of the dictatorship of the proletariat was explicitly raised. Cole was the key figure in this debate, trying vainly to formulate a reasonable position between the two extremes. 'Cole suggested that the question was one of expediency rather than principle and that the safest course would be to turn down both resolution and amendment [opposing the dictatorship of the proletariat]; both were in due course turned down, the amendment by a large and the resolution by a small majority.'[2] Thus he kept the N.G.L. from endorsing the Communist position, but he could not repair the damage done by the issue.

Cole's opposition to the dictatorship of the proletariat brought out his temperamental and philosophical differences from the Communists. In his *History of Socialist Thought*, Cole commented:

Unlike some of my friends and colleagues in the Guild Socialist movement, I was never under any temptation to become a Communist, because my attitude was basically pluralistic and libertarian, and I was repelled by the Bolsheviks' conception of a social philosophy based on rigidly determinist principles and involving the unquestionable class-correctness of a single, unified body of doctrine, regardless of considerations of time and place.[3]

Despite his militancy and his urge to transform society, Cole clung to the liberal values which were his 'sticking-points'. But he did not make

[1] Ellen Wilkinson, 'With the Revolutionaries', *The Guildsman*, No. 41 (May 1920), pp. 5–6.
[2] S.C.L., 'The Annual Conference of 1920', *The Guildsman*, No. 42 (June 1920), pp. 5–6.
[3] G. D. H. Cole, *A History of Socialist Thought*, IV: *Communism and Social Democracy* (London, Macmillan, 1958), 1, p. 7.

them the grounds for a formal rejection of Communism. Rather, he subjected the Communists' dogmas to a practical analysis.

The immediate effect of Communist agitation was to divide the Labour movement into rigid revolutionary and constititionalist factions. Cole detested this, for he knew that without unity Labour could get nowhere. For the same reason, he generally refused to be drawn into 'red-baiting'; Communism attracted militants who had to be encouraged to work with the rest of the Labour movement, rather than be driven to destroy it by ideological quarrelling. Temperamentally, Cole was a 'Centrist',[1] and refused to do anything that would widen factional splits within the Labour movement.

Communist theory offered no benefits that could justify splitting the Labour movement. He found it devoid of new ideas suited to British conditions. 'Certainly there could hardly be a less inspiring programme than dictatorship of the proletariat, the Soviet system (interpreted almost solely as an instrument of dictatorship), and adhesion to the Third International . . .'[2] The Communists relied totally upon revolution, in a way that Cole found 'somewhat hysterical'. Cole retorted that revolution was at best a means to an end, to be judged pragmatically rather than made the goal.

Guild Socialists do not regard either the man who says, 'I want a revolution,' or the man who says, 'I do not,' as possessing an adequate philosophy. The question remains, 'What kind of revolution, and for what purpose?' and even 'at what time?' 'Any old revolution' at any old time is emphatically not good enough.[3]

Any call for a revolution had to be placed in the proper perspective – the goals of Guild Socialism and the Labour movement generally, and the preparedness of Labour. A revolution could only occur if economic events created a Labour movement that was strong and knew what it wanted. 'To-day we could not even destroy capitalism, much less put a new and better social system in its place.'[4] Certainly an immediate revolution would be of no use, although it would have to be supported if it did occur. The call for a revolution had to be postponed until the proper conditions prevailed.

[1] G. D. H. Cole, *A History of Socialist Thought*, IV, 1, 12.
[2] CC, 'Notes of the Month', *The Guildsman*, No. 43 (July 1920), p. 2.
[3] CC, 'Notes of the Month', *The Guild Socialist*, No. 60 (December 1921), p. 3.
[4] CC, 'Notes of the Month', *The Guildsman*, No. 43 (July 1920), p. 2.

Many of us who are not Communists believe that at some stage in the transition from capitalism to Socialism there must indeed come a catastrophic break, but we take the view that it is important not that this break should come as early as possible in the transition, but that before it comes, every year and every month should be used by the working classes themselves, not simply for the stimulation of revolutionary enthusiasm, but for the building up of a constructive alternative to capitalism based on the original working class movement.[1]

In Cole's mind, a revolution was not a trial of strength, but a coherent attempt to substitute one system for another. The workers would have to construct as well as destroy; this was one of the strongest arguments for encroaching control. Encroaching control would provide the workers with an apprenticeship that would prepare them to govern themselves.

In these circumstances, despite the difficulties in the theory of encroaching control, Cole felt justified in trying to preserve the National Guilds League as an independent propaganda body. 'For the present, therefore, we see more hope in a continuance of the preaching of Guild Socialism than in any attempt to create a revolutionary instrument which will inevitably be based neither on a clear community of idea and purpose, nor on an appreciation of the essential interaction of will and economic forces.'[2] Cole thus tried to maintain the integrity of Guild Socialism as a force on the left, pointing out the way in which society could be reorganized, rather than being pushed back into embracing Parliamentary reformism. 'It will not be a comfortable position, or an easy one to sustain; but for all that it may be the right one.'[3]

The position certainly was an awkward one. The intensity of the quarrel between Communists and Labourites made a thorough-going Centrist policy impossible. Revolution ceased to be a practical issue for the Labour movement; well before the General Strike; Cole realized that the English working class simply would not revolt. In November 1920, he wryly wrote:

[1] G. D. H. Cole, 'Guild Socialism and Communism', 'Manuscripts and Proofs', Box 1, folder 4, Cole Papers, Nuffield College. He appears to have given a version of this paper on 23 February 1921 in the N.G.L.'s Mortimer Hall lecture series; the copy in 'Manuscripts and Proofs' is dated May 1921.
[2] CC, 'Notes of the Month', *The Guildsman*, No. 43 (July 1920), p. 2.
[3] G. D. H. Cole, 'Guilds at Home and Abroad', *The Guildsman*, No. 47 (November 1920), p. 9.

There have been at least half a dozen occasions since the Armistice on which the observer, who knows not his England, would have been justified in expecting, though not actual revolution, at any rate a profound disturbance of the whole body political and economic, leading to far-reaching reorganizations and adjustments. On these occasions, the lions on both sides have roared in the most approved fashion, and also the cocks have crowed and the hens clucked; but on each occasion the end of it all has been only that 'the first lion thought the last a bore,' and that the hen has had to own up to not having laid a real egg after all.[1]

The issue of revolution had always been more real to Labour militants than to British society as a whole. Labour intellectuals, in defining their attitudes towards revolution, ran the risk of exiling themselves from the main body of the Labour movement. This was the long-range importance of the debate over revolution but it had had some short-range importance while the heady atmosphere of reconstruction lasted. A major strike for the nationalization of coal, for example, would have set a precedent for industrial direct action in political questions that might have changed the basic outlook of the Labour movement.

But the idea of revolution possessed this kind of reality only while Labour was on the offensive after the war; by 1921 the 'trade slump' forced Labour back on the defensive. The miners and the railwaymen both gave up their hopes of achieving nationalization with joint control by representative bodies of workers and the state. All over Britain men were being forced to accept wage cuts, and the unemployed numbered more than a million. In a sense, Cole's war-time predictions of post-war unemployment and Labour weakness were now coming true. He did not attempt to hide his disappointment at the shape of the world. 'Truly, the world seems sinking back into the darkness of the nineteenth century; the *laisser-faire* economists are returning happily to their own vomit; and the Labour movement hastens to wallow in the mire.'[2]

Cole prepared to face 'the lean years under the blind guidance of our capitalist rulers'. The difficulties facing any attempt to advance towards Guild Socialism multiplied, as unemployment destroyed the militancy of the Labour movement and improved the employers' bargaining

[1] CC, 'Notes of the Month', *The Guildsman*, No. 47 (November 1920), p. 1.
[1] CC, 'Notes of the Month', *The Guild Socialist*, No. 55 (July 1921), p. 1.

position. 'In these circumstances, it is at the moment much more difficult to believe in the sort of transition, gradual and uncatastrophic as it seems to be, which I have tried to put forward . . .' Cole wrote as he prepared a new edition of *Chaos and Order in Industry*. Workers' control looked more and more like a 'might-have-been'.

I have no doubt at all that, if Labour had been adequately prepared in 1919 with a policy of encroaching control, it could have wrung from Capitalism concessions, not merely substantial in themselves, but definitely capable of leading on to other and greater concessions, and of paving the way to a complete transformation of the economic system.[1]

In such a climate, Guild Socialism withered. The National Guilds League announced at its Annual Conference in April 1921 that it would have to cut back on its optimistic plans for a permanent staff. Cole and the remaining Guildsmen fought a sort of rear-guard action to maintain their agitation for workers' control, their voluntary lectures and pamphlets, and their hopes of permeating the unions. They recognized that their only hope for success lay in local action, rather than in any dramatic national advance. Cole frequently reiterated his belief in Guild Socialism, but increasingly it sounded like 'whistling past the graveyard'.

I am, however, not convinced that appearances are conclusive, or that the policy of 'encroaching control' has been proved to be impracticable . . . as the bankruptcy of the capitalist system becomes plainer, and as it becomes clearer, even to the capitalists themselves, that their chances of re-establishing firmly the social order which they understand and in which alone they can believe, are practically non-existent; Labour's opportunity will come again.[2]

However, the real problem for him lay not in preparing to meet Labour's opportunity a second time, but in preventing the worsening conditions from destroying its chances for ever. He had to turn his attention more towards Labour's defence and the use of new techniques to meet the new problems of unemployment and falling incomes.

In this mood, he was tempted to postpone his ambitious hopes. Perhaps it would be better to abandon direct agitation for the time being and devote one's attention to the new generation:

[1] G. D. H. Cole, 'Introduction to the 1921 Edition (of *Chaos and Order in Industry*)', in 'Manuscripts and Proofs', Box 7, folder 86, Cole Papers, Nuffield College.

[2] G. D. H. Cole, 'Introduction to the 1921 Edition (of *Chaos and Order in Industry*)', in 'Manuscripts and Proofs', Box 7, folder 86, Cole Papers, Nuffield College.

We say that if this force is to be enlisted on our side and against capitalism, it can only be by a change of heart, and not being economic fatalists, we do not despair of a change of heart beginning before the old system crashes about our ears ... The problem before us is that of producing a new generation with other ways of thinking, not merely upon economic questions, for 'capitalist mentality' is certainly not confined to that subject, and of seeing that the large number of individuals (including practically the whole human race) who act on instinct and reason about it afterwards shall find their instinctive reactions leading in a direction different from that to which they are accustomed. Our problem, in fact, in the largest sense, is one of Education.[1]

But Cole did not turn directly to education. Just as he was undertaking his first analyses of unemployment, one last outburst of activity held his attention to Guild Socialism.

In January 1920 a group of Manchester trade-unionists, under the guidance of S. G. Hobson, had formed a Building Guild.[2] At almost the same time Malcolm Sparkes' efforts in London also produced a Guild, and others sprang up rapidly. They were made possible by the post-war condition of the building industry. There was a definite shortage of houses, but capitalists were wary about building because rents were still controlled. At the same time, Lloyd George had promised 'homes for heroes' in the 1918 election, and Parliament had passed 'Addison's Bill' which made money available to local authorities through the Ministry of Health. The contractors who received contracts for municipal housing had made sizeable profits for houses which were not the best, and the demand was still unsaturated. The Building Guilds offered to build houses for less, on a cost-plus basis, and the Ministry of Health, after much delay, agreed on a trial of twenty contracts. The Guilds were freed from the necessity of finding capital, which had always been the crucial barrier to co-operative producers' movements, by the fact that the municipalities which signed contracts with them, and the Government indirectly, agreed to provide advances that took the place of working capital.

Guild building incorporated several of the principles of Guild

---

[1] CC, 'Notes of the Month', *The Guild Socialist*, No. 58 (October 1921), p. 2.

[2] On the Building Guilds, see G. D. H. Cole, *A Century of Co-operation* (Manchester, Co-operative Union Ltd, 1944), pp. 284–90. Nuffield College has copies of *The Building Guildsman*, December 1921–February 1922, April–June 1922, and there is useful material in the J. P. Bedford MSS. at Nuffield College. Frank Matthews of Hull University, who is writing a thesis on Guild Socialism, supplied me with useful information, including access to papers collected by Fred Dalley and J. Henry Lloyd.

Socialism. There was to be no profit; when the Ministry of Health changed the basis of the contract to a fixed-sum bid, the Guilds guaranteed to use any surplus equally for price-reductions and working capital. The cost-plus contracts in particular made the introduction of 'pay' for wages possible. The workers would be maintained on 'continous pay' even in the absence of work, and a charge of forty pounds per house was made part of the cost-plus contracts. The Ministry of Health and the building contractors were especially annoyed by this, for it undercut the cherished principle of making unemployment less desirable than any sort of employment. It was the first real application of the idea of 'industrial maintenance'. Finally, the projects were to be governed democratically. Foremen were elected, and efforts were made to get architects and other white-collar personnel to join the Guilds. The work appears to have been well done, and it was not difficult to produce better houses at a lower price when the Guilds started building in the summer of 1920. In 1921, Hobson seemed to gain a further triumph, when the London Building Guild was brought into association with his National Building Guild Ltd; a National Guild was in being, although the amalgamation was never completed.

Cole did not immediately become heavily involved in supporting the new organizations. The more immediate problem was the struggle over the Soviet Resolution. In addition, he had already argued against forming working guilds. They would be a form of co-operative production, something which he felt could not work under capitalist conditions. A co-operative enterprise would either have to adopt capitalist methods and morals, or it would be destroyed by capitalist boycotts, under-cutting, and political harassment. Producers' co-operatives had been tried in the nineteenth century; they had failed as a means of rebuilding society, and had generally decayed into workers' capitalism. The Building Guilds were not the Guilds of the future, for all their efforts to embody Guild principles; so Cole discounted them in 1920, when he devoted his attention to the means of attaining a full Guild society. He found them premature, and overambitious.

None the less, *The Guildsman* welcomed the National Building Guild with some enthusiasm. It was a welcome sign of working-class involvement. Cole kept himself informed on the development of the Guilds, especially after they had overcome the initial delays imposed by the

Ministry of Health. He reported on them in his column 'Guilds at Home and Abroad'; soon he became a propagandist for them to the outer world.[1]

Cole's doubts did not disappear; but increasingly, after the beginning of 1921, he felt compelled to come to the support of the Building Guilds, and of other Guilds which had sprung up in emulation. In December 1921, Cole signalled the conversion of the bulk of the energies of *The Guildsman* and *The Guild Socialist* to the support of the working Guilds movement.

It is true that Building Guilds are not Guild Socialism. No one ever imagined that they were. You cannot have Guild Socialism in a non-Socialist society, and the Building Guilds, like all pioneers, have had to make certain inevitable concessions to their surroundings. But the fact remains that they do exist, and that they are Guilds, and that they have done more to spread the ideas of Guild Socialism among the rank and file – and thus to bring them within sight of realization – than generations of propaganda. It is too often forgotten that it is not merely the capitalist or the middle-class man who regards democratic control of industry as a dream; it is the worker himself who, bred in an industrial atmosphere which directly discourages freedom and responsibility, misses by his own lack of self-confidence the opportunities he might grasp. But the very existence of the Building Guilds is a powerful suggestion to the workers in other industries . . .[2]

Guild Socialism had come to depend on the 'box of bricks'. The Guilds were the only aggressive force in the Labour movement; they alone brought socialism down to reality, away from the counter-claims of parliamentary socialism and revolutionary communism. Now he saw the Guilds to be a standing refutation of what the capitalists said about the impracticability of the ideas of social ownership, service, and workers' control. He admitted that the Labour movement was tired of propaganda, but argued that something as practical as a Guild could still gain attention. Cole also conceded a new point. The existing Guilds could develop into units of the new society, although they could not create that society. He anxiously warned that 'We must

---

[1] For example, 'Practical Socialism in Great Britain: The Building Guilds at Work', in 'Manuscripts and Proofs', Box 1, folder 4, Cole Papers, Nuffield College, dated 26.10.21; 'The Guild Movement in Great Britain, Its Position and Recent Progress', Box 1, folder 4 (spring 1922); article in *The New Republic*, Vol. 22 (3 March 1920); article in *The International Labour Review* (August 1922).
[2] CC, 'Notes of the Month', *The Guild Socialist*, No. 60 (December 1921), p. 2.

never mistake the Guilds of to-day for the Guilds of to-morrow, or forget, in our anxiety to forward the immediate development of the Guild movement, the wider task of social destruction and reorganisation apart from which the Guilds are meaningless and futile'.[1] But in practice, Cole did have to forget the 'wider task', for Labour's general position made agitation for a major change in society useless. He perforce turned his attention to helping the Guilds.

What Cole could do to help the Guilds was limited. He could not start them or restrain them; he had no large amounts of money for them, or influence that could provide desperately-needed capital. Margaret Cole expressed their position well in the 1922 Draft Annual Report of the N.G.L.:

> It is not the business of the N.G.L. to set up Guilds, which can only and should only be done by the workers in each industry; the part of the N.G.L. is to help and advise those who have formed or are forming Guilds as regards the best way to set about it and the obvious pitfalls to be avoided, to supply them with literature and news of other Guilds, and generally to keep what have been described as 'the larger issues' before the minds of the several sections of the Guild movement – since the declared object of the N.G.L. is the establishment not of Guilds merely, but of Guild Socialism.[2]

Cole accepted the limitations entailed by his being a middle-class intellectual, a brain worker.[3] His main task was to purify doctrine and to seek to make the principles behind the Guilds understandable to those actually creating them. He used *The Guild Socialist* to communicate news about the Guilds to each other and to other sections of the Labour movement; but *The Guild Socialist* never had a mass circulation.[4] He wrote 'Notes on Forming Guilds'[5] which was later published as a pamphlet, to present the principles of the movement and details on the legal and financial status which they should accept. But he undoubtedly found *The Guild Socialist* and the N.G.L. insufficient

[1] CC, 'Notes of the Month', *The Guild Socialist*, No. 68 (August–September 1922), p. 2
[2] Margaret Cole, 'Draft Annual Report of the N.G.L., 1922', *The Guild Socialist*, No. 63 (March 1922), p. 7.
[3] See 'Introduction to the 1921 Edition (of *Chaos and Order in Industry*)', 'Manuscripts and Proofs', Box 7, folder 86, Cole Papers, Nuffield College; CC, 'Notes of the Month', *The Guild Socialist*, No. 69 (October 1922), p. 2.
[4] 'The Annual Report of the N.G.L.', *The Guild Socialist*, no. 74 (March 1923), gives the total sales for 1921 as 15,552; for 1922 as 12,779 (only 11 issues appeared in 1922, because of a strike in August 1922); or some 1,200 copies an issue.
[5] 'Notes on Forming Guilds', *The Guild Socialist*, No. 60 (December 1921), pp. 7–10.

vehicles for his mission to the working Guilds. In April 1922 he helped set up a body to take over the task, the National Guilds Council, which was formed at a meeting held jointly with the N.G.L. the following month. Such a body could more efficiently distribute advice and try to prevent imposters from using the Guild name without its principles, and shifted more of the burden on to the working classes themselves, as Cole had always felt necessary.

The establishment of the Guilds Council looked like a major advance. The T.U.C. appointed two representatives to sit on its Executive when it was finally completed, and it looked as if the official Labour movement might take effective notice of the movement. Cole had a further success when, with Clifford Allen's help, self-government in industry was written into the I.L.P.'s new constitution. But financial difficulties coupled with problems in management pulled down the most successful of the Guilds, Hobson's National Building Guilds Ltd. After the Government decided to approve no more Guild contracts, and even refused to allow the Guilds to fill all the twenty test contracts agreed upon in the summer of 1920, the Guild had gone on producing houses, but on a tighter market. It had great difficulty in obtaining working capital, for the Co-operative Wholesale Bank refused to provide money for non-Government contracts. In addition, there seem to have been cases of over-manning and of abuses in the maintenance of pay; and Barclays Bank, one of its new creditors, called for a receivership. This effectively killed the movement, although it lingered on much longer than Cole later liked to think. In his *History of Socialist Thought*, Cole wrote that '. . . the remaining Guild Socialists decided to wind up the movement rather than await its gradual dissolution.'[1] Actually, the Guild Socialist movement dragged on for over a year after the collapse of the National Building Guild Ltd in November 1922. For several months Cole continued to write articles and organize meetings with the aim of putting the movement to rights, despite his growing doubts.

He continued to produce ideas for reforming the Guilds beyond the point, one feels, at which anyone was listening. In April 1923, he started a series on 'Next Steps in the Guild Movement', which was an interesting if pathetic effort to rebuild the Guild movement along his

[1] IV: *Communism and Social Democracy*, i, 453.

Guild Commune lines. 'What, then, if we were to found in each district neither a Building Guild, nor a Tailoring Guild, nor a Furnishing Guild, nor a Guild of Engineers, but a single and all-embracing Guild Society, appealing to every worker, and taking powers under its constitution to promote Guild enterprise in every industry carried on in the district.'[1] But no one rose to the bait, and the whole Guild movement slid downhill. By the summer, the financial condition of the N.G.L. itself had become hopeless, and the Coles wound it up, merging it with the National Guilds Council. The resolution to merge the two bodies

... was virtually a decision that the two organizations ... were not now both necessary to the movement, whose progress in the future would be identified with the work of the Guilds themselves, together with the movement within the trade unions, co-ordinated and helped wherever possible by the work of the National Guilds Council.

... it was pointed out that the financial difficulty of carrying on was overwhelming and that there was nothing to indicate a probable revival of active co-operation and support ... Our existence as a League was no longer radiating outwards; we were no longer doing effective propaganda work, and such propaganda as was being done could be as effectively done by individuals working on their own account ...[2]

Soon after this, the Coles also had to end *The Guild Socialist*.

In a sense, Cole seemed to be relieved at the failure of the Building Guilds. He undoubtedly had had to put up with various compromises, especially the decision to pay interest on loans, and was glad to be free of Hobson's efforts to create a large centralized organization. In April 1923 he commented: 'If we had retained a little longer the optimistic illusion of success, we might have been committed irrevocably to a wrong method of organization.'[3] But even if one takes into account their dissatisfaction, one must admit that Cole and the remaining Guildsmen made an honest decision at a point where many political groups have tried to drag on. As one speaker remarked at the final N.G.L. Conference, 'it was a most difficult thing to end an organization, even when the soul had gone out of it'. The decision was more than the end of an organization. For Cole, it was virtually the end of

[1] 'Next Steps in the Guilds Movement', *The Guild Socialist*, No. 75 (April 1923), p. 4.
[2] S.C.L., 'The Annual Conference', *The Guild Socialist*, No. 77 (June 1923), pp. 10–11.
[3] 'Next Steps in the Guilds Movement', *The Guild Socialist*, No. 75 (April 1923), p. 3.

ten years of work on the concept of workers' control. He had built up a movement, only to see it collapse, dragged down by an institutional form which he had not created.

With the collapse of the Guild Socialist movement, Cole needed both a focal point for his practical energies and a revised picture of the institutions and methods which could carry his ideals. In the next chapter we will discuss the positive choices he made; here we should notice what he came to feel Guild Socialism lacked. For one of the reasons which led Cole to 'wind up' the National Guilds League was a growing dissatisfaction with aspects of Guild Socialism. This was shown both in frequent editorial questioning on whether the movement should continue, and in the need for frequent reiterations that the movement was worthwhile.

In the Preface to *The Next Ten Years in British Social and Economic Policy*, which Cole published in 1929, he described the slow erosion of his Guild Socialism:

Long before I became fully conscious of this difference I had grown aware of something wrong. The first hint came, I think, from a sense of malaise on the platform. While I was making speeches an inner voice began to say to me, 'Do you really believe that? Oh yes, I know you believe it in general. But do you believe just what you said? Aren't you saying just that because it is what you have said before, and what they expect you to say? Are you really sure that is what you mean? My dear good man, isn't what you are saying this instant rather rubbish – rather high-falutin' nonsense? Unless you do believe it, you know, you haven't any right to go on making speeches, and leading these people up the garden path. You don't find it easy to answer? Come now, you must answer. Do you believe it? Yes or No?'

My guardian angel, or my tempter – it was hard to tell which – spoke to me like that again and again – and spoke with so much insistency that I found the making of propagandist speeches more and more uphill work. At length I practically gave up making them; I have made hardly any now for some years . . .[1]

What made Guild Socialism 'nonsense' was, firstly, that it failed to satisfy his need for practical policy. He felt that the world could no longer afford the expenditure of energy on utopianizing which Guild Socialism had demanded. It had been the creature of perfectionists, unwilling to act without being assured that all their ideals would be

[1] *The Next Ten Years*, pp. viii–ix. The 'difference' referred to in the first line is that post-war Socialism could not afford to insist upon perfection and careful long-range plans.

satisfied. Guild thought had also been utopian in another sense; parts of the theory had got out of hand. He confessed

... the later excesses of Guild Socialist system-making, for which I accept my full share of the blame. Guild Socialism took the wrong turning when it ceased to be an idea and aimed at being a system. Then the life went out of it, and, after a brief period of really formative influence, it faded rapidly away.[1]

The most important distortions of the Guild idea came from the theory of the Guild Commune, which Cole came to feel was 'a theory of representation run mad'. Formally, the Commune depended much too much on elaborate schemes of representation.

We must not set up committees for their own sake, or suppose that effective workers' control increases with the number of committees we succeed in getting established ... a society which has reduced its need for representative institutions to a minimum will not be of necessity less democratic than one which is a honeycombed with them.[2]

His suspicion of the representative institutions he had envisaged led him to question his values. Perhaps he had overestimated self-government, making it good in itself rather than one among several ideals. He felt that he had insisted upon self-government far beyond the average citizen's desires. Yet, even in his most self-critical moment, he could not repudiate self-government. People should be free; they should even be forced to be free.[3] What he repudiated was the logical rigidity with which he had clothed the idea. He detected puritan over-tones in his work. He had made self-government a duty, a kind of moral discipline. He had extended it into most corners of a man's life, trying to make men take an interest in their work which he later felt they were right not to take. If one's work were dull, then there was no reason to take as much interest in it as an artist took in his. Similarly, he came to criticize Guild Socialism's emphasis on service as a human motive and as a source of human pleasure. By 1929 he had retreated to a sort of political Benthamism, arguing that happiness was the goal and that service and self-government had to be subordinated to it.[4]

All of this implies a more 'realistic' or sceptical view of human

[1] Ibid., p. 161.
[2] Ibid., p. 171.
[3] Ibid., p. 160.
[4] Ibid., pp. 16–21.

nature. Cole sought to reduce his expectations of human beings. He sought a theory of democracy which would call for less effort from them, without sacrificing the richness of a democratic society. But he did it for an essentially democratic reason, which lies at the junction of his 'bolshevik soul' and his 'Fabian muzzle'. On the surface, it looks opportunistic – the workers did not accept our Guild utopia; therefore we must recast our ideals. What he clearly meant was that as the workers had rejected workers' control in the advanced Guild form there must be something wrong with the concept. As expressed, it was unlivable. Too much was demanded of human beings. Freedom and self-government had been placed in frameworks which impeded their actual spread throughout society. Cole decided that actual freedom and self-government, in limited but bearable amounts, were more important than ideal elaborations which might conceivably have given fuller self-government in a hypothetical future.

In his soul-searching Cole retreated too far, retreated from the values which made his utopia worthwhile. He had been picturing a set of goals which could have made work more worthwhile, especially if they had been coupled, as he predicted, with a reduction of the amount of disagreeable work in society. He could not help modelling this society on his own wishes; and his own wishes and pleasures were noble ones. In order to have something positive to say, he had to return to the basic insights into human values which he derived from his own desires. In a lecture he gave to the Morris Society in 1957, he said, 'I refuse to believe that people are so far different from my-self . . .'[1] Nor had he conceived these values in a tyrannical fashion, despite his self-doubts in 1929; we have seen how he had blurred the outlines of Guild society to make room for other instincts. But during the late 1920s his idealism seems to have been at a low point.

Despite the harsh criticism which he offered, Cole did not really abandon Guild Socialism. He clung to as much of the Guild idea as possible, as much of it as looked practical. He still believed in the broad ideals of self-government, fellowship and democracy. He still protested against the injustice and the insult involved in reducing a man to the level of a hand; and he tried to retain the concept of workers'

[1] G. D. H. Cole, 'William Morris as a Socialist', Transactions of the William Morris Society (London, 1960), p. 17.

control, in a modified form, as a short-term goal for Labour. What disappeared were the institutions and policies designed to put these ideals into effect. A gap opened up between theory and practice which led him to underestimate the theory. Self-governing Guilds yielded to a pale shadow: the nationalized industry run largely by experts, with protest powers granted to the unions. The detailed applications of the principle of function largely disappeared; with it vanished much of Cole's fascinating effort to balance man's life as a producer against his life as a consumer, one of the finest concepts in the system. The whole delicate theory of encroaching control disappeared, leaving Cole to cling to a political tool in which he did not fully believe. He adjusted to a grimmer world; and with this adjustment much of the life and the attractiveness which had gone with the Guild Socialist idea disappeared.

It has been said that Guild Socialism was Cole's 'one idea', and that this early period was the one in which he did his most important work. I shall try to demonstrate that this is an unfairly limited outlook. But Cole's Guild Socialism deserves much attention from a generation which must ask what should come 'Beyond the Welfare State'. Cole's final historical judgment deserves quoting:

in my opinion, for what it is worth, the Guild Socialists did make the outstanding contribution to non-Communist theories of Socialism during and immediately after the first world war.[1]

I would go much further. Guild Socialism, particularly in Cole's versions, had touched a permanently sore spot to which thinkers who were not Socialists also had to respond. Advanced Liberals, including the authors of the 'Liberal Yellow Book', found it necessary to answer Guild Socialism both by emphasizing the community's overriding rights in production and by conceding a degree of workers' participation. Tory reformers such as Harold Macmillan and Robert Boothby made an obvious effort to counter Guild Socialism with the slogan of 'self-government for industry'.[2]

[1] G. D. H. Cole, *A History of Socialist Thought*, IV: *Communism and Social Democracy 1914–1931*, i, 25.
[2] See Ramsay Muir, *Liberalism and Industry* (London, Constable, 1920); *Britain's Industrial Future, being the Report of the Liberal Industrial Inquiry* (London, Ernest Benn, 1928); Robert Boothby, Harold Macmillan, John de V. Loder, and Oliver Stanley, *Industry and the State. A Conservative View* (London, Macmillan, 1927); Harold Macmillan, *Reconstruction: A Plea for a National Policy* (London, Macmillan, 1933).

Cole's Guild Socialist works continue to raise important points about the nature of a free, self-governing society. They tried to push the rational construction of such a society beyond the compromise which has been accepted over the last fifty years – a compromise which divides life into work and 'play', unfree and free areas, and accepts 'one vote every five years' as democracy. Not only did Cole examine ultimate values; he sought to construct a society around them, and to plan how that society could be achieved. This is a significant feat; and perhaps we shall be able to take up the challenge it poses.

CHAPTER 4

A NEW SOCIALIST LIFE

After the withering away of Guild Socialism, Cole built new relationships and new ideas, trying to satisfy the energy, the fellowship, and the ideal of service to the Labour movement that Guild Socialism had allowed him to express. In the 1920s, he had to reorient his social and political thought to come to terms with a Labour movement that became increasingly parliamentary and increasingly concerned with the problems of governing in an age of unemployment. He had to work out the sorts of reforms that he considered acceptable within a capitalist society. Gradually he also came to see the need for a socialist economics which would justify reforms and solve unemployment in a pre-socialist society. Not until the end of the decade did he begin to write extensively and creatively on some of the elements of an unorthodox, reformist economic policy. He was thus one of the precursors of New Deal and Keynesian economics; but he stopped short of a full-blooded Keynesianism, in part because of changes in the mood of the Labour movement. The failure of the Labour Government to implement an unemployment policy in 1930 drove Cole to join with other 'loyal grousers'. They created two organizations, the New Fabian Research Bureau and the Society for Socialist Inquiry and Propaganda, which provided Cole with the fellowship and the co-operative investigation and criticism that had helped make the Guild Socialist years productive.

In this way Cole also solved the problem of how he could most effectively serve the Labour movement. He became a socialist educator. His political role was that of the semi-independent researcher and publicist – half in academic Oxford and half on the fringes of political London. He tried to identify the problems of economic policy and political tactics that would bedevil the movement, and to work on them systematically with his friends in the N.F.R.B. No other group of socialist intellectuals provided this level of research.[1] Cole continued

[1] E. Eldon Barry, *Nationalization in British Politics* (London, Cape, 1965), p. 382.

to have broader connections with the industrial side of the movement than any other Socialist intellectual. These personal connections undoubtedly helped him serve as an effective political educator, but they were too fragile to allow him to be directly and obviously influential.

What Cole lacked was a focus for concentrated pressure. His influence is therefore hard to discuss. It was considerable, but diffuse; it tends to vanish when one tries too hard to say just what it was. It came from his effectiveness as a popularizer, using media that ranged from surveys of contemporary conditions to articles for the *New Statesman* and for more specialized Labour magazines. Cole and Laski were the two best-known socialist intellectual publicists, and in the 1930s they were joined by Kingsley Martin and John Strachey, and supported by the numerous writers for the Left Book Club. These commentators helped raise a generation of socialists on high-level political thought. They could convert those whom the traditional party machinery could not touch, and they could argue a case in more detail than the professional politicians might want to. They created a new set of political commonplaces and brought much of the political discussion on to their own level; the next generation of Tories could not escape this reshaping of the political vocabulary. Their constant elaboration of notions like full employment, the need for a larger social expenditure, and the absurdity of deflationary economic orthodoxy, prepared the way for 1945.

Kingsley Martin edited the *New Statesman*, which may have been the most influential medium in the murky process of changing people's minds about political goals. Richard Crossman points out very aptly that in the 1930s the *New Statesman* reached 'a coherent compact body called "well-informed public opinion" which needs to prove its broad-mindedness by reading a bilious weekly.'[1] This audience was less sure of itself, more willing to accept well-argued new ideas, and larger in the 1930s than it has been since the Second World War. During the 'Twenties' and 'Thirties,' Cole averaged some forty articles a year for the *New Statesman* and helped set the tone of the paper. But it was still Martin's; Cole had failed to become editor in 1931. He never had an organ of his own. If the Society for Socialist Inquiry and Propaganda

[1] R. H. S. Crossman, 'Martin's Weekly Medicine', *New Statesman*, LXXIV (3 May 1968), 584.

had not been rivalled by, and then merged with, the rump of the I.L.P. in 1932, it would have been the ideal medium for Cole as an influential publicist for Labour Party militants, supplementing his *New Statesman* articles, his books, and the New Fabian Research Bureau. The success of 'Zip' would have made him a more formidable and individual influence within the Labour Party; but we must not overestimate the opportunity for such an influence. He could only have presented ideas which reflected what others were thinking and which conformed with visible needs. He could not have remade the Labour Party in his image of an ideal party. And so one must not conclude that this is the only thing which would count as influence, and declare him uninfluential because it did not occur. One does not make socialists in the way that one makes car bodies, or invent a concept such as economic planning and then force it upon a political party; a mechanistic notion of influence does not work. Cole was an important member of the Socialist world of the 1920s and 1930s, helping people develop their thoughts about a better society, providing facts and arguments, not always 'original' but useful.

Cole was content with this 'limited' but broad and very influential role as a socialist commentator and intellectual. Temperamentally, he seems to have matured and mellowed. He left behind him much of the fierceness and intransigence with which he had attacked the Webbs, without 'going soft'. He had given up personal ambition. He wanted to put forth his thoughts, and did so, almost compulsively; but he did not insist upon orthodoxy. The most striking example of this tolerance is the 'self-denying ordinance' of the N.F.R.B. which the Coles also insisted upon in the reconstituted Fabian Society. By making it clear that the N.F.R.B. has no collective policy beyond a broadly defined faith in socialism, the Coles kept it from being a political football – and a road to individual power for themselves. Its influence, of course, was all the greater, training numerous people who became Labour Party candidates and allowing young middle-class intellectuals to avoid the distrust and anti-intellectualism which Cole had always to face.

Cole's health helped 'limit' him to a career of influence rather than one of personal leadership. It is hard to remember that he was a sick man. In 1931, doctors finally diagnosed his recurrent illness as diabetes. Margaret Cole described how they endeavoured to cure him by dietary restrictions without using insulin, reducing him to a skeleton breaking out in sores (like a tramp in a workhouse ward), and filling the house with the horrible stench of a substance made principally, so far as I remember, of seaweed, which was designed to give him the illusion of eating something without the reality.[1]

He recovered from this, but for the rest of his life had to take great care with insulin.

Cole's diabetes had something to do with his decision not to run for Parliament, and with the end of his London tutorial classes. It limited his appearances in Labour politics, and probably helped keep him in Oxford. But other than this it is hard to see how it decreased the amount of work that he performed; it may even have increased it. 'Cole explained his enormous output not as verbal diarrhoea, but as a function of the diabetes that kept him from leading a normal life',[2] writes Kingsley Martin. Cole appeared to withdraw energy from other parts of his life and to put it into his work. He did have to be more careful, physically; he had to give up the walking tours which he had loved, although he found other means of touring. Certainly he did not pamper himself. As he later wrote, 'my body is a machine which I hope to wear out doing useful things'.[3]

In addition to working out a new relationship to the Labour movement, Cole also had to choose a career in the 1920s. This decision came more easily; by the early 1920s, his choice was hardly in doubt. He had not become a Labour official, even when the Labour Research Department had shared offices with the Labour Party in 1918–19. Nor had he become a full-time socialist journalist. Education, the third stream in his active life, now began to absorb a larger share of his energy.

During his Guild Socialist period, Cole had taken part in education through the Workers' Educational Association. The W.E.A. had been founded by Albert Mansbridge in 1903. Co-operating with the Universities through a Central Joint Administrative Committee, it made university-trained tutors available to the working-class; Oxford dons such as Sidney Ball and A. J. Carlyle took the lead on the University

[1] Margaret Cole, *Growing Up Into Revolution* (London, Longmans Green, 1949), p. 141.
[2] Kingsley Martin, *Father Figures* (London, Hutchinson, 1966), pp. 196–7.
[3] G. D. H. Cole, 'What I Believe', in 'Manuscripts and Proofs', Box 8, Cole Papers, Nuffield College.

side, and R. H. Tawney taught the first two tutorial classes in 1907. The W.E.A. recruited the students, who largely determined what they were to study. It was not a degree-granting institution; it sought to give the intellectually active members of the working class a chance to learn and discuss matters that concerned them. Consequently, most of the three year tutorial classes dealt with economics, economic history, and similar subjects. Discussion naturally played a large role – the tutor's lectures were restricted to half each two hour session – and in addition, the W.E.A. required written work, in order to improve the men's powers of self-expression. The W.E.A., at its best, provided a stimulating form of democratic education in areas untouched by other educational institutions.

Cole joined this movement in its infancy. In 1913, he lectured on Rousseau to the W.E.A. Summer School at Oxford. At the time, he was attempting to write a book on Rousseau, in addition to preparing the Everyman edition of the *Social Contract*. From the beginning, then, Cole gave the W.E.A. his best work. In the next year, he lectured widely for it, in addition to teaching philosophy at Armstrong College, Newcastle:

I spent a great many evenings lecturing and talking to W.E.A. branches and classes in the Northumberland and Durham coalfield. I went into Scotland too, talking to miners in Midlothian – difficult audiences that listened intently, but gave few clues to their feelings – and the engineers and shipbuilders on Clydeside – who left me in no doubt at all about their views.

Then I taught cotton operatives on the border of Lancashire one night in the week, and a very mixed bag of students in that popular, South Coast watering-place, Bournemouth, another night . . .[1]

This variety of experience undoubtedly helped make him one of the best-informed members of the Labour movement. It offset the limitations of his formal education, which had taken place in the South of England; it helped him establish valuable acquaintanceships in key trades and to understand what each trade involved.

The W.E.A. offered Cole an opportunity to serve the Labour

[1] G. D. H. Cole, 'Recollections of Workers' Education', in 'Manuscripts and Proofs', Box 4, folder 53, Cole Papers, Nuffield College.

movement on its own terms. 'We wanted to work with them in order that they might become better Trade Unionists and Co-operators, better members of the various working-class movements to which they belonged, as well as better educated persons in a purely academic sense.'[1] This broad but practical conception of education suited Cole perfectly. It satisfied both his social and educational idealism and his sense of practicality. He believed passionately in education, as opposed to propaganda. Many other young left-wingers sympathized with the Central Labour College, which emphasized the teaching of Marxism; Cole, however, believed firmly in assembling facts and arguments in as unbiased a fashion as possible. Propaganda had a place, but it should come after the development of the individual's mind so that he could tell good arguments from bad ones, and judge for himself on the basis of reliable information.[2] The W.E.A. thus appealed to him, for it offered the broadest, most liberal sort of real education. It did not convey facts for professional reasons, or worship them for their own sakes. At its best, it was a genuine education for citizenship and life, avoiding the defects of purely technical education, purely intellectual education, and propaganda.

The democracy and fellowship inherent in the W.E.A. appealed to Cole.

The greatest thing about it all was the founding of a group, not merely of lecturing to so many individual students . . . The real strength of the W.E.A. lay in that group character of its membership; in the fact that it was not merely a weekly meeting, but a continual process, going on through the daily contact between the students.[3]

The tutor thus had to build up a strong student movement. He had to participate with them in order to bring out their needs and abilities. Tutors, Cole wrote, 'are not merely instructors, but essentially partici-pators with their students in a common social purpose – the strengthen-ing of the working-class for the intelligent mastery of its problems and

[1] G. D. H. Cole, 'The Tutor and the Working Class Movement', *Adult Education*, XXXI (Spring 1959), 298. First published in the same journal in 1939.

[2] See G. D. H. Cole, 'The W.E.A. and the Future', *The Highway*, XVIII (Summer 1925), 97–101, for his acceptance of both propaganda and education, while placing education first.

[3] Verbatim report of a lecture Cole gave to a Conference of the British Institute of Adult Education, September 1938; in 'Manuscripts and Proofs', Box 4, folder 53, Cole Papers, Nuffield College.

the improvement of the quality of the working-class life'.[1] The W.E.A. sought to break down the barriers between teacher and student, to create equality and a common purpose. One cannot underestimate how much this appealed to Cole's democratic spirit.

From all the evidence, Cole appears to have been a great tutor, and the qualities that made him a great tutor later enabled him to become an outstanding teacher at Oxford. E. M. Hutchinson, the Secretary of the National Institute of Adult Education, told me that Cole is still remembered as a model teacher. Fortunately he left important records of his methods in his 'Tutor's Manual'.[2] Cole was very kind and painstaking, without being patronizing. One story which he loved to tell illustrates this well:

I remember, for example, one student who began by telling me that he couldn't possibly write a paper, with whom I dealt, knowing that he was a public speaker, by telling him to make a speech on the subject in question. He made the speech and I took it down and showed it to him. 'Here,' said I, 'is the paper. You made it, not I. Now go away and do another.' He did, and thereafter he became quite a regular writer as well as an active participant in class discussions.[3]

Cole clearly brought out the best in his students. He inspired devotion as many reports show,[4] without forcing his will on them. He left them with their individuality, raised to new levels of knowledge and self-expression.

In addition, Cole was a learned and imaginative teacher. He knew concretely what he was talking about; when he taught economic history, for example, he could discuss technical processes and historic

---

[1] 'The Tutor and the Working Class Movement', *Adult Education*, XXXI (Spring 1959), 301.

[2] Association of Tutorial Class Tutors, 'The Tutor's Manual', ed. G. D. H. Cole (n.p., n.d.). It was first published around 1923.

[3] G. D. H. Cole, 'The Tutorial Class in British Working-Class Education', *The International Quarterly of Adult Education*, 1 (November 1932), 143.

[4] See, for example, Hugh Gaitskell, 'At Oxford in the Twenties', and Stephen K. Bailey, 'What Cole Really Meant', in *Essays in Labour History*, ed. Asa Briggs and John Saville (London, Macmillan, 1960). These are the most detailed records of his students' responses. Although both deal with his teaching at Oxford, talking with William Lowth, the District Secretary of the W.E.A. for London when Cole was staff tutor, convinced me that Cole taught in the same manner then, with similar response. Jack Pavey of the University of London Extramural Department made the 'Minutes of the Joint Committee for the Promotion of the Higher Education of Working People' available to me, along with other interesting material.

inventions, about which many teachers are vague and unconvincing. He employed group projects with great skill, long before political scientists discovered simulation games. In 'The Tutor's Manual', he described how he turned one tutorial class into a Railway Tribunal for several weeks.

For these reasons, Cole's reputation grew. He began to work in the London tutorial class movement during the First World War, and, when the London Tutorial Committee decided to appoint its first staff tutor in 1922, Cole was appointed. As staff tutor, he was a resounding success. He used his position to develop a summer school and advanced classes for the best students who had finished three-year classes. His practical pioneering in London was complemented by broader activities in the Workers' Educational Association. He had helped found the Tutors' Association; during the war he and Arthur Greenwood kept it alive. After the war it agitated on two fronts. The first was for the W.E.A. to commit itself more explicitly to class education; the second was to make it possible for a good teacher to afford to stay in adult education.

Cole's loyalty to the W.E.A. continued long after he left the service of the London Tutorial Committee. When he left London, he wrote a lengthy report making suggestions for the strengthening of the roles of the tutors and the W.E.A. in London tutorial class education.[1] He helped establish the W.E.A.'s Oxford District. As a national Vice-President of the W.E.A. until 1938, he sought to keep the needs of the working-class from being overwhelmed by the problems of general adult education; he resigned largely because he did not feel that he was playing an active enough role to justify retaining his position. Nor did Cole want to play an executive role, with others doing the actual teaching. He conducted a W.E.A. class in London until his diabetes forced him to stop in 1931.

In 1925, Cole returned to Oxford as University Reader in Economics and Fellow of University College. The appointment of such a well-known radical caused a stir; so did his introduction of question periods

[1] 'Some Notes on the Organization of the W.E.A. and Tutorial Classes in the London District', in 'Minutes of the Joint Committee for the Promotion of the Higher Education of Working People for the Session 1926–27', University of London Extramural Department. One of his suggestions, the creation of a full-time Director of Studies, was accepted; Barbara Wootton was given the post.

into his lectures. He brought with him the attitudes and abilities that had made him a good tutor. The famous 'Cole group'[1] in particular carried on the W.E.A. tradition of free, informal discussion. Members of successive Cole groups later rose to prominence in the Parliamentary Labour Party – among them were Hugh Gaitskell and Michael Stewart. Of equal importance were those who became trade union research secretaries, W.E.A. or local education officers, or otherwise played essential but generally unnoticed roles in furthering industrial and political democracy. Many of these people, like John Parker, M.P., went on to work for the New Fabian Research Bureau and the Fabian Society and participated in Labour's triumph in 1945. The Cole group continued to function until Cole's death in 1959.

The Cole group was recruited each year from the Oxford University Labour Party and Ruskin College by the previous year's group. Like a W.E.A. tutorial class, it met one evening a week during term-time, and discussed the social, economic, and political ideas and problems that interested the members. Many students found it the most exciting part of their education. As a good, democratic teacher, Cole helped the members of the group to clarify their own positions; he did not seek to impose a particular line on them. And so his influence through the Cole group was considerable, but diffuse. Its short-term effect was great, introducing young socialists to the problems of the day and helping them become involved in the Labour movement. Its long-term influence was more subtle. The members to whom I have talked retain few specific reminiscences of what they learned; this is inevitable, as the issues of the 1920s and 1930s recede into the past. But they vividly remember Cole himself, his goodness and his ability, the feeling of fellowship, and the way he contributed to their own self-realization. One may say, in addition, that the Cole group reinforced two of the dominant tendencies of the British Labour movement. Cole apparently implanted a belief both in his own liberal values and in getting the facts; he also helped prevent radical people from following the Communists into the political wasteland.[2]

Cole devoted a considerable portion of his last thirty-four years to

[1] See Margaret Cole, *Growing Up Into Revolution*, pp. 113–14, for the best published description of the 'Cole Group'.
[2] Neal Wood, *Communism and British Intellectuals* (London, Gollancz, 1959), p. 28.

education at Oxford – lecturing, tutoring, hosting the 'Cole Group', doing research in labour history, and serving on committees. Yet his academic career did not dominate and unify his life in the way Guild Socialism had. From the mid-twenties onwards, his life broadened out. Instead of consisting of a circle of activities – theoretical, practical, propagandistic, and leisured – around Guild Socialism, his life resembled an ellipse with two foci – Oxford and London. In London were concentrated his political and propagandistic interests, *The New States-man* and many of his friends in the Labour movement. Cole's many-sided partnership with his wife also came to centre upon London, especially after they bought a home in Hendon. Margaret Cole had been unhappy in Oxford, which she felt did not give her enough scope for her own activities.[1] Oxford was unhealthy, and it did not treat her as an equal – two good reasons for establishing the household in London. Throughout the 1930s Cole spent half of each week in term time at Oxford and half in London.

This partial geographical separation, with Douglas centering a large part of his life on Oxford and Margaret working out of London, reveals how different the Cole 'partnership' was from that of the Webbs, with whom they are inevitably compared. The Cole partnership was much more a partnership of independent equals. Margaret Cole described it well:

We are, in fact, pretty different; though we happened to be 'joined together, in the same depressing building [the Fabian Society offices] as the Webbs' we are emphatically not complementary to one another in the same way as that unique personality; and the occasional description of us as 'another Mr and Mrs Webb' is only true in so far as that, politically, we have pursued broadly the same end – Socialism – by broadly the same means – writing, organization, and propaganda – and that we have both worked pretty hard at it.[2]

Their partnership allowed Margaret Cole to become an important figure in her own right. As Secretary of the N.F.R.B. and then of the Fabian Society, she could take a closer interest in the day to day work of the Society; she had her own work in education, first with the W.E.A. and then with the London County Council. Her books on

[1] Margaret Cole, *Growing Up Into Revolution*, p. 110.
[2] Ibid., p. 77.

Beatrice Webb and on the Fabian Society will outlast most of her husband's long list of publications.

One could argue that this independence increased the Coles' influence and scope, while not diminishing the effectiveness of their joint work in various organizations and as writers. Together they edited *The Guildsman* and *The Guild Socialist*; Margaret Cole worked with Douglas on several books, including most of the 'Intelligent Man's Guides' through which Cole sought to educate a mass audience. Unlike the Webbs, their basic procedure was to outline a book and divide it into sections, sharing out the responsibilities for writing. Margaret Cole wrote in her autobiography that

as a writer he cannot really collaborate, partly because his pace is much too fast for anyone else to keep up, and partly because the shape of his thought and the turn of his phrase resent being mixed up with anyone else's. I do not mean that he cannot take criticism – far from that, but it has to be incorporated by him, at his discretion, in his own words and in his own way; he does not want another mind interfering with and deflecting *his* book.[1]

Undoubtedly Cole owed much to her criticism and suggestions; the effectiveness of their collaboration makes it difficult to point to places where Margaret Cole influenced Douglas, or to say that any one theme was uniquely hers.

Probably the most pleasing of the Coles' collaborations is the series of murder mysteries which they published between 1923 and 1946. They started writing them while Cole was recovering from a serious illness, and continued them as a profitable diversion. In the 1920s and 1930s they were among the most popular mystery writers, and joined G. K. Chesterton, Agatha Christie, Dorothy Sayers, and other practitioners of this very fashionable style in the Detective Dining Club. As members of this Club, the Coles subscribed to a code that outlawed the use of twin brothers, secret passages, and mysterious Chinamen, as well as supernatural and intuitive solutions to their puzzles. These rules had been designed to ensure a rational contest between the reader and the writer; the game was to spot the genuine clues and fit them together, with no unfair advantage being taken by the author.

The 'English formula' within which the Coles wrote not only limited the tricks that could be used to complicate the plot; the formula also

[1] Ibid., p. 78.

effectively restricted the writers to an upper or middle class milieu. The murder must take place within a closed circle of suspects; it was easiest to isolate the suspects by placing them in a country estate or in a private school or university. It is strange to read a murder mystery by two socialists which accepts such class-bound conventions; it illustrates their position within the 'intellectual Establishment'. The Coles were least convincing when they employed the most typical conventions of an upper class setting, such as the device of the nice, unemployable (or leisured) amateurs who confuse the police – perhaps because they had little patience with their own creations. Often their efforts to introduce humour into these settings had a strong undercurrent of distaste. In *Poison in a Garden Suburb*, they underlined the feudal pretensions of Mrs Freemantle, the patronness of the 'Literary Institute of Medstead Garden Suburb'. A more satisfactory solution was to vary their settings, describing environments and characters that were more palatable to them. Among the characters for whom they showed warmth were a shop steward and a science teacher in a progressive school.

Often the characters in mysteries written in the 'English formula' are wooden. The Coles took more than usual care to give their characters reality by relating them to the social and political questions of the day. One of the more appealing characters in *Scandal at School*, a Jewish sculptress, was made to describe her flight from Vienna when the Social Democrats were suppressed. In *The Murder at the Munition Works*, Cole presented spokesmen for the varied opinions within the Labour movement concerning the Second World War, then in the 'phony war' stage. Interestingly enough, *The Murder at the Munition Works* was not relevant in the crude sense of the word. The Coles did not turn that book into an impassioned plea for the war effort, and avoided the clichés of espionage and treason that many mystery writers mistook for being up to date.

Despite their effort to be realistic, the Coles did not create vivid characters. Their characters were not pathologically complex; they had no depth of obsession or paranoia. Even the criminals against whom the Coles developed the most feeling were ordinary people gone wrong. Elisha Dawes, the religious fanatic and businessman killer of *Dead Man's Watch*, was revealed as having a perfectly rational motive:

insurance money that would save his struggling bicycle shop. Nor were the Coles' descriptions of criminals and crime particularly violent. Elisha Dawes is noteworthy among the Coles' creations for committing two murders and attempting a third. Of his three crimes, one is deduced long after the event; a second is announced by a brief item in a newspaper; and only in the third case are we shown a decomposing body that has washed up on the bank of a river. Violence was exceptional in the world they described, and so was vengeance. Often the Coles allowed their criminal to commit suicide rather than be apprehended and executed.

One might expect the Coles to have described the police as the brutal foundation of middle-class society. Instead, the manuscript of a radio talk, fortunately preserved in the Cole papers,[1] shows how much they enjoyed creating their principal sleuth, Inspector Wilson. Wilson was polite, patient, and hard-working; he reassured suspects by his normality, resembling a bank manager. Wilson respected the civil rights of his suspects. Socialist suspects often began by showing hostility towards him, but ended up respecting and cooperating with him. Some ambivalence crept into the Coles' books when they described Wilson's relations to other policemen. He had conflicts both with inspectors and with the Chief Constables of counties; but these conflicts normally arose when local policemen failed to notice evidence or were satisfied with the first suspect who crossed their path. The police were often stupid and class-ridden, but not malevolent or imperious. Wilson himself constantly insisted upon fair play. 'A public servant has no right to get rattled when an intelligent member of the public points out his omissions.'[2]

The Coles' mysteries come alive when they let their personal preferences show through. *Death of a Millionaire*, their second mystery, was written during the 'Red Scare' election and naturally had a Russian suspect, who was cleared. In that story, the Coles smiled at the antics of a robber-baron sort of speculator, whom they apparently could respect – and only chastised the sort of 'worm' who, as a second-generation businessman, chanted cant phrases about honesty in busi-

[1] 'Manuscripts and Proofs', Box 6, folder 75, Cole Papers, Nuffield College.
[2] G. D. H. and Margaret Cole, *Dead Man's Watch* (New York, Doubleday Doran and the Crime Club, 1932), p. 68.

ness. Another of their best mysteries is *Corpse in Canonicals*, where they pointed out with evident glee that a clerical collar provides immunity from suspicion – revealing two 'clergymen' as criminals. They combined the two types in *The Big Business Murder* – published in the same year as *Principles of Economic Planning* – providing a bishop as the director of a fraudulent company who murdered to conceal his theft of the savings of innocent widows and children. One can feel the Coles' pleasure in writing these books – and a few more people may have learned some rudiments of politics and economics in a painless way.

There might seem to be considerable tension between the foci of Cole's intellectual life. Oxford and London, academic work and murder mysteries, the impartial dissection of academic economic and social thought competing with partisan propaganda – what could unify these activities and perspectives? Beatrice Webb, for one, thought she discerned an unbearable tension between Oxford and his commitment to the Labour movement. In September 1928 she recorded in her diary that Cole wanted to leave Oxford to teach in London and to devote more time to the movement.[1] She may have been right; perhaps Cole would have left Oxford, if diabetes had not intervened.

But one may argue instead that the tension among Cole's activities was more apparent than real. In the first place, Cole did not need the monotonous uniformity of the fanatic's life. He welcomed diversity; and his mental agility and energy permitted him to engage in several activities within a short time-span. Secondly, he created for himself a role that integrated his academic and political work, and even left its mark on his murder mysteries – the role of a socialist educator. This integration was made possible by Cole's belief that even propaganda had to respect the facts revealed by research. Cole came to spend a considerable part of his time in communicating the results of research to the intellectually active Labour or uncommitted voter. He showed this audience that new economic thought led to socialist policies. As a popularizer, he simplified subjects without being patronizing; he had a real gift for untangling complex subjects and creating a clear narrative. Cole covered a broad range of subjects, without pretending to give the final word on any, acknowledging difficulties instead of obscuring

[1] 'The Diary of Beatrice Webb', Vol. 42 (11 September 1928), 125.

them. Even as a propagandist, he sought to elucidate problems rather than to indoctrinate. Cole's style invited the reader to think along with him, and provided the reader with the facts he might want to use. *What Everybody Wants to Know About Money*, *The Intelligent Man's Guide Through World Chaos*, an article for *The Highway* or *The New Statesman*, and a talk to a W.E.A. branch were all part of his efforts to educate the whole Labour movement.

At the same time, much of his academic work concerned the Labour movement and assisted his rethinking of Labour's position, now that Guild Socialism was exhausted and massive unemployment was at hand. In 1923 Cole wrote three volumes for the Carnegie Endowment for International Peace, dealing with workshop organizations, labour relations in the munitions industry, and the coal industry during the First World War. Then he turned to two early nineteenth-century men with whom he sympathized deeply. William Cobbett and Robert Owen appealed to him because of their strong moral commitment to a better society, their humanity, and their love for the common people. Interestingly, in the early days of the Second World War Cole similarly turned to the study of democratic radicals and Labour pioneers; he then wrote Fabian pamphlets on Keir Hardie, John Burns, and Richard Carlile, in addition to his *Chartist Portraits*. One could say that in writing biographies, Cole reaffirmed his basic loyalties.

It took Cole the better part of a decade to rethink his position. Between 1923 and 1929 he struggled to arrive at a consistent conception of socialism within which he could become creative. He found it impossible to satisfy both the ideals and the militancy that made up his 'Bolshevik soul' and the practicality of his 'Fabian muzzle'. He kept up a steady flow of political journalism which adds up to a running commentary on tendencies to which he was unable to commit himself fully. In the months leading up to the first Labour Government he approached reformism warily, then recoiled into an intransigent pose. By the summer of 1925 he had swung over to an extreme partisanship close to the I.L.P's 'Socialism in Our Time'. After the General Strike he veered back towards reformism. By 1929 he had worked out a list of socialist reforms that satisfied him enough to become the basis of a book, *The Next Ten Years in British Social and Economic Policy*. But this reformism satisfied his Fabian sense of practicality more than his socialist ideals, and the second Labour Government exposed the fragility of purely reformist politics. After 1931, he settled on a fuller conception of reformism within which he worked through most of the 1930s. Some of his reforms, such as the National Labour Corps vanished from his writings, while planning and a more aggressive attitude towards the use of power rounded out his politics.

Rethinking his position meant first of all adjusting to the dominant currents within the Labour movement. Cole never worked in a vacuum; he always sought to describe practical policies that would articulate and strengthen what an advanced section of the movement was striving for. He would have liked his thought to develop in close connection with the practices of the industrial side of the movement. However, he lost many of his connections with militant trade unionists as the shop stewards' movement waned, as Guild Socialism broke up, and as the Communist Party was formed. His position had become more nearly that of a sympathetic outsider.

As the 1920s wore on, the unions showed fewer tendencies on which Cole could build an aggressively socialist policy. He was deeply disappointed by their inability to organize the unemployed.

> ... we have to think out means of handling the unemployed as human beings, of organizing their resistance to oppression, of mobilizing them, as well as the employed, against the forces of capitalism. I say deliberately that the Labour movement as a whole has *funked* this job. Too many Labour people have been frightened of mobilizing the forces of the unemployed, for fear they might not be able to control them. Official Labour has left the unemployed to the Communists; and they, and the local Labour people who have tried to tackle the problem here and there, have only touched the fringes of it.[1]

This stand kept him from attacking the National Unemployed Workers' Movement, although he never had much good to say about its efforts. He refused to be upset by the prevailing fears of Communist domination of the unemployed; but at the same time he accepted the verdict banning the parallel Minority Movement from affiliation to the Labour Party. His own solution would have called upon local Trades Councils to organize sections for the unemployed, who would still retain their rights as members of individual unions. However, inter-union jealousies

[1] G. D. H. Cole, 'Workshop and Mine', *The New Leader* (6 October 1922).

and suspicions of the Trades Councils scuttled this proposal. Cole continuously proposed new tasks for Trades Councils between 1913 and 1925, and as continuously saw them rejected.

Cole instinctively supported any trade union that refused to accept wage cuts; he knew that they would reduce purchasing power and thus reduce the amount of goods that could be sold. But this reaction could not teach him much about the expansionary economic policy that would have been the only effective opposition to Tory orthodoxies. As he came to see that unemployment was a national problem, he gave up looking for a wave of strikes like that of 1910–14. He could repress neither his liking for militant measures nor his discouragement.

Even should the fight prove hopeless, the only alternative was the immediate swallowing of all that the mineowners and the Government chose to demand; and we still think a fight, even a losing fight, better than a tame submission. But the plain fact is that industrial action on a falling market is useless in the end; it only serves the employers' ends, and though a *beau geste* is better than no *geste* at all, it is the duty of people who are thinking out policy to find a better way.[1]

In the summer of 1923 he even came to argue against strikes. They might imperil the slight signs of trade revival on which Cole pinned some hope for reducing unemployment.

In Cole's eyes, the worker had come to be a different sort of person. He seemed less wedded to a craft, less likely to seek self-expression in his work. Cole changed the emphasis he placed on various aspects of freedom. Where he had placed the emphasis on abolishing wage-slavery, now he put more weight on the abolition of poverty and on personal liberty. Only a minority would actively seek self-government, in work or in politics. Cole could only hope that the workers would show enough loyalty to allow the political side of the movement to grow. In politics, if at all, resided the expanding forces with which Cole had to come to terms.

Many of the articles that marked steps towards coming to terms with political action are coloured with a bitter attempt at humour, as if to ease unwillingness or embarrassment. In July 1921 he wrote, 'The only course for Labour at the moment is to run its own anti-waste campaign and to send men to Parliament – yes, to the effete bourgeois

[1] CC, 'Notes of the Month', *The Guild Socialist*, No. 55 (July 1921), p. 1.

Parliament – pledged to cancel the claim to unearned income based on the war debt at the first opportunity . . .'.[1] This proposal was essentially the common Labour notion of a capital levy; a repudiation of the national debt would leave more money for unemployment benefit and for various social services then under attack by Tory 'economisers'. But in his search for new directions, Cole was not above seizing and twisting a catchy Tory slogan such as 'anti-waste campaign', even though its deflationary parentage must have been repugnant to him.

When he urged workers to vote Labour in 1922, he felt a bitter relief that a Labour Government could not be elected. 'Our first inclination is to say "Damn the Election!" . . . If we have any choice between the various execrable Governments now offered to us as alternatives, on the whole we choose the worst . . .'[2] In the 1923 election he responded to the left-wing argument that Labour should not accept office as a minority Government. When MacDonald did, he urged him to provoke defeat on a major issue and appeal to the country for a mandate to introduce major changes into the economy.[3] This step makes clear how incomplete was his acceptance of political action. He could not yet believe that a Labour Government would attack unemployment. The first measure which significantly threatened to alter the legal pre-dominance of the propertied classes would create a national confronta-tion, in which Labour would back down. This scepticism undercut his rethinking of his Socialism. It perhaps made him too ready to accept the pleas of politicians that parliamentary tactics precluded an aggres-sive effort to provide work, houses, or social benefits. Thus one article before the 1923 elections pinned a desperate hope on the fact that a Labour Government could help the working class immediately by restoring cuts in educational spending and by reversing Tory efforts to save on the unemployed by changing administrative regulations.[4] These policies would not test the legislative prowess and resolve of the Labour Party at all, but would be a sign of good faith.

[1] CC, 'Notes of the Month', *The Guild Socialist*, No. 55 (July 1921), p. 1.
[2] CC, 'Notes of the Month', *The Guild Socialist*, No. 70 (November 1922), p. 1.
[3] *New Standards*, No. 4 (February 1924), 97. *New Standards* was the successor to *The Guild Socialist*, trying to combine the remnants of the Guild Socialist movement with the workers' education movement. Twelve issues were published.
[4] G. D. H. Cole, 'What a Labour Government Could Do', *New Statesman*, XXII (15 December 1923), 294–6.

The MacDonald Government failed to make even the sign of good faith, and Cole swung back towards political intransigence. It is surprising that he did not become a leader in the I.L.P. campaign for 'Socialism in Our Time' in 1925–6. The I.L.P. was a likely home for Cole. He wrote for its official *New Leader* in 1922–23 and for *Lansbury's Labour Weekly* in 1925. Many I.L.P. supporters shared his basic moral values and his desire for a viable militant policy. The I.L.P. chairman, Clifford Allen, had known Cole since their days in the University Socialist Federation and had been a Guildsman. He probably discussed the ideas that grew into 'Socialism in Our Time' with Cole in 1922–3. The central idea of demanding a living wage appears in several of Cole's articles, and Allen reportedly wanted to run a 'Now for Socialism' campaign then.[1]

But Cole was not at all sure that the I.L.P. had solved the problem of the intellectual's place in the Labour movement. 'The I.L.P. . . . has so far tried to . . . combine the characteristics of a constitutional party with those of a Socialist society of propaganda on the old lines. Naturally it is finding this position more and more difficult to maintain, and is being forced more and more to sacrifice its street-corner Socialism to its political aspiration.'[2] Cole ultimately solved the problem by eschewing personal political ambition, while the I.L.P. went off in the other direction.

'Socialism in Our Time' did not strike Cole as a real programme, a new unified conception of socialism. It was a myth, in Sorel's sense. It was a way of organizing Labour's demands intellectually. Allen wanted to take the demand for a living wage, make it the central demand in socialist propaganda, and lead the workers to realize that only the socialization of finance and industry could redeem the promise. Cole seized on the impossibility of paying such wages and providing high enough family allowances in the beginning, and hinted that the slogan was misleading.[3] He saw much more difficulty in reorganizing British industry and gaining foreign markets, even under socialism; these concerns led him first towards more limited reforms and eventually to economic planning. Cole used the slogan in a few articles for *Lansbury's*

[1] G. D. H. Cole, *A History of the Labour Party from 1914* (London, Routledge and Kegan Paul, 1948), p. 150.
[2] G. D. H. Cole, 'A Socialist Dilemma', *New Statesman*, xxv (18 April 1925), 4–5.
[3] G. D. H. Cole, 'The I.L.P. Conference', *New Statesman*, xxvi (10 April 1926), 796–7.

Labour Weekly in the summer of 1925, but soon let both the slogan and the newspaper slide. The emotional intransigence of this section of the Labour left, in the General Strike and in 'Socialism in Our Time', offended his Fabian practicality.

The deficiencies of the left virtually forced Cole to turn to parliamentary reformism. Socialism had become practical politics. A Labour Party with genuine hopes for a parliamentary majority had replaced the little band of representatives that Cole had scorned in 1913 and 1922. Even the Tories borrowed socialist forms when they nationalized the wholesale operations of the electrical supply industry and set up the B.B.C.

However, desperation, to a greater degree than hope, shaped his reformism.

'Socialism is best' said the pre-war Socialist; but now he calls for Socialism as men call for water in a burning house. And, in the latter mood, he is far less likely to grumble if only muddy water can be got.[1]

He still felt that it would be delusion to expect much from parliamentary reformism. Labour would have to begin with a programme short of Socialism. He had to come to terms with the motives and limits imposed by working within capitalist society. 'I say, as a Socialist, that Socialists are not yet ready to do away with profit-making in industry, and that accordingly they must take steps to make the capitalist system work more efficiently.'[2] Moderation, sobriety, self-restraint, even dullness, turn up as words of praise in his articles. These desperate admissions amused Mrs Webb, who found Cole bobbing up to the right of herself and Sidney as they moved towards their flirtation with Soviet Communism.[3]

As Cole grew more sure of his reformism, and more desperate about unemployment, he thought of leaving Oxford to serve the Labour movement on a full-time basis. In July 1930 the King's Norton division of Birmingham adopted him as their prospective candidate for Parliament. When Cole accepted the candidacy, he prepared to contest a seat Labour hoped to win. King's Norton had seen Labour's first victory

---

[1] G. D. H. Cole, *The Next Ten Years in British Social and Economic Policy* (London, Macmillan, 1929), p. viii.
[2] G. D. H. Cole, 'The Cure for Unemployment', *Everyman* (10 October 1929), 253.
[3] 'The Diary of Beatrice Webb', Vol. 50 (20 July 1936), 95.

in Birmingham, in 1924. When it returned to the Unionists in 1929, it gave them only a 491 vote plurality. Both the industrial and the co-operative sides of the movement were building important bases at King's Norton – the unions at Cadbury's and at Austin's Longbridge plant, the co-operators through the Ten Acres and Stirchley society.

Cole's decision logically followed his change of opinions, but logic did not make him like the idea of entering Parliament. He wrote to his supporters that 'I regard parliamentary politics as a demoralizing business ... very liable to undermine the faith of those who successfully engage in it in the practicability of really drastic measures of social change'.[1] After the fall of the second Labour Government, Cole and his friends converted this distrust into an effort to spell out the measures a Labour Government would have to take to avoid being demoralized. Cole's own resistance was never put to the test. After diabetes had been diagnosed, he gave up the candidacy. One suspects that the illness offered him an acceptable way out of an unpleasant situation.[2]

Cole's sceptical attitude towards Parliament has led many observers to feel that he lacked the qualities of a parliamentary politician. Edward Hyams, in his history of the *New Statesman*, asserted that 'Cole was no compromiser, no politician ... He could have been an embarrassment to any editor with a definite party attachment.'[3] An inability to compromise, or a lack of political skill, was not the problem; the real problem was that Parliament had no place for Cole's particular skills. Participating in the feeble Labour opposition of the 1930s would have been a waste of his abilities as a teacher, a researcher, and a propagandist. He might have been tempted to carry on a one-man campaign like Cripps', out of frustration and impatience at Labour's impotence in the parliamentary process.

The tensions that might have been disastrous in Parliament became creative outside Parliament. He successfully trod the path of a 'loyal grouser', when other intellectual and political critics found themselves outside the party. He tried to find grounds for a genuine consensus between the official Labour Party and other people on the left, both in

[1] G. D. H. Cole, 'Is Unemployment a Non-party Question?', *King's Norton Labour News*, New Series, No. 11 (July 1930), p. 1.
[2] See Hugh Gaitskell, 'At Oxford in the Twenties', in *Essays in Labour History*, p. 18.
[3] Edward Hyams, *The New Statesman: The History of the First Fifty Years 1913–1963* (London, Longmans Green, 1963), pp. 108, 93.

the *soi-disant* left wing and in other democratic forces. The core of this consensus had to be reformism, but its spirit had to be socialist. He sought to turn a collection of reforms into a rational and coherent programme aiming towards socialism. He attempted to assign priorities to the considerable number of potential acts which Labour Party Conferences had approved; he sought to infuse as much of the socialist spirit as he felt the electorate and the problems of the times could bear, and the Labour Party could be persuaded to fight an election with. This effort was something more important than a compromise. It was an effort to make something creative out of the tension between his strong socialist ideals and his desire to be practical in the political terms of the day.

Cole's willingness to modify his position, for reasons of party loyalty and practicality, has been overlooked – perhaps because every time he moved towards the right, the Labour Party moved farther right. He often obtained the worst of two worlds. It often seems that no matter what he did, he would have looked irresponsible to those who had learned to distrust him as a Guild Socialist. He worked closely with Bevin and Citrine on specific projects, but they easily reverted to suspecting him of disloyalty.[1] Other party stalwarts expressed fears that the New Fabian Research Bureau might come to support Mosley or create dissension. Yet Cole's loyalty prevented him from going out on his own, so that he could never appear as a fully original thinker, the systematic creator of a policy. Stafford Cripps made his reputation in this way, challenging the party leadership throughout the 1930s with policies whose coherence may be questioned. Cole didn't try to create a 'Cole policy' for a dissident wing; instead, he worked with what was at hand. The successive works that embody his efforts to clarify Labour's policy have the ephemerality of party documents, yet one can often see in them the strength of his mind.

If one lists the proposals that he wrote about, or chronicles the fluctuating militancy in his articles, Cole may appear inconsistent or irresponsible. Harold Laski, according to Beatrice Webb, accused Cole

---

Walter Citrine, *Men and Work* (London: Hutchinson, 1964), pp. 293–301; Alan Bullock, *The Life and Times of Ernest Bevin:* 1, *Trade Union Leader 1881–1940* (London, Heinemann, 1959), p. 531 ff.

of gambling with various proposals in 1930[1]. But this criticism misses two basic patterns of self-control in Cole's experimentation with new ideas and new slogans. First, Cole largely avoided the most romantic efforts to rally the left wing – the I.L.P's 'Socialism in Our Time' campaign and its secession from the Labour Party, the Minority Movement, and the Socialist League's crusades under Cripps' leadership. More fundamentally, behind these oscillations of attention and emphasis lay a unity of perception similar to that we found in his Guild Socialist period. The foci were his perception that Britain's economy needed rational planning and reorientation, that the problems of unemployment and finance were the keys, and that they could be approached only through an evolutionary, parliamentary socialism. Cole thus worked for some fifteen years with a collection of short-term proposals and more basic concepts that came close to being a complete picture of Britain as it was and as it could become. The picture offered him scope for intellectual progress; it even took on an institutional form with the creation of the New Fabian Research Bureau.

One issue, more than any other, drove Cole through his periodic changes of policy and mood in the 1920s and 1930s. Unemployment was the intolerable fact whose persistence challenged every policy. It also made socialism practical politics, if socialists would only work out their answers. We can see Cole moving from common Labour slogans to an expansionary reformist economics in 1929. The development of his thought brought him close to Keynes; but a combination of unsolved problems and socialist militancy kept Cole from arriving at a full-blooded Keynesianism.

Fundamentally, unemployment outraged Cole as a human being and as an economist. He felt anger at the human effects of unemployment. He detested the callousness people revealed while talking about, or forgetting to talk about, two million unemployed people. However, he generally avoided charitable mawkishness. In a partially detached, somewhat ascetic way, he looked beyond physical suffering to the feelings of shame, frustration, uselessness, and inferiority that came with unemployment. He was appalled by the waste of skilled men and women who were losing their mental and physical agility through enforced inaction, who were rotting away. Cole's outrage at this waste

[1]'The Diary of Beatrice Webb', Vol. 45 (8 May 1930), 48.

of people was humanitarian; and it had a nationalistic strand. The disintegration of Englishmen offended the part of Cole that had responded to Cobbett and Defoe, as well as to Morris.

The economic absurdity of large-scale unemployment was equally infuriating. It was 'a sheer waste of the power to produce good things.'[1] Talk about over-production irritated him, for there were innumerable needs to be filled. It made obvious sense to employ the workers to use existing productive capacity to fill these needs; any deflationary economics was simply nonsense, because it abrogated this common sense. It was equally ludicrous to pay dole to men who could make things. It would pay society to hire a workman, even if he could not produce an amount equivalent to his maintenance. 'For he has to be maintained, whether he produces or not',[2] Cole told his constituents at King's Norton. Employing a workman would, at worst, save part of the cost of his maintenance, while providing more goods for the nation. Cole summed up his understanding of the sham economics of unemployment and derisory doles for the Royal Commission on Unemployment Insurance in 1931:

The direct cost of providing work is, of course, found to be larger than the cost of unemployment benefit. But (a) there is the value of the work to set against the cost, (b) the work will prevent the deterioration of the unemployed, and save many of them from becoming unemployable, and a permanent charge on the State, (c) the effect of providing work rather than leaving men in idleness will have important psychological reaction, not only on the unemployed, but on the whole community, and especially in the depressed areas.[3]

The Labour movement provided two stock answers to the problem of turning this common sense into a policy. The first was the slogan that only socialism could cure unemployment. As Robert Skidelsky has argued, this slogan paralysed Labour thinking.[4] The paralysis is clear in Cole's 1923 study, *Out of Work*. The slogan remained a reflex that could be activated when the compromises Cole was faced with

[1] G. D. H. Cole, *The People's Front* (London, Gollancz and Left Book Club, 1937), p. 233.
[2] G. D. H. Cole, 'The Madness of Unemployment', *King's Norton Labour News*, New Series, No. 13 (September 1930), p. 1.
[3] *Minutes of Evidence Taken Before the Royal Commission on Unemployment Insurance* (London, H.M.S.O., 1931), 19th Day, Tuesday, 31st March 1931, p. 745, para. 72. Cole's written testimony.
[4] Robert Skidelsky, *Politicians and the Slump: The Labour Government of 1929–1931* (London, Macmillan, 1967).

became intolerable. The American New Deal triggered the response: 'Under Capitalism, the more Mr Roosevelt now succeeds in getting men back to work by monetary reflation and by a control which does not really put the key positions into the hands of the state today, the more widespread and disastrous the succeeding crash is certain to be.'[1] If one wanted to support Cole's argument, he might cite the recession which occurred in 1938 as soon as the American Government reduced its spending.

Cole's anti-depression speculations always had a degree of ambivalence about them; he proposed what are now orthodox Keynesian remedies, but feared, and hoped, that they would not work. There always was the possibility that a depression might bring capitalism down. Cole wanted the end of capitalism, but could not bring himself to desire a general collapse of the British economy. Consequently he tried to derive a workable policy from the second traditional socialist slogan, 'work or maintenance'. The policy offered at least a theoretical way out of a deflationary spiral, in particular if the more attractive idea of providing work were emphasized. But, as Skidelsky shows, the Labour movement failed to think the policy out. In practice, 'work or maintenance' became a call for improving and maintaining unemployment benefits, and was extremely vulnerable to traditional notions of 'economy'. Cole's experience with the idea largely confirms Skidelsky's judgments, although at several points we can see that he came close to a workable version of the idea.

Providing work attracted Cole more than maintaining the unemployed. It appealed to his humanitarian urge to restore creativity and self-respect to the workers. Early in the inter-war slump, he concentrated on showing that a number of feasible projects were visible. The expansion of electrical supply, the electrification of the railroads, and a vastly expanded programme of house building all caught his eye. But he could not develop the idea in any great detail; he could not even answer his own suspicion that providing work within capitalism would only be a palliative. What he lacked was a solution to the problem of financing these developments. First he looked for ways to get industry to spend its reserves. The Government

---

[1] G. D. H. Cole, 'The Battle of Hastings', *New Statesman and Nation*, VI (30 September 1933), 377–8.

should force the railroads to electrify, he argued in 1923. In three early articles, one in November 1923 and two in the summer of 1925, he called for a 'great national loan for the enlargement of the nation's productive capacity.'[1] He guessed at a possible total of £100 million in one of the 1925 articles.[2] He presented the idea tentatively – it isn't clear whether he was asking for £100 million a year for several years, or merely for a total of £100 million – and drew no response from readers. He lacked any way of making an expansionist policy palatable to middle-class taxpayers and property owners. From the Labour point of view, Keynes later filled the gap with the theory of deficit spending, making ideas expounded by J. A. Hobson and various socialists an accepted part of fiscal theory. Lacking deficit spending and R. F. Kahn's multiplier, Cole could only appeal to profitability and to anti-deflationary common sense.

In *The Next Ten Years in British Social and Economic Policy* (1929), Cole returned to the provision of work with new enthusiasm. He came closer to a financial solution and provided greater organizational detail. He described a National Labour Corps, which would take on tasks better suited to temporary work than the public works projects he had described in 1923. The National Labour Corps could 'clean up Britain', removing the scars of the industrial revolution and destroying slums. They could undertake capital projects beyond the reach of industry, such as the electrification of the railways, and build houses, roads, and other amenities where business and organized labour were unable or unwilling to take up the task. Unfortunately, the whole conception was too dramatic for any of the major interests in the country to accept it.

Membership of the National Labour Corps would be entirely voluntary. Cole insisted that men should not be forced into it, and that they should be able to leave at any time without imperilling their right to National Assistance. On the issue of pay, Cole found himself hemmed in by the strongly-held belief that relief work should be 'less eligible' than other work and by the fears of the unions that public works might further undercut their bargaining position. He explicitly repudiated the principle of less eligibility and sought to replace it with a minimum

[1] G. D. H. Cole, 'The One Thing Needful', *New Statesman*, XXII (24 November 1923), 201–3.
[2] G. D. H. Cole, 'The Way to Deal with Unemployment', *New Statesman*, XXV (1 August 1925), 440–1.

income, but in *The Next Ten Years* he pegged the minimum below what he considered an adequate rate for a family, urging that family allowances be added. Consequently, the rate offered would have been below union scales unless the whole income structure of society were overhauled at the same time. He made an obeisance to vested interests in the Labour movement by agreeing that the National Labour Corps should not undertake to supply the labour for a project if an existing union could provide it.

The National Labour Corps was an obvious expedient. Cole may well have been the first to work it out, but I am not aware of his proposal exerting a direct influence on later versions such as Roosevelt's Civilian Conservation Corps. It is interesting that Cole lost faith in the idea just when Roosevelt adopted it, in the depths of the depression. For Cole it had only been a palliative, although a far-reaching one. During the depression the level of unemployment seemed to get beyond the point at which the National Labour Corps could make an impression. When unemployment fell in the late 1930s Cole felt able to return to the idea. However, he continually believed that the ultimate prevention of unemployment would rest on other policies for the reconstruction of British industry through State planning of credit and investment.

In *The Next Ten Years*, Cole came closer to solving the problem of finance than he had in 1925. He divided the National Labour Corps' projects into those that were commercially feasible and those that would not show a commercial return. The Treasury would be asked to provide for non-commercial projects out of the national Budget. Cole estimated that £100 million a year could be provided for the National Labour Corps, in addition to a similar amount for family allowances. Defence spending should be cut, by a sum starting around £32 million and rising to £54 million. He projected some £85 million in additional taxation of high and unearned incomes, using proposals current within the Labour Party. He hoped for another £50 million from a revision of death duties, referring specifically to Hugh Dalton's proposal to tax away inherited capital over three generations.[1]

These budgetary speculations are half-practical, half-amateur fiddling with figures. They were different enough to be offensive to a Snowden,

[1] *The Next Ten Years*, p. 408.

but probably not drastic enough to eliminate unemployment. Their amateurishness appears in the juggling of defence figures and in the expectations from taxes on high incomes and estates. As he admitted, the increase in the total Budget from about £760 million to £921 million would sound terrible.[1] The second MacDonald Government could not have seen these proposals as practical politics; even if Snowden had wanted to accept them, he would not have defended them against the inevitable opposition of bankers and industrialists. Paradoxically, Cole's efforts to be practical in political terms would probably have made his proposals ineffective against even the level of unemployment of late 1928. This roughly calculated Budget was balanced. New borrowing was placed outside the Budget, and Cole assured his readers that it would not be inflationary.

In 1929, Cole was not prepared to bring commercial investment into the Budget, nor to place all commercial investment under public control. He left out of his calculations the capital that British industries accumulated out of their reserved profits.[2] To bring other forms of investment under control, he borrowed a device from the Liberal economists' *Britain's Industrial Future* – a National Investment Board. Like many other economists, Cole realized that Britain could not go on exporting capital at a high rate; he wanted the National Investment Board empowered 'to prohibit or license, according to the national interest, not merely public loans raised in this country for overseas use, but all loans so raised'. Cole went on to propose extensive tasks for the National Investment Board in stimulating development at home.

It will act, in the first place, as a great reservoir of new capital from which public bodies and statutory undertakings of every sort – from municipalities to public utility housing societies and the like – will be able to draw, on easy terms, the capital required for productive developments of national importance ... Its more novel and constructive function will be to help the development of industries generally, even where they are not conducted by a public body or specially constituted statutory undertaking.[3]

In this last proposal we can see how far Cole had gone towards accepting a 'mixed economy' in which the Government would help private, profit-making concerns.

[1] Ibid., p. 411.
[2] Ibid., p. 84.
[3] Ibid., pp. 77–8.

In order to supply public and private projects with capital, the National Investment Board needed a sure source of funds. Cole suggested two sources. One was the nationalization of insurance, and the other was the chartering of a Government investment trust, which would borrow money and re-lend it to businesses for development purposes. The latter expedient could yield a measure of state control without nationalization of businesses, by providing state directors of companies using Government funds. Most aspects of this policy have proved too advanced for British politicians, although the Industrial Reconstruction Corporation created in 1966 tried to perform some of the same tasks.

Cole made no effort to work out the volume of capital that the National Investment Board would have to distribute in order to end unemployment. Writing just before the slump was overtaken by the depression, he did not want the Government to increase the total amount of money available for investment immediately. More capital would be available if other measures succeeded in raising the national income. His target was the wastefulness of private, uncoordinated investment. Naturally Cole found speculation wasteful; but he was equally concerned with the erosion of previous public and private investment in factories, schools and amenities in the depressed areas. Waste was a social category rather than a matter of a monetary return on capital; it concerned the social usefulness of particular projects. Cole could not abstract 'capital' from its specific uses in the way Keynesians do. He had no notion of calculating a total capital budget for a mixed economy. He would have retorted that one did not have to wait for elaborate calculations – there was unused money and unfilled needs, and it would be ludicrous not to bring them together.

Cole's approach to the control of credit similarly emphasized strategic and institutional considerations. Again he stopped short of calculating a national budget for credit. His approach to the problem of credit was basically defensive. Cole insisted that 'clearly the banks and the City can, as matters stand, make the position very difficult for a Government of whose policy they strongly disapproved.'[1] Consequently he recommended that the Government nationalize both the Bank of England and the joint stock Banks. Each had specialized functions, and each

[1] Ibid., p. 226.

could slow up or distort the expansion and direction of credit. The Bank of England largely controlled the volume of credit, and the joint-stock banks dominated the directions in which it flows. As a result, nationalization of the Bank of England alone would be inadequate, for the joint-stock banks could refuse to grant credit to firms the National Investment Board sought to encourage, and thus defeat the purpose of a general expansion of credit. However, Cole did not suggest combining the management of the joint-stock banks and the Bank of England, much less combining both of them with the National Investment Board. In addition, he seemed more eager to guard against the 'currency cranks' than to expect great dividends from the nationalization of the banks.

In general, Cole preferred to use the term 'socialization' rather than nationalization in the late 1920s, and with it went a surprisingly moderate political policy. E. Eldon Barry refers to it as 'his curious intermediate stage between Guild Socialism and state socialism'.[1] The position itself is not curious; many reformists have used it to avoid bureaucracy and state monopoly. What is curious is that Cole went over to such a mild reformism. He argued that what mattered was not a change in ownership, but a change in control. Public ownership could come gradually, through progressive taxation; control of policy had to come earlier. Cole felt that Government regulation and control of monetary policy would suffice; he even proposed, in the case of coal (the industry generally proposed for nationalization), to limit Government intervention in the first instance to financial reorganization and control of marketing.[2] For a person of Cole's standing on the left of the Labour Movement, this acceptance of the Conservative model for the nationalization of the wholesale operations of the electricity industry is quite surprising. Cole's realization of the tremendous difficulties involved in taking over an entire industry within capitalist society may account for his caution. The first problem arose from the shortage of parliamentary time, which meant that only a few complicated measures could get through Parliament in any one session. Nationalization further involved carefully detaching an industry from other operations carried on by the same companies, finding competent experts to run it, and pay-

[1] E. Eldon Barry, *Nationalization in British Politics*, p. 203.
[2] *The Next Ten Years*, pp. 141–2.

ing large sums of money. But Cole revealed a more basic reason for his hesitance when he said that 'Socialists themselves cannot afford to take over industries which are in a state of decay'.[1] In fact, the only industries which have been taken over have been those which are no longer profitable, and this has subjected the whole concept of nationalization to the sort of strain Cole feared.

In talking about 'socialization' instead of all-out national ownership, Cole showed his habitual distrust of centralized ownership, bureaucracy and civil service control. This libertarian side is one of the most appealing things about Cole, yet it often made him draw back at the crucial points. He felt that

the less the State has to do directly with its detailed administration the better. The Socialist State will have quite enough to do without cumbering itself with a single function that can be safely left to any other organization or person in the community. Its greatest danger is that of becoming top-heavy, through the accumulation of too many detailed functions on its hands.[2]

In this instance too, in 1929, Cole was still thinking in institutional terms. He argued that civil servants were not expert enough to run an industry, especially one that was in any difficulties, and that Parliament could not hope to exercise any adequate supervision over their actions. In other words, he thought in terms of the qualities which certain kinds of administration – civil service, public corporation, and 'private' management – introduced into industry, and in fairly emotive terms at that. He had more to say about the processes of decision-making than he had about the decisions themselves.

To a fair extent, this was a legacy of his academic background and of his Guild Socialist enthusiasms. It is clear that Cole had had no real enthusiasm for economic theory at the start of his career. At the 1919 Conference of the N.G.L., for example, he admitted that he would have liked 'to bring about a system of society in which economic power does not predominate in society ... He was only interested in economics in order to get them out of the way ...'.[3] Like Marx, he found it necessary to study economics for social reasons, and impressively taught himself the subject. I feel, however, that he retained some degree

[1] G. D. H. Cole, 'The Cure for Unemployment', *Everyman* (10 October 1930), 253.
[2] *The Next Ten Years*, pp. 134–5.
[3] A.E.B., 'Guildsmen in Conference', *The Guildsman*, No. 26 (July–August 1919), pp. 9–11.

of distaste for economic theory; he continued to think in ethical and institutional terms. His later books fall flat stylistically where they 'talk economics', whereas Cole wrote attractively in those historical works where he could obtain a personal rapport with his subjects (especially with Cobbett, Owen and the Chartists), and in his Guild Socialist polemics. His distaste for economic theory was not entirely a handicap. The reverse of the coin is that Cole retained the crucial perception that economics was a tool, a means to human and social fellowship, and this helped him avoid the absorption of the orthodox economists, who let their economic theories dictate inhumane passivity to them.

With the publication of *The Next Ten Years*, Cole had stated many elements of an unorthodox, expansionary economics. He had embedded his instinctive expansionary bias in a coherent reformism. He had come to grips with the concept of providing work. He had increased his understanding of national finance, capital and credit. He had labelled some of the machinery which could be used to run an expansionary policy. But what that policy was he did not know. He was uncertain whether to strike out for consumption-led or investment-led growth. On the one hand, consumption was too low, as J. A. Hobson had said, and so it made little sense to increase the proportion of the national income retained as capital. Cole's instinctive sympathies with the unemployed and the poor impelled him in this direction. On the other hand, Britain needed to build new industries, both for home use and for exports, and to improve her social capital. Keynes was soon to integrate this need for expansion of capital goods into his short-term policy, by pointing out that the capital goods industries were sensitive areas in expanding and contracting employment. Cole had seen this, as early as 1923,[1] but failed to make use of it, since he had not approached the problem of unemployment from the angle of the trade cycle. He had no way of making this choice between alternate strategies of growth, because he lacked any device similar to R. F. Kahn's multiplier. He had not worked out relationships between capital and national production, and tended to deny that any such relationships existed. The precision and simplicity of this part of Keynes' argument gave him a considerable advantage over his socialist predecessors.

[1] G. D. H. Cole, *Out of Work: An Introduction to the Study of Unemployment* (London, Labour Publishing Co., 1923), ch. IV.

It is only fair to Cole to say that many more advanced socialists are coming to see that a simple reliance on macroeconomic weapons does not reach deeply depressed areas and classes. Once again it is becoming clear that political intervention on behalf of these groups is necessary. In another ten years, Cole's economic writings – *Principles of Economic Planning* more than the earlier *The Next Ten Years* – may appear less outdated. In *Principles of Economic Planning* Cole came up with a clearer solution to the problem of choosing between competing proposals for development.

The gaps in Cole's economic unorthodoxy left him nearly as vulnerable to the depression as more orthodox reformists such as Snowden. Reformists had their economic policy dictated to them by the fact that they had accepted the basic outlines of capitalist society. It seems to have been virtually impossible to conceive of another set of economic rules, much less to apply one. Cole was free from one of Snowden's particular constraints, a dogmatic belief in free trade, but he uneasily felt that he could not dispense with other orthodox rules. He asserted in *The Next Ten Years* that

It is now scarcely profitable to discuss whether we were wise to return to the gold standard or not. We have done it – in my view, if not wrongly altogether, at any rate in the wrong way – and the case for price stability and stability of international monetary conditions is so strong that no Government is likely at present to reverse what has been done.[1]

This practically ruled out any sort of expansionary economics with its traditional invocation of the fear of inflation.

In one case Cole's acceptance of capitalist assumptions had disastrous consequences. In July 1930 he became chairman of a special committee of the Economic Advisory Council examining unemployment insurance. He had earlier accepted the assumption that the insurance fund should not pile up deficits; in *The Next Ten Years*, he had felt confident that the fund could easily repay what it had borrowed. Now he agreed that those risks that could be insured on actuarily sound grounds should be separated from non-insurable risks. In the context of 1930, this point was vulnerable to those who wanted to slash unemployment benefit. Cole requested a supplementary fund, drawn from general revenues, for the long-term unemployed. The Government

[1] *The Next Ten Years*, p. 241.

was totally unwilling to consider either increased Governmental contributions or a non-contributory scheme of unemployment relief,[1] so Cole's proposals merely contributed to the pressure for lower unemployment benefits. For those workers who had exhausted their insurance rights, he was willing to accept both a means test and a test of the individual's willingness to seek work; this further undercut Labour's defence of the unemployed.

Cole uneasily admitted that capitalist conditions restricted the amounts of money available for social services and economic development.

We cannot, however, take the entire surplus of the larger incomes over the owners' needs as the upper limit of taxable capacity . . . because the large incomes are, under the existing conditions, in part the response to the opportunity of securing them, and, if this opportunity were destroyed by taking them away, a substantial part of them would not be realized at all.[2]

All very practical and reasonable; but in this way, a socialist Government would have to leave basic economic inequality untouched, and could easily be led into courting capitalist 'confidence'. With the Bank of England in private hands, and no exchange controls, the need to protect the sacred Gold Standard could lead to drastic deflationary measures, with a Labour Government deepening a depression by 'economies' in wages and unemployment benefits. In fact, this is what happened, and Cole gradually liberated himself from the assumptions which had made this ghastly paradox possible.

Cole's further development was retarded and complicated by the fact that a Labour Government was in power when the futility of his reformist synthesis became apparent. At first, the Government's dilemmas seemed to open the way for greater influence for Cole and for other Labour economists. Beatrice Webb recorded in December 1929, that Arthur Henderson talked to others in the Government of putting Cole on to an emergency committee to attack poverty. In January 1930 MacDonald announced the formation of an Economic Advisory Council. At the first meeting, Cole joined Keynes on a committee appointed to diagnose the nature of the slump; but their recommendations were countered by Sir Arthur Balfour and Sir John

[1] Robert Skidelsky, *Politicians and the Slump*, p. 238.
[2] *The Next Ten Years*, p. 202.

Cadman.[1] MacDonald's and Snowden's own unwillingness to consider dramatic responses to the depression, coupled with the wide range of opinion on the Economic Advisory Council, prevented Cole from obtaining Government recognition of his first steps towards an expansionist policy.

In public, Cole remained as loyal as possible, and muted his criticisms of a Government which often carried on the unimaginative policies of its predecessor. He realized the obstacles the Government faced and the opposition powerful interests (such as the Bank of England) would make to any hint of unorthodoxy. The breaking-point, for Cole and for the whole Labour movement, came on the issue of unemployment. By the summer of 1929, Cole could see that J. H. Thomas was not going to initiate any major programme of work for the unemployed, but the tone of his articles in the *New Statesman* remained remarkably mild. It was not until February 1930 that Cole accused Thomas of imbibing the Tory and civil service attitude that nothing could be done for the unemployed.[2]

Meanwhile, by the autumn of 1929 a new offender had been added to the list – Philip Snowden, Chancellor of the Exchequer. Cole was unhappy when the Bank Rate was raised, making credit more difficult to obtain. He admitted that under orthodox rules of banking there was no alternative. But he argued for a departure from orthodoxy. If the ratio of gold reserves to currency were altered, then Britain could afford to let gold leave the country and could avoid a restriction upon credit. He did not yet dare tamper with the Gold Standard directly, but he called for a managed currency as opposed to the traditional 'automatic' currency.[3]

As budget time came round, Cole offered Snowden useful advice on how to find an expansionary solution to his problems. He pointed out that the amount which had been projected for the Sinking Fund to abolish the War Debt would cover the estimated fiscal deficit for the coming year. He argued forcibly that 'the advance of the social services

[1] Robert Skidelsky, *Politicians and the Slump*, pp. 142–5.

[2] G. D. H. Cole, 'Mr Thomas and his Colleagues', *New Statesman*, XXXIV (15 February 1930), 593–4.

[3] G. D. H. Cole, 'The Problem of the Bank Rate', *New Statesman*, XXXIV (12 October 1929), 4–5; 'Second Thoughts on the Bank Rate', *New Statesman*, XXXIV (19 October 1929), 45–6.

cannot be put back' and that 'industrial development and reconstruction are the only way of escape'.[1] He advocated borrowing for national development, a first step towards deficit financing. But deficit spending was inevitably a less attractive picture for a socialist than for Keynes, for borrowing would tend to give capitalists claims upon the Government which could prove confining later on. It also raised the hoary question of 'confidence', so annoying to a socialist government. And Cole had not totally escaped from the orthodox belief in balanced budgets. He rather assumed that Snowden would have to find new sources of tax revenue. But on one point he was sure: a deflationary budget would only lead to further problems. In another year he would put these points more bluntly: 'Nothing very dreadful would happen, even if Mr Snowden were to decide against raising any additional revenue at all, and were, for the moment, to suspend all attempts to reduce the net volume of the National Debt . . .'[2]

In this way, Cole's revolt against economic orthodoxy had come close to being a revolt against the Labour Party's acceptance of this economic orthodoxy. Mosley was drawn from the one into the other; Cole managed to avoid this mistake. The next step in his development was a collective, Fabian one, rather than an individual challenge to the Party's leadership. It took the form of the creation of two new bodies, the New Fabian Research Bureau and the Society for Socialist Inquiry and Propaganda.[3] Both groups grew out of a series of informal meetings held at Easton Lodge, the home of the Countess of Warwick; Margaret Cole has described the process in her *History of the Fabian Society*. The meetings started towards the end of 1930, with the Coles[4] the focal point for the disparate elements who felt that Labour's policy needed rethinking. Clement Attlee, Ernest Bevin, Colin Clark, H. L. Beales, R. H. Tawney, William Mellor, C. M. Lloyd, G. R. Mitchison, and W. R. Blair of the Co-operative Wholesale Society were among those who took part in the Conferences and in the organizations which had

[1] G. D. H. Cole, 'Mr Snowden's Problem', *New Statesman*, XXXV (12 April 1930), 4–5.
[2] G. D. H. Cole, 'Mr Snowden's Problem', *New Statesman and Nation*, I (28 March 1931), 172–3.
[3] See Margaret Cole, *The Story of Fabian Socialism* (London, Heinemann, 1961), pp. 222–42; 'Society for Socialist Inquiry and Propaganda', Cole Papers, Nuffield College; Box 15 of the Fabian Society's records.
[4] The idea of S.S.I.P. first came from Margaret Cole, along with H. L. Beales and C. M. Lloyd, and had to be 'sold' to Cole.

grown out of them by February 1931. Bevin became the chairman of S.S.I.P., while Attlee was the first chairman of N.F.R.B. The N.F.R.B. in particular provided a valuable outlet for the 'loyal grousers' to turn their discontent into research. It offered training and criticism for the young socialists coming out of Oxford and the other universities, and often put them in contact with the non-intellectual kinds of power and facts which they needed to know about. Many of the young men of the N.F.R.B. entered Parliament in 1945; they broke down much of the habitual Labour suspicion of intellectuals which had hampered Cole at the start of his career. One also suspects that many of Labour's policies and programmes would show the slow, steady, unspectacular influence of the thinking and writing carried on under the auspices of the New Fabian Research Bureau. In *A History of Socialist Thought*, Cole argued that the Labour Party's wartime Reconstruction Committee drew heavily on N.F.R.B. work in preparing the fourteen reports from which its 1945 manifesto was prepared.[1]

The two bodies form a unit in the same way that the National Guilds League and the Fabian Research Department did around 1915. There is the same sort of apparent division between research and propaganda, which is incomplete because the same people were generally involved in discussing the same problems. The basic attitudes behind the new organizations were simple. Cole and the other people who met at Easton Lodge insisted on fundamental loyalty to the Labour Party. Only Labour Party members could be full members, and, in order to avoid any suspicions of creating a new party, 'Zip' could not sponsor candidates as the I.L.P. and occasionally the Fabian Society had. Transport House was informed of the formation of the new organizations. The inaugural meeting of the New Fabian Research Bureau took place in Henderson's rooms at the House of Commons, and Ramsay MacDonald was even asked to serve on its advisory committee. The 'loyal grousers' sympathized with some of the points over which Oswald Mosley had resigned from the Government, but they refused to be drawn into negotiations with his supporters. C. M. Lloyd wrote to Beatrice Webb that John Strachey was roundly criticized at a S.S.I.P. meeting in December 1930 for his efforts to obtain support for Mosley's

---

[1] G. D. H. Cole, *A History of Socialist Thought*, v: *Socialism and Fascism 1931–1939* (London, Macmillan, 1960), p. 91.

Manifesto.[1] One other principle deserves special mention: the 'self-denying ordinance' which made it clear that pamphlets were individual efforts and did not bind the societies. This was a powerful defence against any individual making one of them his sounding-board, as Cripps later used the Socialist League.

Both S.S.I.P. and the N.F.R.B. have the general appearance of 'ginger groups', but they succeeded in avoiding the cliquishness and self-righteousness of most ginger groups. They disclaimed any new revelation of Socialist gospel; Cole often said that the Labour Party had approved the essential features of a socialist policy which simply needed more thought and careful application. This attitude offset the dangers latent in the impressive scope of the task which these thinkers took upon themselves:

> It set out to study, systematically and conscientiously, with the aid of all available expert opinion, the long-range problems of Socialist policy, whether economic, political, national, or international; its object being to provide on the one hand a body of information being likely to be useful in the subsequent framing of policy, and on the other a stimulus to individual thought in the detailed working out and restatement of Socialist principles.[2]

Behind this ambitious programme, rapidly applied by N.F.R.B. committees according to plans drawn up to a large extent by Cole, lay the practical realization that a socialist party in power had to know much more about what it intended to do. It had to calculate the effects of its policies and decide how it could really put its ethical imperatives into practice. An undated, unsigned manuscript in the possession of the Fabian Society puts this 'tough-minded' attitude bluntly:

> They assume that the old socialist postulates are inadequate to the present necessity of scientific planning in Socialist methodology. Its ethical urge may always be the fundamental source from which Socialism draws its strength, but its moral claim to political and industrial democracy, equality of opportunity, a living wage, and so on, are no longer sufficient. The ends it seeks will only be realized by scientific reorganization of social and industrial life. The question that all socialists have to answer therefore, is not whether their claims are morally just, but whether they are scientifically possible. The claims

---

[1] 'The Diary of Beatrice Webb', Vol. 44 (10 December 1930), 174, letter from C. M. Lloyd to Beatrice Webb.
[2] 'First Annual Report for the Year Ending 31 March 1932', in 'Society for Socialist Inquiry and Propaganda', folder 'Annual Reports', Cole Papers, Nuffield College.

of socialism must be the end of scientific organization, not the assumption of political philosophy.[1]

The formation of 'Zip' and the N.F.R.B. thus entailed an effort to restudy socialist policy in a practical, expert way which must not be underestimated. One may argue that if the 'Bevanites' of 1951 had approached their problems in the same way, they would have done much more worthwhile work. Working with the other members of the New Fabian Research Bureau provided the right sort of background for Cole: Strong, stimulating discussion and criticism which he could use in rethinking old ideas such as workers' control and in moving on to new ones such as planning.

But little of this rethinking was completed before the 'bankers' ramp' and MacDonald's 'defection'. In the General Election which followed, Cole's socialist militancy outran the reformulation of his economic policy, in a way which took him away from the development of an unorthodox policy to follow within capitalism. The old emotional rhetoric still had a strong appeal to him. He saw the Election as a straight battle between socialism and capitalism.

The main difference between Cole in 1929 and in 1931 is more than anything else a change in mood. He was clearly tired of the reformist pose, compromising with destructive unemployment for the benefit of bankers' 'confidence'. He wrote that he felt 'elation and escape'[2] at the purification of the party because of MacDonald's defection, despite Labour's heavy losses in the General Election of 1931. However, this increased militancy was not reflected in a more unorthodox policy. He found it necessary, during the election, to soothe the fears that Labour would be inflationary; his unorthodoxy took the form of suggesting expedients for balancing the budget which would not weigh heavily upon the workers. He suggested, for example, that the Government owed the holders of the National Debt 'not a bit more than we owe the unemployed fair maintenance'.[3] As an exercise in social priorities this was undoubtedly true, but one wonders how he would have put it into effect.

[1] In Box 15, folder 'S.S.I.P. Circulars, Rules, Meetings, etc.', Fabian Society.
[2] G. D. H. Cole, 'The Old Labour Party and the New', *New Statesman and Nation*, II (14 November 1931), 601–2.
[3] G. D. H. Cole, 'National Government and Inflation: Six Little Talks on Politics', S.S.I.P. pamphlet (London, 1931), p. 16.

The important point is that this burst of Labour militancy, which came over the whole party for something like a year after 1931, was basically a change of mood, not a change of policy; the more basic rethinking was to come later in the 1930s, out of the N.F.R.B. programme of research and parallel activities by other Labour theorists. For Cole, this short-term aggressive attitude probably culminated in the Leicester Conference of the Labour Party in 1932, at which 'Zip' members succeeded in imposing more radical resolutions in favour of nationalizing the joint stock banks and in favour of workers' control upon the Labour Party Executive. After the Conferences, Laski wrote Cole a letter of congratulations: 'I think you in particular, and S.S.I.P. in general, deserve warm congratulations for Leicester. Clearly for the first time you have got socialism moving in the country.'[1] Laski was wrong; the burst of enthusiasm of 1931–2 was more a reaction to a grievous wound than a genuine show of life. Soon the aggressively socialist energy of various militants was dissipated in Cripps' Socialist League, while the Labour Party settled back to 'MacDonaldism without MacDonald'.

In this burst of militancy, the left-wingers came right up against the crucial question for reformist socialists. How could they make a revolution by peaceful means; how could they rapidly take control of the nation's political and economic life and prevent a repetition of the blockage and defeat of 1931? Both the MacDonaldites and the Russians argued that one could not succeed in this manner; the 'centrists' or the English left-wing have generally failed to make their answer clear enough and convincing enough to establish a real identity. Well before the 'crisis' of 1931 N.F.R.B. and 'Zip' members had been debating this problem, and they settled on a list of actions which are the closest thing to a solution that any democratic socialist group has put forward. Assuming a Labour victory, they presented the following list in 'A Labour Programme of Action':[2]

1. The taking of emergency powers to prevent a possible financial crisis.

---

[1] Laski to Cole, 10 October 1932, in 'Society for Socialist Inquiry and Propaganda', folder 'Friday Group Folder', Cole Papers, Nuffield College.

[2] 'A Labour Programme of Action' was prepared by a group of S.S.I.P. members and circulated to the Policy Committee of the Labour Party before it was given a wider circulation by hand. There is a copy in 'Society for Socialist Inquiry and Propaganda', folder 'Friday Group – Memoranda and Minutes', Cole Papers, Nuffield College.

These will include the emergency control of the banking system, the foreign exchange, the issue of new capital, and speculation in stocks and shares.

2. If necessary, the immediate abolition of the House of Lords – a step which will be taken in any event at an early stage – and the reform of the procedure of the House of Commons and the methods of legislation.

3. The assumption of power to bring any or all land, minerals, or industrial property under public ownership and operation, and to set on foot a comprehensive policy of agricultural development . . .

When those powers had been taken, it would be possible to 'put in hand . . . comprehensive schemes of national economic development', about most of which Cole had speculated before. Housing and slum clearance, public works, and the reorganization of coal, iron and steel came high on the list. Effectively, the economy would be run on socialist terms, although enclaves of private ownership would survive for a while.

One may attempt to criticize this policy in many ways. One may argue that it would never win an election, or that the resistance of influential sectors could make a mess of it. It would take a degree of resolution and a willingness to use force which Cole himself probably did not have; the Labour Party as a whole certainly has never had it. The dilemma remains to be solved by any group which tries to change the structure of society peaceably.

In terms of his own development, Cole had decided in favour of a rapid jump to socialism, and against a reformist unorthodox capitalist economics such as Keynes was in the process of developing. A change of ownership was the first step to be taken, rather than a change in economic policy. The escape from 'MacDonaldism' had reinforced his tendency to think in terms of institutional change.

For Cole fundamentally lacked the faith in Britain as it was which lay behind Keynes' work. He did not feel that a purified capitalist system could avoid depressions and end unemployment. We have already quoted what he said about Roosevelt's New Deal: 'Under Capitalism, the more Mr Roosevelt now succeeds in getting men back to work by monetary reflation and by a control which does not really put the key positions into the hands of the state to-day, the more widespread and disastrous the succeeding crash is certain to be.' And, equally important, Cole did not want the existing order to survive;

one of his students in 1931 remembers the perfectly calm way Cole wound up a meeting by saying, 'Of course, we don't want capitalism to survive'.[1] He was willing to write his quarter of a million words telling people what changes had to be made in order for Britain to revive; when they didn't listen he moved on to another aspect of socialist theory:

... I have done my small part in trying to suggest to people how they ought to set about patching it up. Although it is theoretically and physically possible to patch up the situation, it involves so much intelligence, that it is impossible to expect statesmen to rise to such a state of reasonableness.[2]

And so he turned towards the leading concept of the 1930s, economic planning, in an effort to clarify the alternatives to the status quo.

[1] Interview with Christopher Hill.
[2] Speech given at National Peace Conference on 'The World Economic Outlook', 9 December 1932, 'Manuscripts and Proofs', Box 3, folder 28, Cole Papers, Nuffield College.

CHAPTER 5

PLANNING

'Planning' was the seminal idea of the 1930s, as Syndicalism had been just before the First World War. It was the growing edge of socialism, the new departure and the new slogan with which many ventured to experiment. The leaders and the models in many ways were the Russians, with their Five Year Plan. But similar ideas had been occurring to European socialist leaders for different reasons. The concept of planning was an indispensable, if often unvoiced, part of socialism, which had always claimed to substitute the will of the community for the anarchy of capitalist production. Planning inevitably had to be discussed when it came to moving from criticism to socialist action. The depression added new force and urgency to the cry. Many of the continental socialists who took it up were sceptical of Russian claims and achievements. Continental plans, unlike the Russian one, were largely a series of economic and social measures to combat recession with the help of liberal capitalist parties. They were more antecedents of the Popular Front than of socialist planning as Cole interpreted it; he tended to agree that Soviet planning provided an example of socialist planning.[1] This acceptance of a physical, statist planning model was much stronger than we now realize. Socialists tended to accept it; and wartime necessities forced the British Government to apply physical controls to manpower and raw materials. As Samuel Beer points out, it was not until 1947 that Keynesian planning became the dominant form in Britain.[2]

In 'le Planisme' Russophiles, Social Democrats, and liberal capitalists might be reconciled. The concept had a promising vagueness and impressive overtones of prudence and rationalism – a sort of reasonable, solid ring – and was thus an ideal slogan. As *S.S.I.P. News* commented as early as January 1932, 'the most recent universal remedy

---

[1] G. D. H. Cole, 'Socialist Planning – The U.S.S.R.', *Practical Economics* (Harmondsworth, Middlesex, Penguin, 1937).
[2] Samuel H. Beer, *British Politics in the Collectivist Age* (New York, Knopf, 1965), p. 200.

is apparently contained in the word "Plan"'.[1] Characteristically, they immediately added: 'We must have a better understanding of what this word means before we use it from our political platforms.' Yet Cole himself accepted one of the most pernicious of the confusions implicit in the popular use of the word. He used it both to describe short-term political programmes (e.g. *A Plan for Democratic Britain*) and the economic planning of a socialist society. It is this latter meaning that we will discuss in this chapter.

Cole joined the hunt as soon as the word entered English politics late in 1930. His Guild slogans concerning 'the coordination of supply and demand' foreshadowed his acceptance of planning, but we have seen that the path from 'coordination' to 'planning' was by no means direct. In particular, the short-term problems of a Labour Government drew him off the path. After the General Election of 1931, he was somewhat freer to turn his attention towards a new sort of economics. Essays in his collections of 1932 and 1934[2] lead on to *Principles of Economic Planning*, in which Cole published his fullest investigation of the nature of socialist planning.

Cole recognized the variety of claimants to the word, and was forced to spend a large portion of his time showing the defects or ineligibility of would-be capitalist planners. The essential defect, he felt, was that capitalist planning was inherently restrictive. To Cole, this restriction on potential output was morally wrong, and moral outrage was not the least part of his reaction. 'A planned system which involves the widespread restriction of output by powerful sectional monopolies is necessarily wrong and anti-social.'[3] Wrong, because it was stupid; wrong, because it was harmful to individuals. For restricted output led to underconsumption and to a deflationary spiral. Cole argued that restricted output was implicit in monopoly capitalism, and in any sort of 'planning' which made large companies the planners. He assumed that a company aimed at 'the highest total profit and not the highest production compatible with covering social costs'.[4] This meant that a

[1] *S.S.I.P. News* (January 1932), pp. 1–2. Copy in 'Society for Socialist Inquiry and Propaganda', folder 'S.S.I.P. Bulletins', Cole Papers, Nuffield College.

[2] G. D. H. Cole, 'Towards a New Economic Theory', in *Economic Tracts for The Times* (London, Macmillan, 1932); 'Towards a New Economic Theory', in *Studies in World Economics* (London, Macmillan, 1934).

[3] G. D. H. Cole, *Principles of Economic Planning* (London, Macmillan, 1935), p. 165.

[4] *Principles of Economic Planning*, p. 402.

monopoly, or any company strong enough to create 'imperfect competition', would restrict output, at the expense of employment. Monopoly capitalism simply could not distribute enough purchasing power at the peak of a boom to prevent companies from acting in this way, nor could it find a way out of a slide it had started.

Nor did Cole feel that Government action could solve these dilemmas permanently within private ownership of the means of production. 'If scarcity pays the monopolist better than plenty, it is not easy for the State to compel him to pursue plenty, as long as it leaves him to conduct the actual business – especially if the State itself is largely dominated by capitalists.'[1] The state would run the risk of offending that mysterious growth, 'confidence', with the result that it would be met by passive resistance or worse. Or, at the bottom of a depression, businessmen would accept a Roosevelt, but when trade improved, they would seek to return to their disastrous ways. The alternative, a Fascist system, dispensed with the need for high wages in return for full employment and a destructive economic nationalism; the pressure of a lack of purchasing power caused by high profits and low wages could only be siphoned off by the absolute waste of armaments. Thus the Fascist solution was inherently instable, and would either collapse or lead to war.[2]

'True' planning stands out sharply against these alternatives. 'Socialism, as an economic system, involves the planned distribution of the available resources of production in such ways as will best serve the welfare and happiness of the people as individuals.'[3] Here again, we see how Cole defined socialism just as much by its goals as by its methods. Effectively, socialist planning meant expanding output as much as was possible without damaging individuals; '. . . the object of national planning will be to secure the fullest possible utilization of the available productive resources'.[4] Cole insisted that this meant the fullest utilization of all resources, rather than artifically ensuring full

---

[1] G. D. H. Cole, *Practical Economics*, p. 22.
[2] *Principles of Economic Planning*, p. 222; 'Fascist Planning – Germany and Italy', in *Practical Economics*.
[3] G. D. H. Cole, *The Machinery of Socialist Planning* (London, Hogarth Press, 1938), pp. 10, 20.
[4] *Principles of Economic Planning*, p. 360.

employment by keeping the level of technology low.[1] However, I feel that had he been faced with a case in which all conceivable resources other than men were being used to the utmost, he would share the work out to avoid unemployment. That is, he thought of men as the crucial scarce resource which had to be used fully, and added the other provision to prevent wasteful ways of reaching the main objective. He strongly emphasized avoiding waste and attaining maximum output, trying to reduce the distance between current output and the provision of a decent standard of life for all. 'All income, and not profit income alone, is from the social standpoint a gain, and all usable products that people want at any price are worth producing, if the alternative is to produce nothing.'[2] He drew only one limit to this, admitting that there was a point at which people would want to have more leisure instead of increased consumer goods; but he would not accept any level of production below this point. In one important way, Cole did not envisage a society like our own. He desired more production to meet needs, and avoided the paradox which demands an ever-increasing amount of goods simply to keep men at work. He would have agreed with Galbraith: 'Among the many models of the good society no one has urged the squirrel wheel.'[3]

A planned economy would be a state-planned economy, in which the state would be the sole producer – or at least the sole major producer.[4] In this sense, his notion of planning differed profoundly from the way the word is used today. Western governments use it to mean a kind of forecasting which allows elements of a mixed economy to predict demand because of the interlocking estimates provided by these elements themselves. Cole thought of planning in a statist or physical manner. The state would control directly the essential economic variables – production, investment, incomes, and prices – to achieve

---

[1] G. D. H. Cole, *The Means to Full Employment* (London, Gollancz and The Left Book Club, 1943), pp. 22–3.

[2] G. D. H. Cole, 'Towards a New Economic Theory', *Economic Tracts for the Times* (London, Macmillan, 1932), p. 197.

[3] John Kenneth Galbraith, *The Affluent Society* (Boston, Houghton Mifflin, 1958), p. 159.

[4] G. D. H. Cole, 'Towards a New Economic Theory', *Studies in World Economics* (London, 1934), pp. 250–1. In the 1950s Cole, like many Socialists with a radical background, turned against an extensive expansion of the nationalization following the 'public corporation' model. In *Socialist Economics* (London, Gollancz, 1950), pp. 92 ff, he assumed simply that the nationalized sector would be large, and made the procedure of planning correspondingly indirect.

maximum production. This concept of planning would set the government a more difficult task than is normally undertaken by current planning agencies. These agencies leave action on the basis of their forecasts up to other agencies and to firms. Conversely, the individual company's planners assume a level of demand and correlate production to it. Cole, however, saw that statist planning would not be able to make one factor constant and correlate the other factors to it.

In effect, the answer to each question would be bound up with the answers given to the rest; and in most cases the finding of the right answers would involve, not arbitrary decision by a central planning authority, but constant adjustment of decisions in the light of actual experience and changing conditions, and constant collaboration between the central planning agencies and the sectional bodies – local as well as national – directly concerned with the actual execution of the various parts of the plan.[1]

Ironically, now that western governments have given up physical planning, it has become more feasible because of the input-output analysis developed by Wassily Leontieff.

Cole could not leave the concept of planning at this level of confusion, and so, in several works, he sought to outline steps which a socialist government would be likely to follow. At each step he evolved principles which differ strikingly from current practice.

'The first step in the making of the plan will be to schedule all the available resources, with indication of the degree to which they are capable of being used for the making of alternative products, or are to be regarded as non-transferable, or transferable only at considerable cost or loss.'[2] This thorough-going inventory of Britain's resources was a feature of Cole's thoughts on planning only through *Principles of Economic Planning* (1935); in his later studies, his concentration upon transitional problems, his emphasis upon the representation of consumer interests, and his awareness of the difficulties of a rigidly planned system prevented him from returning to the point. But the concepts that he had developed by beginning with the notion of an inventory of resources continued to give substance to his descriptions of the way planning agencies would make decisions concerning incomes,

[1] *Machinery of Socialist Planning*, p. 24.
[2] *Principles of Economic Planning*, p. 180; *Economic Tracts*, p. 194.

prices, and consumption, and would evaluate investment in new forms of production.

Cole insisted that this inventory, and any other analyses of the economic process, had to be made in real rather than in monetary terms. In sharp contradistinction to the dominant conception of economics, which has been to focus upon the problems of production through monetary terms, Cole argued on the lines which economics texts call 'Robinson Crusoe economics'.

For the basic problem for a Socialist economy is, like Crusoe's problem, simply that of discovering the best practicable distribution of the available productive resources; and this problem has to be faced, as it had to be faced by Crusoe, not in terms of money costs, but directly in terms of efforts and sacrifices, the expenditure of scarce productive resources, in relation to the satisfactions to be secured from the products of economic activity.[1]

The inventory of resources, and the decisions to be made from it, thus had two aspects. On the one hand there had to be an estimate of the value to be gained from the use of human and material resources in alternate ways; on the other hand, this value had to be compared with the social costs of production. In each of these terms Cole proposed conceptions which deviated from orthodox economics.

In the first case, Cole sought to find a better estimate of value than demand. Demand, as the classical economists used it, took the existing distribution of income as a given. Thus classical economics was unjust and did violence to the fact that production creates incomes. Cole, as we shall see later, sought to separate income from production; such a step, incidentally, would have made classical operations more viable. Cole argued that demand and value were two very different things, which orthodox capitalist economists assumed were equated by monetary demand. Surely this was placing the cart before the horse; the problem was to calculate value and then adjust monetary demand to it.

Ricardo and Marx had sought to obtain a criterion of value through the amount of labour used in producing a product. This quickly proved untenable in a crude form, and even Marx's elaborate calculations of 'socially necessary labour time' did not satisfy Cole. The divergence came out clearly in *Studies in World Economics*.

[1] *Studies in World Economics*, pp. 253–4.

The 'value' of any sort of labour, from the standpoint of a Socialist economy, is the 'value' of the utilities which it can be employed to produce. This 'value', unlike Marx's 'value of labour-power' under Capitalism, is accordingly determined not by the amount of labour required to produce it, but by the amount of final utility which it can produce.[1]

But calculating the value of labour in terms of the final utility only pushed the question back one step. How could one calculate utility? For Cole, the central variable was *need*:

The need for bread will take precedence of the demand for cake, up to the point at which the entire community is in a position to consume enough bread to satisfy all reasonable needs. More broadly, the need for a generally diffused supply of all things which can be regarded as necessaries of civilized living will constitute the first overriding claim upon the available resources of production. A satisfactory minimum of food, fuel, clothing, housing, education and other common services will come before anything else, as a social claim that a planned economy must meet.[2]

Asserting this accomplished the crucial aim of putting real wants – necessities – first, instead of profits and effective demand. It restored a sense of priorities to economics. It was here that Cole had the most to offer professional economists, who often work with their models and descriptive concepts without questioning the human values that economics must serve. Cole sought to create another kind of economics; he approached economics from a moral perspective, and tried to make his democratic values the basis for economic institutions.

The main problem which a theory of need must meet is that of making its criteria objective. Cole argued, and I think rightly, that basic needs can be seen objectively.

The basic needs are neither highly subject to individual caprice nor very liable to rapid change. What each individual demands will vary; but the law of averages will afford, over a large part of the field of production, a fairly safe and accurate guide . . .[3]

The task becomes harder when one reaches social services such as education; but in general Cole's principle was to allow the political process and consumers' organizations to try to make need articulate and therefore objective. The task would be made easier, and could be

[1] Ibid., p. 263.
[2] *Principles of Economic Planning*, p. 224; *Studies in World Economics*, p. 261.
[3] *Principles of Economic Planning*, p. 237.

translated into measurable terms, by the fact that, under conditions of full employment and a guaranteed minimum standard of living, the process of calculating needs would be quite similar to that of estimating the demand for bread, houses, and so forth. This would not be changed by Cole's willingness to distribute certain goods free of charge, for the elasticity of demand for necessities is fairly rigid. Cole, I feel, realized this; he certainly emphasized the way in which previous consumption patterns and trends in distribution would be at the planners' disposal. It was not a case of planning from scratch.

Once necessities had been calculated, the planners would have the task of establishing guide-lines for the production of 'substitutable necessities' and of luxuries. That is, many more goods were 'not necessities for everybody', but *in toto* 'form a necessary part of a tolerable standard of living . . .'.[1] Here the planners would rely almost exclusively on traditional methods, estimating demand with the help of a price mechanism. Cole showed surprisingly little concern for the difficulty this would cause for an inventory of the goods that could be produced. He remarked that any effort to calculate the demand for substitutable necessities would depend on the society's incomes policies. More basically, he felt that he had made the most important point, by establishing the correct order of priorities.

The second half of the process of calculating what would be produced was that of estimating real costs in terms of necessities consumed. By calling for a comprehensive concept of social costs, Cole was trying to avoid the destruction of man's environment that competitive capitalism has brought.

The social valuation of the 'costs' of any service has to be made ultimately in terms, not of its prices, but of the amount and quality of the labour and real capital resources which it uses up, the quality of the life which it affords to the labourers . . . the indirect effects of the particular uses to which the labour and capital are put – e.g., such effects as pollution by smoke, the promotion or destruction of the employee's intelligence or vitality, the disturbance of amenities as well as values caused by a particular localization of an industry, and a hundred other considerations which will not directly admit of money measurement.[2]

In such a manner labour could be assigned a utility-value which could

[1] Ibid., p. 225.
[2] *Economic Tracts*, p. 189.

be compared with what was actually produced. The central concept, here, for Cole, was 'the amount and quality of the labour'. Cole agreed with the critics of the labour theory of value in asserting that various kinds of labour were worth more than others. He attempted to calculate these graduations in value by the utilities which each sort of labourer could produce. One could argue that this underestimates the importance of real capital in productivity, and also introduces a sort of circularity that reduced calculation of the costs to the same thing as the calculation of values. The scarcity of a particular sort of labour did not affect his notion of its value, but did impose additional limits on approving a particular sort of production. Finally, capital could be evaluated both on the amount of particular sorts of labour it contained and on the presence of other limited factors, such as land.[1]

Many of these decisions would involve the development of quantitative criteria of judgment, perhaps to a greater degree than Cole realized. He could have translated these qualitative social costs into numerical terms to some extent through the existing concepts of marginal pricing.[2] In the case of capital, he was even ready to allow the purely formal calculation of interest as a device for estimating the value of new increments of capital.[3] But Cole always distrusted those who sought to make economics a pure 'science', an adjunct of sophisticated mathematics. He argued that the basic choices in any economic system were choices about values and the nature of a good life. Consequently, the stages in planning which he envisaged dealt more with the qualitative aspects of planning; monetary and other quantitative costing systems had to be subordinated to these qualitative aspects. Many of the numerical components of costs would be fixed by society – such as incomes – and so any numerical expression of costs would to a large extent only express qualitative decisions which had already been made.

From these qualitative and quantitative estimates of the value that could be produced and the social costs of making it, one could evaluate a particular project. One could contrast the amount of goods produced and their relative degree of essentiality, coupled with what society

[1] *Studies in World Economics*, p. 264.
[2] *Principles of Economic Planning*, pp. 54–7.
[3] *Studies in World Economics*, p. 259.

indicated it desired, with the amount of scarce resources used in making it.[1] Certainly the process would be difficult, but I feel that Cole was right in saying that it would not be impossible, and that in fact we do attempt to introduce these basic conceptions – need and social cost – even into our market economy through state intervention. The results might look somewhat poorer in monetary terms, but Cole felt that the active consideration of people, their needs and their conditions of life and work, would maximize human happiness.

Since such a large part of the calculation of needs was also a calculation of demand, a forecast of incomes was essential to making actual decisions about production. In this sense, the planning of incomes came first. Several times Cole made statements to this effect; in *Studies in World Economics*, for example, he said:

The logically first task of a Socialist Planning Authority will be to plan the distribution of incomes in the community, because, until that is planned, it cannot settle in what proportions the various classes of goods ought to be produced.[2]

But he followed this sentence with another which indicates that the actual distribution of incomes was a secondary aspect of planning. 'What has got to be planned at this stage is not, strictly, the amount of *money* to be distributed, but the proportion in which whatever money is distributed will go to different types of income-receivers – for the actual amounts of money becomes important only when prices are being fixed.'

Cole was clear on the first principle of planning incomes. Every individual had to have enough purchasing power to obtain the basic necessities of life. Some of them would probably be distributed free of charge; the purchasing power necessary to obtain the rest of them would come from a system of social dividends.[3] This phrase bears the

---

[1] Imports would tend to confuse the picture, but Cole felt that they could be dealt with by the same conceptual apparatus. If a necessity could not be produced at home in sufficient quantities, then clearly it had to be imported. Intermediate cases came with 'substitutable necessities' and with goods which could be produced at home, but at a higher monetary cost than imports (*Principles of Economic Planning*, p. 259). Here Cole revealed his dependence upon monetary systems of estimating costs; barter would remove some of the reliance upon mathematical or monetary systems of decision-making.

[2] *Studies in World Economics*, p. 19.

[3] *Principles of Economic Planning*, pp. 234 ff.

obvious imprint of Major Douglas, and certainly Cole had grown more sympathetic towards the monetary aims of social credit since 1920. In an article he wrote for the *New Statesman* in 1932, he admitted that Douglasism's 'approach to economic problems is preferable to the complacent orthodoxy'.[1] Cole's pamphlet, '50 Propositions on Money and Production',[2] accepts as many of Douglas' assumptions as possible; it envisages the use of social dividends within a mixed economic system. One should not over-estimate the influence of Major Douglas. In the idea of a 'social dividend' one can recognize a basic socialist demand, the principle of a 'guaranteed minimum of civilized life', which socialists as disparate as the Webbs and Bertrand Russell had written about before and during the First World War. Cole had dissociated Douglas' phrase from the details of his argument that capitalism was constantly short of purchasing power. Cole used the phrase as he generally used slogans, for his own purposes; in this case, he saw in the idea of social dividends a way of ensuring greater economic quality. Social dividends replaced the earlier device of family allowances, which Cole had espoused in *The Next Ten Years*. The dividend would be distributed according to need, which Cole obviously felt was roughly the same for all people in the same society. He envisaged an equal payment to each adult, with allowances for children that would increase with their age.

But the social dividend would not be the sole means of distributing purchasing power. In *Principles of Economic Planning*, he estimated that about 50 to 60 per cent of purchasing power would be distributed in the form of dividends;[3] the rest would be in the form of wages. Wages would be much less than they were at present, without being equal. For Cole was seeking to undo the worst effect of the wage system, the fear of poverty, without destroying wages or introducing economic equality, although equal incomes had had an idealistic appeal to him in 1918. In *Principles of Economic Planning* he foresaw the use of wages as an incentive even under socialist planning. Relatively

---

[1] G. D. H. Cole, 'The Douglas Theory', *New Statesman and Nation*, III (20 February 1932), 223–5.

[2] Written for the *New English Weekly*, Orage's organ after his return from America; Cole published it as a pamphlet in 1936 and later as an appendix to his *Money, Its Present and Future* (London, Cassell, 1944).

[3] *Principles of Economic Planning*, p. 255.

small wage differentials could induce people to work because they would provide larger amounts of 'substitutable necessities'. However, Cole still retained his desire to keep wage differentials to a minimum, and to use differentials in hours and conditions of work as incentives. He felt that wages would be robbed of much of their destructive power, while still serving as incentives – perhaps a curiously optimistic belief. 'Earnings will become, under such a system, more and more of the nature of "pocket-money", without any loss of the incentives to effort such as absolute equality of incomes would involve.'[1] One may feel that this retention of wages indicates either a more realistic or a more cynical picture of human nature; it does indicate how much less 'utopian' his thought had become.

The essential purpose of incomes was to enable the citizens to obtain all the goods which were placed upon the market.[2] To this Cole added a qualification which complicated the planning of incomes. Incomes were not to be pegged directly to the amount of goods produced; they had to be adequate to purchase all the goods which *could* be produced with the existing productive resources.[3] In normal times, the actual amount of goods would equal the potential amount of goods, Cole hoped; furthermore, he was trying to make full employment of economic resources inevitable by monetary means. He could not assume that full production would always occur, and so he was guarding against abnormal times and providing adequate purchasing power for expansion. This entailed separating incomes from the vagaries of the productive process. There would seem to be one flaw in this; if the actual production of goods fell below the potential production, there would be a waste of purchasing power. Since prices would be fixed, such a surplus of purchasing power could not lead to higher prices – unless some sort of black market arose. However, a waste of purchasing power might lead to some people obtaining less than their full share of scarce goods and services. The danger would be minimized if, as Cole suggested, essential goods were distributed free or in a non-market fashion. Thus it appears that the social institutions surrounding the distribution of incomes could prevent the orthodox inflationary out-

[1] Ibid., p. 236. See also p. 318.
[2] Capital goods would be provided directly by the planning authorities, without purchasing them on the market.
[3] *Principles of Economic Planning*, p. 234.

come of a surplus of purchasing power, while providing useful protection against a deflationary spiral. Cole does not appear to have considered the possibility that the total amount of goods desired would drop below the level needed to secure full employment.

Prices were the third planned factor which had to be adjusted. In a sense, they were the factor which equated production and incomes. 'The total prices charged for all the goods and services available for consumption must, if the economic system is to be in health, balance the total incomes available for their purchase at such a level as to provide for the full use of the available productive resources.'[1] Cole realized that this created an interesting dichotomy between costs of production and prices. Since wages were only part of incomes, the total amount of incomes to be absorbed by the total price of goods was much higher than the amount of incomes arising directly within the productive process. Prices would have to be high enough to cover indirect costs such as the social dividends and the provision of new capital goods. Total prices had to be made equal to the sum total of purchasing power, at least at full employment, in order to allow the Government banks to retain the difference between costs chargeable to an industry and the total paid by the public.[2]

Prices had another function which Cole integrated poorly with the general problem of absorbing purchasing power. Prices also related to individual goods on a market. Cole assumed that consumers would be able to choose what to spend their money on; and prices were naturally an important factor influencing their choices. Thus, if the whole stock of a particular commodity was not bought at its original price, the price could be lowered to clear the market.[3] Manipulating prices for market reasons seems to produce a major difficulty for the main purpose of planned prices, however. If the prices of some commodities had to be reduced for market reasons, would not the prices of others need to be increased in order to absorb the total purchasing power? That is, the general equivalences which Cole sought to establish are plausible, but when one thinks about the actual distribution of incomes and prices when applied to individual men and individual goods, the

[1] Ibid., p. 257.
[2] Ibid., p. 260.
[3] Ibid., p. 229.

task seems overwhelming unless one assumes a stable economic system with relatively little change to disturb decisions already made. This last assumption of course would be one of the main attractions of a planned economy, if it were stabilized at a comfortable standard of living. At points in his writings on planning, Cole did make these assumptions; he was justified in writing about a planned economy as a going concern, rather than as something starting from scratch. But the introduction of a market system, while desirable from the standpoint of the freedom of economic choice, makes these assumptions less plausible.

For it was not simply a matter of solving certain economic problems; Cole hoped to satisfy his strongly-held beliefs in democracy and liberty through planning. Obviously Cole had to settle for a less ambitious concept of democracy than that he had held in 1920. The abolition of classes had become the most practicable part of his earlier conception of democracy; he also had become much more favourably disposed towards parliamentary interpretations of democracy. In the 1930s he took more time to defend the traditional negative liberties than he had done in his Guild days. All of this made for a more traditional picture. There was no longer any prospect of dividing sovereignty; sovereignty had to rest with the Cabinet. This of course did not mean that the Cabinet would be omnicompetent. 'It is unlikely that a body of Cabinet Ministers could take more than the most general responsibility for the planning of production.'[1] The real business of planning had to go on at a slightly lower level, and here we meet the old Cole, trying to separate functions to prevent excessive centralization. He tried to design a set of central institutions which would divide up the functions entailed in planning.

It is necessary at this point to distinguish three functions. The first is that of estimating, as a check upon the estimates formed by the various sectional authorities, the national requirements in the various fields of production, and thus of framing in outline a draft national plan for all industries, with which the various sectional drafts can then be compared. The second function is that of actually deciding, in the light both of this national draft and of the sectional drafts, what the national plan of production is to be, and thereafter of authorizing alterations in it in accordance with changing needs or errors in its execution. The third function is that of supervising the carrying out of

[1] Ibid., p. 307.

the plan from the standpoint of ensuring the highest possible efficiency both in the conduct of the sectional authorities and in their relations one with another.[1]

These bodies were to be a National Planning Commission, a National Planning Authority, and a Department of Economic Inspection. To these he added a National Investment Board and a body to deal with incomes; the other planning functions would be allotted among the three major bodies. In proposing this sort of tripartite division Cole made a concession to his normal predisposition against unitary control, a concession which is not very satisfactory since one cannot see how these divisions either increase social control or provide interstices for personal freedoms not otherwise provided for.

Nor does establishing these various agencies appear to ensure that planning would take place on the basis of an inventory of resources, a calculation of needs, and a careful balancing of the benefits of increased production against social costs. Cole's account charges no particular body with the task of drawing up an inventory of resources or of calculating basic needs. Cole himself apparently felt that the problem was solved by presenting these variables as principles that planning agencies would follow.

In calling for these agencies to deal with central planning, Cole seems to have shifted his attention to providing an adequate mirroring of the community's wishes. In the case of the crucial National Planning Authority, Cole sought it in an interesting way.

Such a body will have, I think, to be constituted mainly on a representative basis. It will have to include persons chosen to represent primarily the interests and point of view of the whole body of consumers.[2]

This involved reversing a number of Guild tenets. Here he was admitting a sort of 'general will', a consumers' point of view which would be represented. The consumers were more or less assumed to be the community, and functional representation was out. To consumer representatives he would add watch-dogs for regional and industrial groups, but made it clear that they were not to be allowed to push their interests to the exclusion of the community as a whole. In keeping with his earlier distrust of nonfunctional direct elections, these representa-

[1] Ibid., pp. 303–4.
[2] Ibid., p. 308.

tives would be chosen, by the Government and by the special interests involved.

Other aspects of procedural democracy could be reconciled with planning. While major planning decisions had to be made at the centre, the preliminary stages of planning could be performed industrially and regionally. Each industry would have its own advisory body, and Cole hoped that various regions of Britain would also seek to coordinate industry and social services on their own. If these bodies became expert at their tasks, much of the effective decision-making would lie in their hands. At the same time, while Cole still believed strongly in decentralization, he did not feel that many would take advantage of it. Politically-minded individuals were inevitably few; it was relatively less important to multiply outlets for them. For Cole, the essential form of procedural democracy still lay in the workshop, to which his firm belief in workers' control still applied; one must not ignore this in totalling up the democratic features he hoped to introduce into planning. But in the late 1920s and the 1930s Cole decided to emphasize the social aspects of democracy, rather than the procedural form. The creation of a sort of classless society, the destruction of unemployment, by a democratically elected Government – these came first. From the destruction of class and unemployment Cole hoped to create a society in which fellowship would flourish, but he no longer said much about it. Where he had previously said that freedom was more important than the abolition of poverty, now he virtually put the abolition of poverty first.

One must not forget the positive increase in freedom that Cole felt would accrue from the abolition of classes and poverty. This would more than offset the commercial freedom of the rich, the freedom to deal in another man's labour – which he would never have considered a freedom. Cole certainly did not consider that the introduction of planning would limit the average individual's choice of goods, and he wanted to retain enough of a market system to register consumers' desires on most goods for which demand was elastic. As in his Guild Socialist writings, Cole hoped to expand this freedom of choice by introducing consumers' advisory councils and representatives, so that one could by-pass the slowness of a market system in demonstrating what was desired or detested. Nor did Cole seek to limit the individual's right to choose his job. He could have argued that the actual number of choices would be greater in a planned economy, since an individual, assured of his social dividend, need no longer accept the first job that came along out of sheer poverty.

Cole's optimism about the freedoms available under planning is open to two sorts of criticism. The first point was nicely made by Barbara Wootton in a Fabian volume, *Can Planning be Democratic?* She said sharply, 'To plan is, by presumption, to plan well and wisely.'[1] The person who writes favourably about planning generally assumes that the planners would be as humane and libertarian as himself, and this assumption may often be violated. This is a separate point from the one made by those who assert that planning invariably involves all the things most dreaded, often legitimately, by the middle-classes: bureaucracy, oppressive uniformity. Certainly sectors of the middle classes would feel the weight of national planning, for their ability to force others into their patterns through monopolistic planning would disappear. The special prerogatives of certain unions would also be jeopardized. But is it true that the centralization of economic planning in the state imperils 'negative' liberties such as freedom of speech? In a way it does, for certain economic practices would have to be made unthinkable. The general Fabian answer was that there was no logical connection between the two sorts of forces, economic and personal. But here the old Guild slogan, 'Economic Power Precedes Political Power', points to a danger which Cole may have shrugged off too easily in the 1930s. A planned society may not leave enough room for alternative centres of power capable of exposing invalid decisions and preventing endemic tyranny and high-handedness. Cole does seem more to assume that they will not be needed, rather than to provide for them; very likely he would have rectified the omission if faced with the task of constructing an actual planned economy.

The period of transition would be the least democratic period of planned socialism. Cole did not feel that workers' representation, on which he put much of his hope, could be brought immediately into play. During the period of transition, there was the need to prevent a strike of capital or other counter-revolutionary action by the possessors

[1] Barbara Wootten, 'Freedom Under Planning', in *Can Planning Be Democratic?* (London, 1944), p. 38.

of property. Cole hoped that a socialist government or series of governments would not have to use its emergency powers, and thus could avoid trespassing on formal democracy. But this elaboration of a planned economy made his speculations about the need for strong emergency powers during the period of transition seem more realistic. He now had a sharper appraisal of what the goal of socialist policy must be, and it could promise to threaten vested interests enough to provoke desperate measures.

From this picture of a planned economy, Cole was led to some revisions in his suggestions concerning short-term Labour policy. A social government had to create some sort of preliminary planning body, under the Cabinet, which could grow into the National Planning Administration. It would have to supervise industries in public hands as well as plan measures involving the public sector of the economy. It, and allied bodies, would begin to interfere more with the distribution of income, capital, and productive resources, and with the price mechanism. But Cole was hesitant about the actual powers such bodies could wield.

An incoming Socialist Government . . . would have no power to determine, in any complete sense, how much should be invested or consumed, or exactly what should be produced, or what prices should be charged for all the various goods and services. It would only be setting about the task of establishing a form of economic organization which could, later on, be so developed as to deal with all those matters in a more comprehensive way.[1]

In this way, Cole built in two directions with the concept of planning. On the one hand he had sketched the final state, and on the other he had seen something of the first steps towards it when he had re-evaluated Labour's short-term policy in 1928–32. The most hazy part of the picture, naturally, was the junction of the two approaches.

Planning was the new element in Cole's theories in the 1930s; but it did not mean that he abandoned Guild Socialism entirely. He remained a Guildsman, in a modified form as can be seen in the pamphlet on workers' control which he and Mellor published through the N.F.R.B. in 1933.[2] The pamphlet was a collective effort. Cole and Mellor drew up a draft after the Leicester Conference had requested the Executive

[1] *Machinery of Socialist Planning*, p. 25.
[2] G. D. H. Cole and William Mellor, 'Workers' Control and Self-Government in Industry' ,New Fabian Research Bureau Pamphlets, No. 9 (London, 1933).

to consider workers' control. They went over it, clause by clause, with a group of Trade Union leaders who were sympathetic.[1] In the process, some of the Guildsmen's pet phrases had to go, and criticism forced them to clarify their thought. Before it was published, it was sent to the Labour Party Executive, which refused to accept it. The incident is typical of Cole's willingness to solicit criticism and support from the trades union. At the same time, it did not lead him to change the document radically, for he had reached the basic position before 1929 – and was to repeat it in his last political book, *The Case for Industrial Partnership*.

The continuity between the Cole of 1920 and the Cole of 1933 is most evident in the basic principles which still made workers' control relevant to him. He still accepted the Guildsmen's account of the motives which had to replace fear and coercion in industry. Service and the conception of joy in work still held their meaning, although he talked about them less. Workers' control became the answer to his legitimate fear that planning would increase top-heaviness, rigidity, and bureaucracy in industry. Cole had no faith in indirect control of industry through Parliament. It is worth quoting a passage on this point in some detail, to demonstrate the continuity of his basic values.

I do not believe that men who have no freedom or responsibility in their working lives will ever be able to perform the task of exerting political control over industry with effect. The process is too indirect to be effective. The citizen has to elect his political representatives. They in turn have to set up a central organization for the co-ordinated direction of economic policy. Out of this central organization have to emerge the separate managing bodies for each industry and service, and out of these again the technical and administrative directors of each separate establishment. By the time this elaborate circuit of delegations has found its way back again to the rank and file worker, by way of departmental manager and foremen, such original impulse as the process of democratic election for the political assembly possessed will have long been completely spent. There will be no freedom

---

[1] Among those taking part in these discussions: Harold Clay, John Cliff and Arthur Creech-Jones (T.G.W.U.); Arthur Pugh (Iron & Steel Trades Confederation); J. W. Bowen (Post-office Workers); George Ridley (Railway Clerks' Association); G. W. Thompson (Association of Engineering and Shipbuilding Draughtsmen); George Parkhurst (A.E.U.); H. N. Brailsford; and Ellen Wilkinson. Many others were consulted. Material relevant to this, such as transcripts of individual sessions, are in 'Manuscripts and Proofs', Box 7, folder 97, Cole Papers, Nuffield College; and in the F. W Dalley Papers, Hull University, which include letters from Cole to Dalley.

in industry, except for a few happy technical directors, free to manipulate their tools, human and inhuman, to their hearts' content. There will be no democracy; for political democracy will be stultified by the autocracy of the economic system.[1]

Thus despite the new prominence which he gave to the abolition of poverty, Cole still vigorously demanded freedom in industry. He had two separate reasons for this; the first assumed in the passage above and in all his writings, was that freedom was good in itself. The second was that freedom and democracy in society as a whole could only be created in a system in which the workers were granted freedom in their work.

Finally, Cole argued that only under a system of self-government could the makers of policy know where the shoe pinched.[2] This argument, unlike the ones above, shows the distance which separated Cole's theory of workers' control in the 1930s from its Guild Socialist predecessors. In the 1930s, Cole was working within a conception of a planned economy which in evitably gave more control to the planners and to the technicians than he had intended in 1920. Workers' control had to be boiled down to fit into this new world; in it Cole felt he had retained the essential claim of Guild Socialism. Around it he reinstated as many Guild claims as possible.

'What is sound finally is the view that to lead men is better than to drive them, that industrial leadership accordingly demands large qualities of human understanding as well as of technical expertness, and that the administrative designs of the technician must be constantly checked and corrected by the reactions of the ordinary man to whom he issues commands.'[3] Cole here saw workers' control as checking the technician, rather than totally controlling him. He had to admit that the argument that the workers could not control industry, and that their efforts would simply hamper efficiency, 'is undoubtedly formidable – far more formidable than I used to admit when I wrote my Guild Socialist books'.[4] People who argued this line contended that, given the highly mechanized and integrated nature of industry, only the technicians and managers could see the process as a whole and could create on the basis of this knowledge. Cole largely admitted this case, but

[1] *Principles of Economic Planning*, p. 329.
[2] *Principles of Economic Planning*, p. 331.
[3] *The Next Ten Years*, p. 162.
[4] *Principles of Economic Planning*, pp. 328–9.

could not let it pass without a counter-attack: Large-scale, mechanized industry increased the prospects for rational collective control through a version of collective contract.

Mechanised production tends to substitute semi-skilled labour for skill and 'unskill' alike. If it lops off some of the lofty trees, it also adds stature to the undergrowth ... It tends to substitute the group for the individual as the unit of job control ...[1]

But Cole also had to make the damaging admission that relatively few workers really wanted full control over their work.

As he made this admission, he had also reduced his anticipations of what was necessary to make industrial democracy work. The average man should find that industry took up less of his time and emotional energy; not every worker had to take an active hand in control.

What is necessary is to create among each body of workers who are called upon to co-operate in a common service a collective sentiment of responsibility and interest in the success and efficiency of their work. This involves no more than that there should arise in each factory and workshop a sufficient minority of active and interested men and women to impress their leadership upon the rest, and to make their spirit and attitude set the general tone.[2]

Cole firmly believed that an adequate number of individuals like this would be released by a system of self-government. But would they be enough to create a truly democratic society?

Given the limits imposed on the principle of self-government by national planning on the one hand and by collective disinterest on the other, Cole concentrated even more on workshop control. The workshop was the place where industry encroached upon the individual, and thus the most important centre for his control. By emphasizing it, Cole could retain something approaching a Guild Socialist functional distinction. While the planners would have to decide what to produce, 'the appropriate sphere for "workers' control", as distinct from workers' criticisms and suggestions, is that of means and method.'[3] And it was here, in the workshop, that the worker could be induced to take an interest in governing himself. 'For, even if the workman is not interested in his work, he is directly and inevitably interested in the

---

[1] G. D. H. Cole, *The Simple Case for Socialism* (London, Gollancz, 1935), p. 144.
[2] *Principles of Economic Planning*, p. 340.
[3] Ibid., p. 332.

conditions under which it has to be done.'[1] The first step would be to provide a works council or workshop organization in every plant and mine. After this should come some mode of choosing foremen, as the Guild Socialists had demanded, although Cole in the 1930s seemed somewhat solicitous of protecting the foremen against 'capricious removal'. Gradually the whole Guild apparatus could grow up within nationalized industry, as more workers were brought into the Guild, until it included the entire personnel. Eventually the representatives of the workers could take over the regional and national boards entrusted with the overall control of the industry. 'After this fashion, or something after the fashion – for I have no wish to be dogmatic about it – I now envisage the coming of Guild Socialism.'[2]

However, Cole made it clear that this sort of workers' control did not extend to control of the day-to-day administration of the industry at the top. He adopted a German device, separating Boards of Control from Boards of Management. The latter would have to be composed of full-time members; and Cole was certain that

... it is practically impossible for any person who becomes responsible as a full-time officer for the conduct of any industry or service to serve at the same time as an effective representative of the workers or any section of the workers engaged in that industry or service on any matter over which a clash is liable to arise between the managerial and the rank and file point of view.[3]

This, of course, did not lead Cole to deny that a worker could rise to become a manager; he simply asserted that when that happened he ceased to be a worker and did not represent them. The elaborate system of representation which he had proposed in 1917 could not survive such an admission.

When this stage was attained, the workers would have some sort of representation at the middle levels of national planning, rather than control of the basic policy of an autonomous industry. 'The guilds can be left to decide for themselves neither what they will produce, nor what prices they will charge, nor what they will pay their members for the work of production.'[4] This did not mean that Cole had given up his elaborate proposals for decentralization and the devolution of decisions

[1] *The Next Ten Years*, p. 163.
[2] *Principles of Economic Planning*, pp. 335–6.
[3] Cole and Mellor, 'Workers' Control and Self-Government in Industry'.
[4] *The Simple Case for Socialism*, p. 153.

The factual information and preliminary proposals for planning would come to a large degree from the industries themselves, on a regional and on a national basis.[1] But Cole insisted, even more than in 1920, that all such sectional plans must be subject to the needs of the community; the delicate balance between the producers and the consumers had disappeared. All sectional plans were to be subject to the codification and scrutiny of a National Planning Authority, rather than a bipartisan Joint Body, which in turn had ultimately to be under political control. By accepting planning, Cole had explicitly repudiated his earliest Syndicalist sympathies.

The 'coordination of supply and demand' had grown into the contention that the whole output of the community had to be planned; this in turn strengthened the state, as the representative of the consumers, i.e. the community. This same growth of the state is implicit in a socialist incomes policy, for the same reason. No sectional interest could rival the claim of the community as a whole. Cole had chosen to make the political representatives of the community supreme, giving up his quest for a society with no sovereign. The state had to have the last word and workers' control was merely the most important way of preventing tyranny.

Admissions such as these marked the high point of Cole's identification of socialism with planning. He never developed the idea beyond what he had written in 1938. On the other hand, he did not formally abandon it. But examining the two principal editions of *Money* (1944 and 1954), along with *Socialist Economics* (1950) and 'Is This Socialism?' (1954), shows that he retreated from a full statement of the ideas contained in *Principles of Economic Planning* (1935) and *The Machinery of Socialist Planning* (1938). While no overt conflicts broke out between planning and Cole's basic libertarian values, the issue affected his thinking. As he indicated in 'Is This Socialism' a general uneasiness about placing too much power in state hands had diffused itself throughout the Labour movement.[2] This uneasiness inhibited the further development of his ideas, in much the same way that the uncertain conditions of 1920–2 made Cole retreat from his Guild Socialist utopia.

[1] *Principles of Economic Planning*, p. 332.
[2] G. D. H. Cole, 'Is This Socialism?', pp. 7–8.

The winter of 1947–8 is often taken to mark the erosion of Labour's confidence in its goals; but Cole's faith in planning had begun to decay by the autumn of 1943. He was no longer able to define away the accusation that national planning necessarily led to autarchy. Having socialist planners would not be enough. Instead, he argued that 'national planning in individual countries involves international planning, unless it is to be perverted into isolationism'.[1] His speculations about international planning reveal a greater awareness of the problems of 'more backward areas', and contain hopes for economic integration in a socialist Europe. At the same time, they made the whole concept of planning more fragile. In *Money* he made only two practical efforts to envisage international planning relationships – the planning of imports, and the planning of world supplies of money (in which he relied on ideas that had been raised in Anglo–American negotiations). A completely planned economy, for Britain alone or for Europe, had become inconceivable.

The experience of the Labour Government increased his uneasiness. In the 1930s, planning had existed in an uncertain balance with Cole's concept of liberty. Workers' control had been a necessary part of that balance. The Labour Government, however, did not make extensive provisions for workers' participation in nationalized industries. This omission created much uneasiness in the left wing, and inhibited the concept of planning. Cole could not repudiate the connection between state ownership and planning. But neither could he show much interest in extending state enterprise. He turned some of his attention to the Co-operative movement, and largely stayed out of the debate over what constituted the commanding heights of the economy.

The institutions he had described in *The Machinery of Socialist Planning* began to vanish from his books. In the 1944 edition of *Money*, Cole retained brief references to a Minister of Economic Development. The 1954 edition deleted all these allusions. Inability to speculate about planning institutions not only ended Cole's utopian writing; it broke up the correlations he had sought to establish between short-run policies and his socialist goals. In the 1930s he had used institutional speculations to connect short-term policies to his overall notion of a planned economy. In 1944 he continued to repeat the proposal for a

[1] G. D. H. Cole, *Money: Its Present and Future* (London, Cassell, 1944), p. 20.

preliminary planning body, to be created whenever Labour took office. The idea vanished from the 1954 edition of *Money*.

One must not read too much into these specific retreats. Many of his earlier institutional speculations remained latent in his mind, and could have been revived if the state of the Labour movement made them practical once again. Thus, he pushed aside the question of political machinery in *Socialist Economics*, and referred his readers instead to *The Machinery of Socialist Planning*.

Deprived of the bulk of his quasi-utopianizing speculation, the concept of planning itself fragmented. In *Money* (1954) and in *Socialist Economics* he made separate forays into a socialist plan of production, the need to plan the overall allocation of credit and capital, the possibilities of planning imports and exports, planning for full employment, and establishing some sort of incomes policy. His proposals on capital will help to show how unwilling he was to abandon his earlier concepts, but he could not express them fully. He continued to assert that Britain needed to plan the total amounts of capital invested, and to call for a National Investment Board. To the 1954 edition of *Money* he added a paragraph that asked

Why should not the National Investment Board, the Investment Trusts, the Building Societies, and the Insurance Companies be taken over as Public Corporations and used as the instruments of a concerted plan of investment, designed to fulfil the requirements of a national policy of full employment?[1]

However, he refused to integrate these corporations into a unitary mechanism for the distribution of capital. He contended himself with references to the need for a common investment policy, led by the National Investment Board. Behind this idea, one can see the conflict between his uneasiness about unitary state control and his firm belief in the need to determine the relative priorities for the development of specific industries.

Most post-war socialists found Keynesianism a satisfactory technique for controlling the economy without creating an overwhelming state. Cole, however, continued to desire a specifically socialist economics. There was a touch of personal pride involved. Cole felt that young socialists praised Keynes excessively and ignored J. A. Hobson's earlier

[1] G. D. H. Cole, *Money, Trade and Investment* (London, Cassell, 1954), p. 265.

explanation of the gap between savings and investment. As an economist, he felt that Keynesianism relied too much on the manipulation of 'global' terms such as aggregate demand that were too far removed from personal reality. Finally, he doubted whether manipulating fiscal and monetary policy could not work by itself. 'For, can the state really, by following the Keynesian prescription, maintain full employment without setting inflationary tendencies to work, unless it is in a position to control, broadly, what is to be produced and when, and what is to be charged for it, and also the broad distribution of purchasing power, as well as its global amount?'[1]

Thus Cole could not abandon his concept of planning. His specific recommendations continued to look like imperfect portions of a planned economy. The retreat left him dissatisfied and unsure of what a socialist society would look like. Cole himself never found another unitary concept of socialism. He could talk about principles, as in *Socialist Economics*, or about Britain's problems and prospects, as in *Money*. But these discussions stayed separate from each other. He was not able to find a new way of relating important middle-level principles, such as basing the economy on need rather than on economic demand, to contemporary problems. After the mid-1950s, we shall see that Cole's uncertainties even lead him to move outside the Labour Party and to call for a new effort to rethink socialism.

[1] G. D. H. Cole, *Socialist Economics* (London, Gollancz, 1950), p. 50.

CHAPTER 6

PROGRESS, WITH JERUSALEM STILL IN THE DISTANCE

Working out the concept of planning required a less complete re-thinking of socialist goals and possibilities than had the concept of workers' control. Cole did not find it necessary to abandon the parliamentary, reformist framework that he had come to accept in the late 1920s. In the 1930s, his discussions of short-term Labour policies included the construction of planning agencies, but constructing these agencies never seemed to lead necessarily to socialism in the same way that encroaching control appeared to make the means to workers' control identical with the goal itself. Nor did the concept of planning point as obviously to a section of the Labour movement that could serve as a carrier for Cole's values and hopes. And, after Cole ceased to develop his concept of planning, no single conception of socialism serves as a continuing core of his thought.

Thus the last thirty years of Cole's life have a less obvious unity than his Guild Socialist period; but, while his work was not integrated around a single slogan or theme, neither did it disintegrate. One focal point was his work at Oxford, which we have described in another chapter; the other focal point was his continuing relationship with the Labour movement, which crystallized in a many-sided career as a socialist educator. What Cole did as a socialist educator – the problems he thought about, the research and propaganda he organized – depended considerably upon the health and needs of the Labour movement. The Labour movement went through one cycle, from weakness and uncertainty to effective opposition to legislation based on the results of the previous phases, during Cole's last thirty years; when he died, it was unclear whether the cycle would repeat itself fully, but Cole was trying to apply the same remedies he had developed to cope with the previous period of socialist uncertainty. Each of these stages set different tasks for socialist intellectuals, and gave them different positions within the movement. While the Parliamentary Labour Party was weakest, in the early 1930s and during the war-time electoral truce, Labour intellectuals participated prominently in the discussion of policy. When the third Labour Government implemented the minimum programme accepted over the previous fifteen years, Cole and other intellectuals largely vanished from public attention. Finally, in those periods when the Parliamentary Labour Party was an effective opposition but not making obvious strides towards power, debates over policy came closest to setting left-wing fundamentalists against the rest of the Party. Both in the 1930s and in the 1950s, the Party regrouped after internal turmoil; but the nearly-disloyal Popular Front movement of the late 1930s both came closer to splitting the movement and contributed more to later electoral success. At this point, it remains unclear whether Cole considered the Labour movement of the late 1950s to be weaker and less socialistic than it actually was, as he came to feel that socialist thinking would have to begin all over again.

Throughout the shifts in socialist fortunes, Cole retained two sets of ideas that guided his behaviour. He continued to see a socialist society as one characterized by the extension of democracy and freedom into all aspects of life. Secondly, at any time when Labour seemed to be losing momentum and purpose, Cole formed groups to study possible policies, from an empirical as well as from an ideological point of view. In the 1930s this technique appeared to work better than in the 1950s. The socialists who had joined the New Fabian Research Bureau in the 1930s were more likely to be or become Cole's personal friends, surrounding him with the fellowship and support that he valued. The N.F.R.B. also attracted young socialists from the universities to a greater degree than the International Society for Socialist Studies, Cole's parallel group for the late 1950s, and was able to give these young people access to other sections of the Labour movement. Whereas the New Fabian Research Bureau did not challenge the rest of the Labour movement, with I.S.S.S. Cole was a lonely figure, coming closer to turning his back on others in the Labour movement as he felt that they were no longer interested in achieving what he meant by socialism.

Part of Cole's effectiveness during the 1930s depended upon his ability to reach different groups of concerned people through his varied activities. Once the wave of socialist fundamentalism that culminated in the Leicester Conference of 1932 had passed, Labour's rebuilding became hard slogging, looking for recruits in every group of concerned or alarmed citizens. At Oxford, Cole was at the peak of his influence upon students, which remained strong at least until the end of the 1940s. Cole approached many specialized non-academic audiences through his political journalism, writing articles for such disparate periodicals as *The Aryan Path* (a Theosophist journal), *The Highway* (the W.E.A. monthly), *Service in Life and Work* (the Rotarian monthly), *Everyman,* and *The Adelphi.* The *New Statesman* was his most common forum for political journalism and Cole played a major role in shaping it. He contributed a major economic article nearly every week, discussed policy as a member of the editorial board, and wrote many unsigned short comments. Kingsley Martin wrote that '... my job was to see that Keynes, Nicholas Davenport, our city editor, and Cole did not contradict each other'.[1]

Cole extended his role as a socialist educator with a new venture into popular education, a forerunner of the immensely successful and important Left Book Club. In 1932 he published *The Intelligent Man's Guide Through World Chaos.*

This book is an attempt, within the compass of a single volume, to give the intelligent and open-minded citizen, who wants to understand how the world has got into its present plight but possesses no special economic training, the means of unravelling in his own mind the tangle of world economic affairs.[2]

This he could do without talking down to his audience; his clear nontechnical exposition was quite suited to the task. Academic critics tend to sneer at this side of Cole. They claim he wrote too much, citing the Intelligent Man's Guides as evidence. But they were among the most significant things he did. While Cole himself could be self-deprecating about them – he once said that the formula for them was to 'take a packing case, fill it with necessary textbooks, go to the Channel Islands, return in six weeks'[3] – they could be done rapidly only because of his great speed and memory. The Intelligent Man's Guides were solid, and crammed with the latest statistics; their arguments were original. They filled an important gap in mass education. Their success

[1] Kingsley Martin, *Father Figures* (London, Hutchinson, 1966), p. 202.
G. D. H. Cole, *The Intelligent Man's Guide Through World Chaos* (London, Gollancz, 1932), p. 5.
[3] Interview with Michael Fogarty, October 1965.

in reaching a mass audience – something that Cole and many other socialists had sought to do for years – demonstrated the existence of a literate population eager for the latest political information at a reasonable price. The lesson was not lost on Victor Gollancz, their publishers; he improved upon the formula with the Left Book Club.

The expansion of propaganda would have been useless if the Labour movement had not been able to put new recruits to work, and if Socialist intellectuals had not continued to try to refine the ideas from which propaganda would grow. Before the fall of the second Labour Government, Cole and his friends had created two organizations that they hoped could convert enthusiasm into solid work. Cole probably intended to co-ordinate the more propagandistic association, the Society for Socialist Inquiry and Propaganda, with the New Fabian Research Bureau in the same way that the National Guilds League and the Labour Research Department had divided tasks between 1913 and 1920. These hopes were only partially fulfilled; the failure of S.S.I.P. and the success of N.F.R.B. illuminate both the divisiveness and the service that the left brought to the Labour movement in the 1930s.

During the wave of socialist fundamentalism that followed the 1931 debacle, S.S.I.P. succumbed to a take-over; it is to Cole's credit that the capture did not mean a new splinter society too. In the summer of 1932, the I.L.P. decided to disaffiliate from the Labour Party and head for the political wilderness. A rump of the I.L.P., led by Frank Wise, in turn separated from the I.L.P. and proclaimed their loyalty to the Party. This created a rival for 'Zip', and many members felt there was no use for two societies fulfilling the same purpose. Cole first thought of sending a letter to 'loyal' I.L.P. supporters, asking them to join S.S.I.P., but Wise, who also belonged to S.S.I.P., foiled this by preparing to organize his rump. Within the Society, pressure grew for an amalgamation with the remnants of the I.L.P. So Cole met Wise to work out terms of amalgamation, in which Cole very likely conceded too much by putting unity first.[1] It is possible that Cole's newly-

[1] See Frank Horribin to Cole, 18 September 1932, in which he expressed gratitude for Cole's 'comradeliness and evident desire to do your utmost for "unity" yesterday', and Bevin to Cole, 24 September 1932; both letters are in 'Society for Socialist Inquiry and Propaganda', folder 'Formation of the Socialist League – Correspondence', Cole Papers, Nuffield College.

diagnosed diabetes weakened his resistance. Wise became Chairman of the new organization; Cole had wanted Ernest Bevin to lead the new Socialist League as he had led S.S.I.P. Bevin was quite offended by being passed over, and this confirmed his suspicions of socialist intellectuals. They were mercurial and disloyal, he felt; but Cole had stood loyally by him until it became clear that Wise would not accept Bevin as chairman. The larger issue was that of the relations between the new Socialist League and the Labour Party. Cole did succeed in making it clear that the new body was not to run candidates; but it did affiliate as a group to the Labour Party, thus assuming the position of a party within a party. This separatism bedevilled almost every effort to form a left-wing sounding board, and only the 'self-denying ordinance' could prevent it. Cole could not help associating himself with many of the aims espoused by Wise and Sir Stafford Cripps, who took control of the Socialist League when Wise died; but Cole found their approach unpalatable in the early and mid-1930s. He suspected them of subordinating issues to personal crusades within the Labour Party, and did not share their assumption that establishing formal alliances with the Communists would strengthen Labour. Consequently he soon gave up the seat on the Executive of the Socialist League that he had received when S.S.I.P. merged with the remnants of the I.L.P.

The other half of the 'loyal grousers' of 1931, the New Fabian Research Bureau, stayed out of the Socialist League and survived to do good work. The Coles remained the most important figures in it, but never sought to dominate it as the Webbs had dominated the Fabian Society after 1914. Cole prepared the memorandum on research into economic policy which guided the N.F.R.B's efforts in the early 1930s, but was not a member of the committee that planned their political research. As Cole's own interests turned in the direction of economic planning, so did N.F.R.B.'s research. Young recruits were assigned specific industries to study, a task which contributed to their political education and their later usefulness to the Parliamentary Labour Party and Transport House. Much of this material ended up in a volume of studies on public ownership edited by W. A. Robson. Reviewing their progress in 1936, the N.F.R.B. Research Committee found that studies of socialization in various industries had outstripped the overall examination of planning machinery; Cole wrote *The Machinery of Socialist Planning to fill the gap.*

But planning was only one focal point for the energies of N.F.R.B. members. Soon after the fall of the MacDonald Government, Cole suggested an expedition to Russia, although he ultimately did not join it because of his illness. A later trip to Sweden, which he did join, also yielded a book of essays – one of the first solid results of British interest in Sweden as an alternate model of socialist development. N.F.R.B. nourished an active International Section, and its Local Government Section became energetic when the Popular Front agitation turned socialist attention towards local campaigns for various social services. N.F.R.B. members co-operated closely with the Fabian Society; Cole participated in Fabian lecture series and contributed to a volume of Fabian essays in 1937. Finally, in 1939, the obvious step occurred; the New Fabian Research Bureau took over the remains of the Fabian Society, now denuded of the 'old gang'.

The N.F.R.B. thus formed a major part of the background to Cole's most solid and most original political thinking during the 1930s. Unfortunately, this research played a less significant role in the most dramatic outburst of Socialist militancy – the Popular Front agitation – and in Cole's own efforts to discipline that militancy. Had the Popular Front been more closely based on continuing research, the Labour movement might have been less unsure of what could follow the minimum programme enacted in 1945. The Popular Front agitation saw an important change in the position Cole and other intellectuals filled in the Labour movement. It shifted the balance of intellectual activity towards propaganda, away from political passivity but also away from the detailed investigation of socialist alternatives. In particular, it threatened to distract Cole from thinking out the concept of planning.

The intellectuals found themselves more visible than ever, way ahead of the Party's leadership. They articulated the worries of a large portion of the British population, instead of playing the role of revolutionary romantics posturing in isolation. Cole in particular faced a considerable growth of the audience he had located via his Intelligent Man's Guides. At the same time, satisfying that audience, and coping with the Fascist menace that had created it, made him reconsider his acceptance of Labour parliamentarianism. Here especially, however, the critic may feel that Cole failed to create a new alternative for the non-communist left. In a sense, he simply used the opportunity to reiterate the minimum programme within which he had worked since 1928, refurbishing it to appeal to his broader audience.

Analysing the Popular Front in *The New Statesman: The First Fifty Years*, Edward Hyams wrote that Cole 'had thought of this Left-tending compromise in the first place.'[1] In this passage, Hyams concentrates on the policies of the American New Deal rather than on the political style of the French Popular Front while assessing the predecessors of Popular Front activity in Britain. If Hyams is right, Cole's originality would lie in earlier conceptions such as the National Labour Corps, which he incorporated into his Popular Front proposals. But Cole's originality in the mid-1930s lay in his effort to get beyond the two competing ideas of how a Popular Front would act. The phrase in itself was not new. The Third International was the first to preach it, in 1920–1. Moscow meant to re-unite the working class against capitalism – which looked suspicously like forcing Social Democrats to accept guidance from Communists who had recently failed to capture control of national working-class movements. The French Popular Front was a far cry from this concept. It was an electoral coalition of Socialists, Communists and Radicals; enthusiasm for this form of Popular Front spread across Europe.

In Britain, the idea of a Popular Front crystallized around the Socialist League. In 1933, the Socialist League initiated a drive for a 'united front' of the Labour Party, the I.L.P., and the Communist Party, which Cripps continued for several years with little success. Initially, Cole was not particularly interested. He suspected that such a campaign would only result in internal chaos for the Labour Party, rather than in the adoption of an attractive radical programme. Thus it was not until the summer of 1936 that he began to make guarded use of the slogans of a Popular Front, articulating what he felt was a growing discomfort in the nation. In January 1937 he was ready to offer moral support to Cripps, who was threatened with expulsion from the Labour Party for Popular Front activities.[2] What had happened to

[1] Edward Hyams, *The New Statesman: The History of the First Fifty Years*, p. 192.
[2] G. D. H. Cole, 'Dedication', *The People's Front* (London, Gollancz, 1937), p. 26.

change his mind, to bring him back to a position where he felt that he might have to become a rebel again?

The rise of Fascism in Spain, coupled with an aggressive German foreign policy, had completed the task of showing Cole the weakness of the assumptions on which any hope of slow progress towards a decent society rested. Cole bitterly wrote that

It was taken for granted by almost everybody that Great Britain, and indeed the whole world, would go on getting, faster or more slowly, more democratic, that there would be more freedom and more opportunity for doing what one liked, that the standard of living would go on rising, and that, on the whole, on account of this progress, men would gradually get more reasonable in the management of their common affairs.[1]

Cole, as a left-wing socialist, had given up some parts of this optimism sooner than others. Even the early stages of depression in the 1920s had made him sceptical of capitalism's power to create more wealth or to yield comfort to the masses through reforms. The rise of Fascism converted his scepticism into grim disbelief. But the crucial part of the assumption, for a political thinker as rationalistic in his appeal as Cole, had been the belief that men would respond to reason when faced with the breakdown of capitalism. Here Fascism provided a crushing blow.

Fascism . . . is not merely cruel and evil and decivilizing in itself . . . Fascism is *nonsense*; and that is perhaps the gravest indictment of all. It not merely is nonsense; it spews sense out of its mouth. It believes in nonsense, believes that the ordinary man is moved by nonsense, *and ought to be so moved*. It not merely deems men fools and irrational, but wants to keep them so. That is a very different thing from admitting that men are in fact largely irrational, while seeking to increase the hold of reason upon them.[2]

Fascism was dangerous in a new way – a malevolent force beyond the reach of Cole's weapons of fact and argument. This kind of wilful, fundamental stupidity irritated Cole more than anything else; he hated the reasons which could lead anyone to choose economic and social insanity. And it was gaining ground, 'threatening to pull down again all that has been so painfully built up, and offering in exchange for the

---

[1] *The People's Front*, p. 144. Compare Cole, *Labour in War-Time* (London, Bell, 1915), pp. 277–8.
[2] *The People's Front*, pp. 145–6, 149–50. The whole of the chapter from which this excerpt was taken is one of the best Cole ever wrote, a polemical description of the moral weakness and economic nonsense of Fascism.

values of democracy and freedom and a rising standard of life an alternative set of values which to me at any rate seems lunatically evil'.[1]

Against this wickedness, traditional Labour politics offered no real hope.

> The Labour Party alone cannot rouse the people to turn out the existing Government and put a Government of the Left in its place. It cannot even force the Government to change its policy under pressure from public opinion. It is manifest that it cannot do these things, or why has it not done them already? Why is it not doing them now?[2]

Cole concluded that the Labour Party's policy was futile in two respects: it insisted upon making opposition to Fascism a party affair like any other, and it made everything depend upon the feeble prospects of winning a parliamentary majority in four years. Cole reinforced his sceptical judgment of Labour's electoral chances with a detailed scrutiny of the 1935 election figures. More ominously, Cole said that 1940 would be too late, even if elections were held.

The dangers to democracy were too urgent to be subordinated to 'politics as usual' in this manner. Assuming that a majority of the British were democrats, he sought to give them a voice before 1940, a voice that would yell for those who shunned the Labour Party as well as for those who already expressed their fears through it. He wanted to reach the people who were

> ... prepared to play their part in the struggle against Fascism and war, to help build up the League of Nations into a real instrument for the preservation of peace and the furtherance of international justice, and to agitate in domestic policy for a sensible immediate programme of social and economic reforms.[3]

The problems lay in two areas. First, all of the passive democrats, who thought of democracy as being left alone and a vote every five years, had to be made to see the danger. Cole was undoubtedly optimistic in feeling that a majority of the British were democratic in any positive sense. It is clear that he had been forced to use the word in a more slovenly sense than ever before – and that he still kept the strong

[1] Ibid., p. 145.
[2] Ibid., p. 26.
[3] Ibid., p. 24.

emotional attachment to it which he had for democracy properly defined as fellowship. Secondly, he and his friends had to convert this perception of a coming struggle between Fascism and democracy at home and abroad into an effective force with a coherent purpose.

The central issue had to be that of restraining Fascism; this negative point became the lowest common denominator of democracy. Here Cole proposed 'a policy of real pooled security, based on effective pledges of common action and involving a joint planning of military measures of mutual defence'.[1] Such a policy would have required international cooperation on a scale hitherto never attempted in peacetime or wartime. It would have gone far beyond the sanctions on Ethiopia, which had caused divisions even among leftists such as Cole, Cripps and Lansbury. Nor could it be worked out within the framework of the existing League of Nations; Cole felt that only if the European nations could create such a pact could they revitalize the League. Such a policy was beyond the capacity of the Baldwin Government, Cole instinctively felt; he argued that the Tories would reject it as 'opening the door to Socialism'. 'For it involves making Great Britain part of a "Left Bloc" in European affairs . . .'[2] – something more fragile than Cole realized. Russia sought such an alliance, until the summer of 1939, but the Popular Front Government in France was a brittle reed.

Perhaps pooled security would have been the only way out, if it had been followed vigorously. But a fatal contradiction falls across Cole's presentation. For, in addition to restraining Fascism, Cole and most of the left saw such a pact as a way of resisting further increases in armaments. 'The Left . . . is exceedingly unwilling either to divert money from desirable social services to armaments, or to resort to armaments to any provocative extent.'[3] Cole here encountered the difficult problem of what sorts of armaments deter and what sorts provoke; in seeking to prevent escalation like that of 1914, he ran the risk of weakening Britain and her partners in a pooled security pact. For he seems to have felt that international cooperation would be virtually a substitute for a large amount of re-armament by the British Govenment. 'Armaments

[1] Ibid., p. 90.
[2] Ibid., p. 181.
[3] Ibid., p. 90.

that may be wholly inadequate for a country which proposes to act in isolation may be fully sufficient if they can be pooled with the armaments of like-minded countries.'[1] All these humane maxims make sense, but were far from solving the problem.

Cole's chosen political weapon, public opinion and a broad-based People's Front to mobilize it, had deep splits which rendered it impotent on precisely this issue. The Socialist League, under Cripps, opposed all re-armament by a non-socialist Government. They had opposed sanctions on Ethiopia, arguing that the Conservatives could not be trusted not to use the powers given them against the left rather than against the Fascists. This was a coherent argument, and Cole's milder predictions that the Tories would only co-operate with left Governments at the last moment certainly came true. But a popular movement which did not trust the existing Government enough to try to influence it could hardly be useful. Another segment of the Labour Party contained outright pacifists such as Lansbury, to whom pooled security was anathema. A far larger number of liberal-minded people would be unable to support a movement which anticipated war. Cole's generation naturally did not relish the thought of another war: it took time to overcome such a pragmatic pacifism. As a result, the left found itself unable to commit itself directly to re-armament, and without a policy. Cole himself was unable to challenge pacifist opinion with a constructive policy of re-armament that would make a pact of pooled security effectives. All he could do was drift towards the inevitable.

Now I am not prepared to oppose some amount of re-armament, even if it is carried out by the National Government. I am prepared to oppose the National Government on all accounts, and to attack its re-armament programme on the grounds both that it is excessive and that the Government has provided no satisfactory assurance of the purpose for which the armaments are to be used, or of the policy to be furthered by them.[2]

His own attitude was passive and confused, and the same thing is true of most of the left. This led Cole to a fascinating piece of half-realism. The left had to win in order to create such a policy of pooled security; but it could not win on such a policy.

[1] Ibid., p. 90.
[2] Ibid., p. 336.

In the first place, the Left includes practically all the convinced pacifists, who will necessarily feel so strongly about pacifism as to talk about it when it is most unpopular ... On re-armament, this makes it simply impossible for the Left, in a country where real pacifism is at all strong, to steal the Right's thunder. If the Left tries to become the party of re-armament, it merely succeeds in looking silly and disunited.[1]

Looking at elements in the Socialist League and other supporters of a People's Front, one may be pardoned for thinking that it was not simply a problem of images.

If 'the Left' could not win on an anti-Fascist foreign policy, it would have to play down foreign policy and win on 'bread and butter' domestic issues.[2] However, the policy Cole had to offer was largely his old minimum programme for a socialist government. The National Labour Corps, for example, received the new title of 'C.U.B. – because I want its special task to be expressed in the words, 'Clean Up Britain.'[3] The financial measures which we saw Cole proposing in 1929 also made another appearance, and indeed the conditions were similar – pockets of long-term depression coupled with reasonably decent conditions in the growing areas of the country.

In this domestic programme, we can see the other basic difficulty of Cole's proposals and of the whole concept of the Popular Front as far as Britain was concerned. The policies comprised a standard reformist socialist minimum programme, which had failed to win elections for the Labour Party. Presenting them in a new guise would not be likely to win over many new recruits, and anything less than a socialist minimum programme had little appeal to Cole and to the militants needed to make the Popular Front vocal.[4] Including the Communists and the I.L.P., as Cripps demanded, certainly would not reassure the faint-hearted or the Liberals. Such a programme could hardly be the

---

[1] Ibid., p. 89.

[2] Ibid., p. 91.

[3] Ibid., p. 241.

[4] Cole admitted this (*The People's Front*, p. 285): 'Clearly, however, the democratic non-Socialists who are potential supporters of a People's Front are not prepared to stand at present for a full Socialist programme. And, on the other hand, a programme of mere social reforms will fail to satisfy the Socialist, or to arouse any enthusiasm among those who believe in the need for a thorough change of system.' But he followed this admission with a sentence which indicated that he had missed the point: 'It is therefore impossible to achieve democratic unity within a single party, however much we might prefer on tactical grounds to achieve it in that way.' A Popular Front would be no more effective than a Party, faced with this division.

basis for a new departure politically; it contradicts Cole's efforts to create a new sort of politics.

The aim of a Popular Front, after all, was to get beyond the limits imposed upon democratic politics by a Labour Party with little hope for a majority and with four years to wait for an election. 'The purpose of both the United Front and the People's Front, as I understand them, is the strengthening and more effective expression of democratic opinion in relation to immediate practical issues of opinion.'[1] That is, Cole sought to mobilize public opinion for pressure upon the parliamentary system. He did not think of a British Popular Front as primarily an electoral coalition. But the general set of aims which Cole had allocated to a People's Front inevitably brought it back into the centre of the political arena. They were too broad for a pressure group to achieve; they depended upon toppling the Tory Government and replacing it with one that would carry them out. In the circumstances, the movement would probably have to force an early General Election. The idea of a People's Front really was a protest against the impotence of the people once a Government had been elected, and as such was bound to be impotent itself.

Thus the People's Front proved incapable of carrying out Cole's hopes for a socialist society. It failed to provide him with a body of people whose actions seemed to make socialism possible, failed to call forth his speculations about socialist values and practices in the way that trade union militance had stimulated his Guild Socialism. The Popular Front movement was too negative, too desperate, too characterless in the hope of gaining recruits, yet too sectarian in the attitudes of some of its main protagonists. Cole's ambitious hopes for a national People's Front dissolved in the basic contradictions between pooled security and pacifism, between blocking Fascism and enacting a socialist minimum programme, and between pressure group activity and the goals of a political movement. By the end of his Left Book Club volume, *The People's Front*, Cole found that his most important task was to puncture unrealistic thinking about what democratic forces could do. This realism, he argued, was a necessary precondition for effective action.

When it came to action, Cole recognized, the People's Front could

[1] Ibid., p. 17.

only be a movement for a People's Front at a later date. It had to work independently to prepare the left and potential allies for cooperation when an election or a political crisis gave it a real opportunity of changing the possession of political power. 'Any movement for unification of the "Left" in face of the present crisis will have for the present to arise without the help or sanction of the official Labour Party and Trade Union leadership, and to win its way, if at all, upwards from below.'[1] This unification could come about if the Labour movement itself became more aggressive and concentrated upon the people's needs instead of accentuating its internal divisions. In April 1937 he even wished for a new strike wave, to integrate militants into the Labour movement.[2] In these ways he hoped to distract them from loud, ostentatious efforts to unite the Labour Party, the Communists and the I.L.P. by allowing the latter two organizations to affiliate to the Labour Party – Sir Stafford Cripps' hope. Such a direct movement would inevitably fail again and again, its leaders already faced excommunication, and the attempt made real cooperation less possible. Yet Cole was drawn to sound similarly rebellious, with his insistence that 'We must ... either convert the present Labour Party leaders, or replace them.'[3] Wherever he moved, the Labour Party's stubborn self-sufficiency impeded him. The Labour Party had to be the core of a People's Front; there was no other real source of members. The Communists were a handful; the Liberals more, but not exclusively libertarian. Obviously, as many of these two groups as possible, and of the apathetic voters, had to be won over. 'We have to recognise that conditions are not ripe for it, and that much more has to be done by way of preparation before it can exist. For the present our task is to familiarize and popularize the ideas, and to build up the habit of collaboration ...'[4] Cole argued that the only way to do this was through local action in good causes.

The first thing is for all democrats, of all colours and persuasions, to get to know one another, and to get used to working together about particular things. It may be the Left Book Club, or Spanish Democratic Defence, or

[1] Ibid., p. 350.
[2] G. D. H. Cole, 'Strikes and Profiteering', *New Statesman and Nation*, XIII (17 April 1937), 627.
[3] *The People's Front*, p. 342.
[4] Ibid., p. 342.

Peace Propaganda, or Milk in Schools, or help for the Depressed Areas, or any of a hundred other things. They are all grist to the democratic mill; they all help to build up the habit of democratic unity. For the moment, our task is to take our chances when they come, and not to cry for the moon.[1]

Support for these and other practical, functional or local activities was probably the most important by-product of Popular Front agitation. Beneath the surface of the Popular Front, and to some degree with its ideas as a focus, Cole continued his service to the Labour movements – articles for various journals, participation in Fabian lecture series, and research. In addition, he took on obligations that related more directly to the Popular Front. He contributed money for a child in Spain. In October 1938 he supported A. D. Lindsay's candidature in the by-election to fill the Parliamentary seat for the city of Oxford. Cole was not responsible for the initial offer to Lindsay to stand for the seat. When he heard of it, he insisted upon finding out the opinion of Patrick Gordon Walker, the official Labour candidate, who was being asked to withdraw in the middle of his campaign. "I could not agree to any step which was likely to involve either a split in the local party or its disaffiliation by Transport House."[2] Walker withdrew, appearing to support Lindsay's candidature, but later denounced it; his opposition obviously dismayed Cole. Lindsay, running as an 'Independent Progressive' backed by both Labour and Liberal Party members, ran well but lost; at the same time, Vernon Bartlett won Bridgewater in a similar protest against appeasement.

Despite an occasional success such as Bridgewater, Cole could find no grounds for hoping to avert another world war and resuming steady progress towards socialism. This hopelessness had its impact primarily upon his most original thinking; Cole's original work on economic planning, for example, came to an end with *The Machinery of Socialist Planning* in 1938, and no new unitary conception of socialism came to take its place in his writing. Cole continued his prolific production of the various forms of socialist education that he had helped create, but with a new grimness. Recording Cole's visits in September 1937 and October 1938, Beatrice Webb found him very critical both of the

---

[1] Ibid., p. 334.

[2] Cole letter, *New Statesman and Nation*, XVI (12 November 1938), 765–6. See also G. D. H. Cole, 'Independent Progressive', *New Statesman and Nation*, XVI (19 November 1938), 817–18; G. D. H. Cole, *A History of the Labour Party from 1914*.

Labour Party and trade union establishments and of many of their pacifist and marxist critics. Mrs Webb felt that Cole agreed with her prediction of coming political decadence for Britain, but that he was unwilling (one might say, constitutionally unable) to be inactive or fatalistic.[1] Instead, he went on warning his audiences of the coming war, testing and discarding the hopes that others put forth for evading war. In each article he tried to strengthen the opposition to Fascism on rational, democratic grounds, so that the war would at least be fought in the proper spirit.

Cole's reluctant acceptance of an anti-Fascist war comes out clearly in 'War Aims', an interesting pamphlet he wrote in November 1939. Cole's reluctance differed greatly from the direct opposition of the members of the Communist Party, who argued that the war was an imperialist venture, once the Soviet Union had signed an agreement with Germany. He pointed out the difficulties involved in fighting Germany in a one-front war: The result would be 'mutual exhaustion up to the point at which Stalin will be left to dictate what terms he pleases to the ruined civilizations of Western and Central Europe'. Rather than 'proceed to this extremity, till nothing is left of our civilization except the smile on Stalin's face', Cole tried to 'think hard and realistically about every possible way of avoiding the greater catastrophe'.[2]

'War Aims' was neither cowardice nor a final gesture of appeasement. It was an attempt to apply foresight to the situation. Where others could fight negatively, to 'stop Hitler', Cole wanted Britain to decide what sort of a world she wanted to emerge from the war. If these war aims were promulgated, perhaps talks would be held on their basis, or perhaps a revolt might take place within Germany.[3] He realized that neither of these possibilities had any real chance of coming about – but the promulgation of war aims would have the effect of committing Britain to a progressive reconstruction of Europe after the war. He wanted Britain to commit herself to a new federal Europe which would unify certain economic services and provide an orderly basis for the

[1] 'Diary of Beatrice Webb', Vol. 51 (11 September 1937), p. 103, London School of Economics.
[2] G. D. H. Cole, 'Was Aims' (*New Statesman* pamphlet, London, 1939), p. 13. The pamphlet went through three editions in November 1939.
[3] 'War Aims', p. 31.

lowering of tariff barriers and for economic expansion.[1] In addition, he demanded that the European countries pool their colonies, with the intention of liberating them as soon as possible.

This emphasis upon reconstruction is thoroughly consistent with his position in the First World War, although this tends to be obscured by his abandonment of pacifism and by his acceptance of new roles redefining his position within the Labour movement. In practice, he separated his new roles from his essential position as a socialist educator, continuing to debate policies through various media. But in some of his wartime work, Cole moved outside the Labour movement. He offered his services to the Government. This offer entailed a partial suspension of his deep distrust of Tory motives; it brought him into situations in which he had to ignore ideas he had supported as a socialist propagandist, and act as a cautious committee-man rather than as a critic or as a source of striking new ideas. He spent much of the war translating into practical goals those socialist ideas that seemed to have gained common currency and mediating between socialism and the consensus reached in the middle of the war.

Cole's services were not immediately accepted. Until Chamberlain was replaced by the Coalition, intellectuals did not find it easy to join the war effort;[2] even then, the obvious Labour intellectuals, who had irritated their own party by Popular Front activities, were at times met with suspicion and had difficulties in finding places where their abilities could be used. Cole started with practical experience in semisocialist planning, and then worked out a position from which he could seek to influence the shape of postwar reconstruction.

Cole first worked under Sir William Beveridge, who had been appointed Chairman of the Man-power Requirements Committee under the supervision of Ernest Bevin at the Ministry of Labour. The conscious decision to distribute workers among the possible employers of labour meant that Britain's war economy resembled the kind of

---

[1] Cole developed these proposals in two books published during the early years of the war: *Europe, Russia and the Future* (London, Gollancz, 1941), and *Great Britain in the Post-war World* (London, Gollancz, 1942). In addition to the arguments cited in the text, these books contained interesting appraisals of how much of Europe would be dominated by Russia, and evaluations of the changes Britain would have to make to compete in the post-war world.

[2] See a letter from Margaret Cole to Beatrice Webb, October or November 1939, in the Passfield Papers, Section II, sub-section 4, group 1, item 42.

planned economy Cole had described in *Principles of Economic Planning* more closely than it resembled the 'Keynesian' variety of planning that came to dominate after 1947. In *Principles of Economic Planning* Cole had treated labour as a key resource whose availability, training and uses should be planned. However, the urgent need in 1935 had been to plan the creation of new jobs; consequently, Cole had not foreseen the establishment of a specific agency to ration the use of labour. Manpower planning employed semi-socialistic, direct physical controls rather than manipulation of the labour market through the availability of investment funds or through a selective employment tax. Certain occupational skills were declared 'reserved' for armaments work or for other essential tasks; male workers in less essential trades such as distribution and retail work were made eligible for military service or retraining. Cole organized a network of volunteer researchers who gathered information about the numbers of workers in various industries, as a basis for the redirection of labour. His Man-Power Survey was conducted rapidly and well, and helped make mobilization and dilution more efficient, yet more equitable than it had been in the First World War.

But this was only temporary work, which the Ministry of Labour took over once the Survey had been prepared. Cole returned to Oxford, where he rejoined Nuffield College, then in the process of being created as Oxford's first college for post-graduate work in the social sciences. Early in 1941 the college decided to operate a Social Reconstruction Survey. This decision obviously owed much to Cole.[1] With the Warden, Harold Butler, working for the Government, Cole carried much weight, and eventually became Sub-Warden for a short time. His concern for creating a decent society found an outlet in the topics

[1] It is unclear whether the idea came first from Cole or from Sir Harold Butler, the Warden. Cole in 'The Nuffield College Social Reconstruction Survey', *Oxford*, VIII, No. 1 (Summer 1941), said that 'the original impetus to our Survey came from the Warden...'; in his 'Report 1941–2' (Oxford, May 1942), he said that 'I therefore proposed to the Nuffield College Committee that, if it cared to entrust me with the work, I would try to organize a Social Reconstruction Survey...'. What really matters is that Cole did the organizing and the work, with Butler busy on other important tasks; the idea was his in its execution. See also G. D. H. Cole, 'The Nuffield College Social Reconstruction Survey: A Description', *Social Welfare* (April 1942), pp. 38–42; G. D. N. Worswick, 'Cole and Oxford, 1938–1958', in Asa Briggs and John Saville (eds.), *Essays in Labour History in Memory of G. D. H. Cole* (London, Macmillan, 1960); and materials at Nuffield College.

Nuffield College chose to investigate. As in the First World War, he found a way of staying aloof from the actual fighting of the war, concentrating instead upon the sort of society which could emerge from it.

In another important way, Cole was able to affect the direction the Survey took. He knew of course the Labour members of the Churchill cabinet, among them Arthur Greenwood, Minister without Portfolio entrusted with the general task of making provisions for postwar reconstruction. On the first of April 1941 Greenwood and Lord Reith, Minister of Works and Buildings, defined the Government's relation to the Social Reconstruction Survey in answer to a question in Parliament. Cole summarized this answer in the following terms:

Broadly, the Survey was given three groups of questions to investigate, together with a fourth reference which in effect defined the general purpose and spirit of its work. The three groups of subjects were: first, the probable future distribution of industry and population in Great Britain; second, the effects of the war on the educational services; and thirdly, the working of the social services, other than education, and the lessons to be drawn for the future from their war-time development and experience. The fourth matter referred to the Survey was to report upon the adequacy of the existing institutions of Great Britain, both statutory and private, for giving expression to the spirit of a democratic community – an exceedingly wide reference, which was clearly meant to indicate a line of approach to the Survey's studies in all their aspects.[1]

Thus Cole and the Survey obtained a broad definition of tasks which was egalitarian in its outlook and offered latitude for interpretation as well as the gathering of facts. This came at a time when most other interested parties were unable to think deeply about their conceptions of what Britain should be like, and when there was general agreement that major changes would be needed to prevent the recurrence of the difficulties of the inter-war period. When the end of the war grew closer and when specific interests were at stake, this consensus dwindled.

The operating procedure of the Social Reconstruction Survey grew out of the Man-Power Survey. A central staff at Oxford directed the work of 'local collaborators in rather more than twenty key areas . . .'. Cole boasted that 'we had assembled a remarkable team of unpaid investigators – in effect mobilising for this important national service a

G. D. H. Cole, 'Report 1941–2', p. 7.

large proportion of the University teachers in economics and kindred subjects who remained at work'. He believed very strongly that this semi-amateur social research 'could accomplish far more than we could possibly hope to do if we worked merely from a single centre'.[1] The concept of the Survey illustrates Cole's inheritance from the Victorian tradition of volunteer service performed by enlightened members of the privileged classes. But Cole adapted this tradition through his experience with the Fabian and Labour Research Departments and the New Fabian Research Bureau. It became part of his fundamental belief in active citizenship in a democracy and his trust in the broadly educated person. Most professional sociologists do not share his faith, and his reliance upon amateurs may have been a factor in the opposition which later developed at Oxford.

The Oxford staff decided how to implement the instructions given to them by the Minister without Portfolio and the Minister of Works and Buildings, and left much of the actual task of obtaining information to the local researchers. The material they assembled was collated at Oxford by Michael Fogarty, P. W. S. Andrews, H. A. Silverman, and others, and used with other material obtained from the Government or from earlier studies. Members of the staff drew up specialized reports, for which Cole, as director of the Survey, took general responsibility. Occasionally he drafted a report himself, with his well-known fluency and ability to synthesize a mass of information.

By the autumn of 1942, the members of the Survey had completed most of the work they had undertaken for the Government. Co-operation from Government departments had never been automatic. As G. D. N. Worswick writes:

It was one thing to have central government approval; it was another to extract statistical and other information from individual Ministries. Some co-operated whole-heartedly. But there were others who had their own ideas about security and who thought that the number of days in the week should be kept a closely guarded secret.[2]

When Arthur Greenwood and Lord Reith left the cabinet, these problems were intensified. In April 1943, the Treasury grants which

---

[1] G. D. H. Cole, 'The Nuffield College Social Reconstruction Survey', *Oxford*, VIII, No. 1, p. 3.
[2] *Essays in Labour History*, p. 32.

had partially financed the Survey were withdrawn; its active work for the Government was over. Worswick makes an intelligible 'guess' concerning the basic reasons for terminating the Government's connections with the Survey:

By 1943 the war economy was under way, and there was time to breathe and to think of the future. The departments began to have ideas of their own. Not that the government's own efforts in the matter of forming and guiding opinion proved ultimately superior. (The Employment Policy White Paper of 1944, for example, compares poorly with the Nuffield Statement.) But anyway they did not want some outside body barging about. Nor can one escape the thought that Cole's avowed socialism might have occurred to some as a good reason for winding up the Survey.[1]

Well before this occurred, the Survey had begun to shift its attention to the more general arena of postwar reconstruction. Their chosen device was the unofficial conference on a particular topic, to which industrialists, trade unionists, academics and government officials were invited.[2] The Survey staff prepared the documentation, and Cole took on himself the essential task of summing up the Conferences. Worswick gives a graphic picture of Cole at work at this:

His extraordinary memory, his intellectual tidiness and his power of lucid exposition were fully displayed, perhaps the most remarkably when the conference had appeared to be least interesting and purposive. Ideas and arguments which had seemed at the time trivial and disconnected were, like the scrappy themes of a symphony by Sibelius, drawn together into a final statement of overwhelming clarity and force.[3]

Cole's hand can also be seen in the drafting of the Statements of these Conferences, without distorting or misrepresenting the work and opinions of those present. For Cole resisted the temptation to use the Conferences for propaganda for his own positions. The progressive social policies outlined in the Statements depended upon the consensus created by the war; this consensus was later revealed in the 1945

---

[1] *Essays in Labour History*, p. 33.
[2] The results of several of these Conferences were published, notably *Employment Policy and Organisation of Industry after the War: A Statement* (London, Oxford University Press, 1943); *Industry and Education: A Statement* (London, Oxford University Press, 1943); *The Open Door in Secondary Education* (London, Oxford University Press, 1943). Copies at Nuffield College. Civil servants and local government officers attended the first conferences, but not later ones.
[3] *Essays in Labour History*, pp. 31–2.

elections. Perhaps the most useful effect of the Conferences was to demonstrate a general willingness to accept the Beveridge plan and the concept of full employment. The war had made national planning respectable, and weakened the resistance of sectional interests to national policies. In a war against Nazism, people were more ready to take democracy seriously. In such circumstances, the average participant was much closer to Cole than he would have been before or after the war, and could be more impressed by his lucid presentation of an argument. But Cole did not abuse this power by trying to force the participants into socialist positions.[1]

The storm which blew up around the Social Reconstruction Survey came from another source – the University. Some thought that the work was not of a high enough quality for an Oxford College; the Treasury had apparently given this as a reason for withdrawing its grant.[2] Undoubtedly the quality of much of the work was erratic, for Cole had had to rely upon people who could not serve in the armed forces and who had not already joined the war effort in another way. Still, both Cole and Michael Fogarty wrote books using material gathered by the Survey. After Cole had resigned, a committee composed of Professors A. L. Bowley, G. N. Clark, and D. H. MacGregor finally exempted the Survey from charges of incompetence, and decided to publish several volumes of articles based upon it.[3] With the approaching end of the war, Cole became vulnerable. His view of the Survey now appeared controversial; it was merged with the general question of what was to become of Nuffield College. Sir Harold

---

[1] I looked carefully into this matter, for it is an angle from which one would expect criticism of Cole; members of all political parties answered that Cole was scrupulously fair.

[2] Worswick, in *Essays in Labour History*, pp. 32–3.

[3] *Studies in Industrial Organisation*, H. A. Silverman (ed.), Nuffield College Social Reconstruction Series, G. D. H. Cole and A. D. Lindsay (gen. ed.) (London, 1946). *Voluntary Social Services: Their Place in the Modern State*, A. F. C. Bourdillon (ed.), Nuffield College Social Reconstruction Survey, G. D. H. Cole and A. D. Lindsay (gen. ed.) (London, 1945). Much of this material was initially prepared for Beveridge. In addition, G. D. H. Cole, *Building and Planning* (London, Cassell, 1945), and Michael Fogarty, *Prospects of the Industrial Areas of Great Britain* (London, 1945), drew on material gathered by the Survey, as did *Britain's Town and Country Pattern*, Rebuilding Britain Series, No. 2 (London, 1943). Publications are only a partial index of the Survey's activities; it is impossible to tell how much the reports made to various Government agencies and commissions succeeded in supporting advanced positions on economic and physical planning, and the development of the social services.

Butler's death added the question of the college's leadership. Early in 1944 Cole resigned as Sub-Warden and as director of the Survey.

The end of the Social Reconstructive Survey must have disappointed Cole. It demonstrated that his war-time efforts to find a new position, working for a less partisan but radical reconstruction of England, had been submerged in political resistance and academic squabbling. The Survey had helped shape the discussion of postwar policy, but it had not led to a dramatic acceptance of physical planning of the location of industry; it is impossible to say whether the Survey's memoranda on education and the health services were used significantly in drafting the Butler Act and in Beveridge's reports. Ultimately, Cole's less formal activities during the war had a greater effect. Before the start of the war, the Coles had merged the New Fabian Research Bureau with the Fabian Society and given the parent body new life. They and their friends kept the Fabian Society going while most political activity had ceased. Individually and collectively, the Fabians, the writers for the *New Statesman*, and the Left Book Club, continued to set the tone of political debate. Despite Cole's work for the Government, he continued important criticism of Government policies, both when they infringed upon civil liberties and when they violated standards of social service that had evolved out of research carried on in the 1930s. Later in the war they used these standards to evaluate suggestions for rebuilding Britain. Cole and his socialist companions organized pressure for the Beveridge Report; they tried to mobilize opinion against compromises that would hinder reconstruction. They focused attention on Beveridge's acceptance of the socialist idea of full employment as necessary to make the various welfare services work; Beveridge had found the idea too controversial to elaborate in his official report. As part of this agitation, Cole produced *The Means to Full Employment* for the Left Book Club. They participated in the war-time adult education programme which brought specific policies and new economic thinking to the attention of a wider part of the population.[1] Cole himself gave several broadcasts to the troops, emphasizing what a government could do to prevent unemployment from returning to the level of the 1930s. Finally, Cole and other socialist intellectuals

[1] Mary Stocks, *The Workers' Educational Association: The First Fifty Years* (London, Allen & Unwin, 1953), p. 122.

continually speculated upon ways in which Britain's foreign relations might be reshaped by a world government, various forms of European co-operation, and closer relations with the Soviet Union. Often the hopes were ephemeral. For example, in the summer of 1941 Cole may be found advocating a Europe divided into three confederations for economic planning, including a central European confederation led by a socialist Germany. Yet these speculations must not be underestimated. They healed some of the antagonisms within the Labour movement caused by the Soviet–Nazi treaty, and they mobilized a common wish to escape the world of power politics.

All these activities helped give the Labour Party in 1945 a majority it had not expected. The official Labour Party had been hamstrung by events. Its overwhelming defeat in 1931 and its failure to regain enough seats in 1935 had prevented it from mounting an effective parliamentary opposition. During the war Labour leaders had accepted office in the Coalition, at the price of ceasing to run official candidates against the Conservatives. This valuable experience, of course, destroyed the myth that Labour could not run the country. But much of the burden of thought and propaganda had fallen on the Labour militants and unofficial leaders. Fifteen years of agitation and thought by Cole, Laski, Martin, Strachey, the New Fabian Research Bureau, the Socialist League, the rejuvenated Fabian Society, and the Left Book Club had raised a new political generation. The socialist intellectuals provided much of the propaganda which erased the memory of MacDonald's failure. They publicized the horrors of unemployment and the need for new standards of health and welfare. The twin experiences of depression and war made social and political action on these questions palatable; these experiences completed the process of changing people's ideas of what a Government could do. The new generation of voters and politicians had a radically different conception of their rights; and Cole and other Labour intellectuals must be given much of the credit for these changes.

After the Parliamentary Labour Party left the Coalition Government and won the 1945 election, these unofficial leaders and Labour publicists had to create new roles for themselves. Many of Cole's pupils and associates entered Parliament. In an obituary notice, A. J. P. Taylor spoke of Cole being left standing on the platform as his students took the train for Westminster.[1] Cole himself found it more difficult to establish a new position within the Labour movement that would use his talents and leave himself the freedom of a 'loyal grouser'. Attlee appointed him to the Economic Advisory Council, but, as in 1929, the Prime Minister made little use of the Council. The author of Cole's *Manchester Guardian* obituary suggested that he was mildly offended by Attlee's failure to use his services on the Council in a more prominent manner,[2] but this suggestion does not agree with other evidence. Cole did run for Parliament in 1945 for the Oxford University constituency, having accepted the candidacy in 1939. However, in his election address he defined his political approach in such a way that we can see that holding office was far from his mind. He emphasized the independent duties of a Member of Parliament representing the Universities, and indicated that educational questions would concern him most.

I hold that the most important tasks for educational reformers are (1) to make an end of the waste of human ability which is involved in present methods of selecting pupils for the higher stages of education, and (2) to break down the barriers which have disastrously separated what is called 'cultural' from technical education. I believe that we must, for reasons of sheer self-preservation as well as of necessary adaptation to the conditions of the modern world, put much more weight on technical (including higher technical and applied scientific) education than we have done hitherto. But I believe that this can be done, not merely without sacrificing the culture that we have inherited from the past, but in such a way as to deepen and enlarge it and to penetrate culture with the spirit of science and science with the best achievements of that older culture.[3]

Prevented from carrying this mission to Parliament, he turned to Oxford to make progress in the spirit of his election address. He expanded the social studies, used them to establish closer relations between the University and educational institutions outside, and sought to tie the social studies together through his concern for the ethical side of social theory.

[1] A. J. P. Taylor, 'His Socialism Was Pure', *Tribune* (23 January 1959), pp. 6–7.
[2] *Manchester Guardian* (15 January 1959).
[3] A copy of this election address is preserved at Nuffield College. See also R. B. McCallum and Alison Readman, *The British General Election of 1945* (London, Oxford University Press, 1947), pp. 223–35.

In these first years after the Second World War, Cole was further from the centre of political development than he had been since the 1920s. The volume of his political writing fell off, although he put out a new *Intelligent Man's Guide* in 1947 and continued to write in the *New Statesman*. There was little that he and other Labour intellectuals could do to affect the Government's course. The propaganda of the 1930s and the war-bred sense of national-purpose, coupled with the success of war-time economic planning, had created a situation in which there was almost no opposition to much of the traditional minimum programme of British socialism. The Government passed several measures which, taken together, gave protection from many of the hazards of normal life. These measures rested on the Government's undertaking to ensure full employment. In building this 'Welfare State', socialists could rely on a strong national determination to avoid the years of stagnation, unemployment and suffering which had followed the previous war. This determination also enabled the Labour Government to act on another traditional goal, by nationalizing the coal industry, the railways, electricity, the Bank of England, and the industrial use of gas. When the first burst of enthusiasm was over, thorough-going socialists discovered that they had not altered the country as much as they had hoped. Economic inequalities still remained; in fact, some of the rich had improved their positions by getting out of unprofitable industries. The basic relation of manager to worker remained the same; despite the incursion of the Government into management, the socialist spirit had not reached the factory. As E. Eldon Barry writes, 'The nebulous desire of millions during the Second World War for a "New World" after the defeat of fascism was allowed to dissipate, under a Labour Government, in a critical appraisal of separate nationalization measures and social reforms that seemed unrelated to any vision of radical change.'[1]

Cole was among the first to notice the promised land slipping away. In April 1946 he wrote a pamphlet for the *New Statesman* on *Labour's Foreign Policy* containing several veiled criticisms. He urged Labour to concentrate on Western European economic integration, and to tell the Soviet Union of this policy in such a manner as to prevent polarization of the two major powers. Other sections warned of the impossi-

[1] E. Eldon Barry, *Nationalisation in British Politics* (London, Cape, 1965), pp. 383–4.

bility of Britain remaining a great power, and criticized efforts to establish a Jewish-controlled Palestine. The first point was aimed at Bevin, but did not attack him personally. Left-wingers, such as the authors of 'Keep Left', grew more alarmed as the Government reached the end of a socialist minimum programme. When the Labour Party held its annual conference in 1948, Herbert Morrison proposed that the time had come to consolidate the gains of the previous two years. He argued that both the voters and the national administration had to be given time to digest what had been accomplished. The Party's electoral strategists feared that further moves towards socialism would drive away marginal voters, while Britain's economic problems precluded for a while further developments of the social services.

The proposal clearly suited most of the Party's leaders. It shelved the fundamental, disruptive question of what to do, now that the basic minimum had become law. The left offered no effective opposition at the 1948 Conference. Left-wingers were caught between their sense of the country's mood and their awareness that political passivity would not win votes. Thus Cole, commenting on the Party statement 'Labour Believes in Britain' in the Spring of 1949, agreed with calling a halt to further nationalizations, although he called for attacks on inequality – in wealth, in work, and in the Lords. As Chairman of the Fabian Society, he turned to his customary policy for stimulating socialist thinking: members of the Fabian Society started to hold conferences and conduct research for a volume of *New Fabian Essays*. Cole himself took special interest in industrial democracy and in the possibilities offered by the cooperatives. But his ideas did not lead to a comprehensive new socialist programme, and he did not shape the research in the way he had during the 1930s. The actual work within the society was done largely by men to the right of the Party, and Cole eventually stopped working with the group who prepared the volume of *New Fabian Essays*, although Margaret Cole wrote one of the essays.

Cole did not follow this resignation with a counterblast announcing his own proposals. He still felt a basic loyalty to the Labour Government and had no personal cause to advance; we may also feel that he had no particular policy to advocate which seemed to lead directly enough to socialism to justify a major campaign within the Party. As a result,

Labour's uncertainty was not expressed clearly and was not dealt with; no other left winger or intellectual stepped in to provide more successful leadership. Within the Parliamentary Labour Party many looked to Aneurin Bevan; but he only became a visible rallying point in 1951, when he resigned from the Cabinet over Gaitskell's Budget.

The debate over the Labour Party's policy was postponed until Labour lost office in the 1951 elections, and then continued in a diffuse manner for several years. Cole largely stayed aloof from it, except for major pamphlets in 1954 and 1956. When he did make a public statement, it reflected dissatisfaction with the whole shape of the debate, finding no one position satisfactory. The initiative largely passed to articulate critics to the right of the Party.

Anthony Crosland presented the most permanent record of the dominant 'new revisionist' position in *The Future of Socialism*, first published in 1956. Crosland discarded the traditional goal of nationalizing the means of production, distribution and exchange. He argued cogently that nationalization had become irrelevant to the human goals of the Labour Party:

A higher working-class standard of living, more effective joint consultation, better labour relations, a proper use of economic resources, a wider diffusion of power, a greater degree of co-operation – none of these now primarily require a large-scale change in ownership for their fulfilment– still less is such a change a sufficient condition of their fulfilment.[1]

For the new revisionists, national ownership was irrelevant because the Welfare State and the 'managerial revolution' had ended many of the inequalities of *laisser-faire* capitalism. It is Crosland's satisfaction with this analysis of society, including an inevitable division into rulers and ruled, that most sharply separated him from the left. Crosland did not find a 'managerial revolution' threatening; he felt that the managers could not dominate political power, and thus were not a true class.[2] Following Hugh Clegg's Fabian report on industrial democracy,[3] he asserted that there were inevitably two sides to industrial questions. The managers had to make decisions, in the interest of efficiency; the workers were not qualified to make decisions, and had no desire to do

[1] C. A. R. Crosland, *The Future of Socialism* (London, Cape, 1956), p. 475.
[2] Crosland, pp. 32–3, 38–9.
[3] Hugh Clegg, *Industrial Democracy and Nationalisation* (Oxford, Blackwell, 1951).

so. Thus Crosland and his fellow revisionists were not ready to offer many changes in economic and industrial life. They agreed with the decay of the idea of planning into an emphasis on forecasting and fiscal policy. The frontier of socialist attacks on inequality had moved into the social services, education, and customs. For Crosland, 'the school system', not the industrial order, 'remains the most divisive, unjust, and wasteful of all the aspects of social inequality'.[1]

No writer on the left offered a comprehensive rival to this brand of reformism, working within the Welfare State for small doses of greater equality. Crosland's strongest weapon was his ability to confront sentimental left-wingers with the flaws in their own dream; and left-wingers like Cole could not deny the force of his arguments against social snobbery and educational inequality. When opposed to Crosland's clear, realistic arguments, books such as Bevan's *In Place of Fear* ritualistically clung to old slogans. The left had lost most of its traditional short-run policy because of the effectiveness of the Labour Government. Left-wingers retained their antagonism to capitalism, and their strong desire to see an entirely different sort of society. Increasingly this became an emotional desire to 'get tough' with the remaining capitalist sources of power. They also tended to put less emphasis on Britain's economic difficulties, which the right at times felt precluded greater expansion of the social services. All these points, however, were more differences of attitude and timing than differences of policy. The most crucial differences between the new revisionists and the left lay in foreign policy. The left wanted Britain to play an independent role, as the leader of the developing nations. They grew increasingly discontented with Labour's willingness to accept America's leadership in a Churchillian cold war policy, together with German re-armament and the Korean War.

Cole felt that both sides were enmeshed in a quarrel that would not lead to a new socialist programme. '... the quarrel as it stands at present is much more between two attitudes than between two policies. Mr Attlee and his group are very conscious of the difficulties that confront them, but seem to me to have no solution for them.' Temperamentally, Cole was closer to Bevan. The Welfare State simply was not socialism, and could not be his stopping-point. But despite Cole's

[1] Crosland, p. 258.

sympathy with Bevan's urge to achieve socialism, he found Bevan too impractical to endorse. 'Mr Bevan sweeps the difficulties aside and calls for more Socialism and more welfare in the same breath; but has he any better idea than his antagonists concerning the means of rendering practicable these excellent alternatives?'[1]

Cole wanted to create a new synthesis between socialist idealism and Fabian practicality, but he could not. Britain's precarious position in the world's economy seemed to make a radical Government impossible. He argued that Britain had to get clear of dependence upon America, whose booms and recessions alike threatened the British balance of payments, and whose support of the British economy allowed her to dictate foreign policy. In this argument socialist realism agreed with a left-wing foreign policy; but its consequence was to deny, in the short term, the possibility of socialism. The Government's first task would be to increase national productivity, creating a larger, more stable national income which could then be divided more equitably. In this way, Cole's *New Statesman* articles in the early 1950s were part of the process by which the left came to accept much of what Morrison, Gaitskell and Crosland had been saying. His hard thinking on Britain's economic position impressed others to the Left of the Party, and fitted in well with the growth of technocratic thinking within it.[2]

Cole's intellectual appraisal of the situation thus brought him close to the 'revisionists'. Like them, he had grown disenchanted with the prospect of further nationalization. However, he still demanded the substitution of public for private enterprise, through a variant of the Rignano–Dalton plan for inheritance taxation and the development of new forms of public ownership. But it would be wrong to see Cole as simply vacillating between intellectual 'rightism' and emotional 'leftism'. He had something substantial to contribute, which went largely unnoticed. He offered his life-long attachment to a truly demo-

[1] G. D. H. Cole, 'After the Shouting', *New Statesman and Nation*, XLIV (6 December 1952), 668.
[2] See John Freeman, 'Challenge to Britain', *New Statesman and Nation*, XLV (20 June 1953), 720–1. In light of Harold Wilson's rise within the Labour Party by combining the temperamental left-wing with technocratic ideas, which he used in both the 1964 and 1966 elections, it is interesting to find Cole praising Wilson for being the only Bevanite to show 'a realistic appreciation of the problems facing the British economy'. 'After the Shouting', *New Statesman and Nation*, XLIV (6 December 1952), 668.

cratic society; he wrote two serious studies of the possibilities of decentralized democratic ownership and industrial democracy.[1]

Cole's conception of industrial democracy in the 1950s was basically the one he had come to in the late 1920s; he never expressed it as well as he had in 'Workers' Control and Self-Government in Industry' in 1933. Cole placed the greatest emphasis on works' councils and other forms of local participation; he rebuked the Labour Government for having dismantled many of the shop stewards' committees which had been established during the Second World War. He wanted collective bargaining extended to cover questions of discipline and the effects of introducing new machinery, with the ultimate aim of giving workers some immediate control over workshop discipline and organization. Foremen could be turned into supervisors elected by the men themselves; only after these local developments could the election of workers' representatives to boards controlling industries have any real democratic use.

The 'new revisionists' answered that the workers did not want this democratic control in the workshop. Their objection is not conclusive. Some versions of workers' control persisted into the 1960s; for example, workers in the aircraft and automobile industries in Coventry worked in 'gangs' that make their own work rules. Proponents of this plan argue that productivity and workshop morale are much higher than in factories run by the traditional hierarchy of foremen and management officials. But Cole's objection to the revisionist position was far more fundamental. He assumed that one had to work to destroy the apathy and resistance which many workers feel at being asked to take part in questions of discipline and manning. Unlike Crosland, Cole felt that there was no good moral reason for being content with inactive industrial citizenship, with the existing division between manager and managed.

This active conception of workers' control predictably did not appeal to political and union leaders. Union leaders were used to a centralized system, largely defensive in nature, which concentrated upon maintaining the workers' relative position in a wage scale. Cole felt that this function would have to be replaced by national collective bargaining

[1] G. D. H. Cole, 'Is This Socialism?' *New Statesman* Pamphlet (London, 1954), p. 29, and G. D. H. Cole, *The Case for Industrial Partnership* (London, Macmillan, 1957).

over what industry could afford to pay, and over the wage differentials needed to recruit men into various industries. In society of full employment, it was wrong to settle wages by a sheer test of industrial strength.[1] His argument for an incomes policy has severely tested the relationship between intellectual reformers and trade unionists in the Labour movement. One could argue that in effect what Cole wanted happened for a time under the fourth Labour Government, with unions restricting their demands to meet national guide-posts and with the majority of strikes being local, unauthorized strikes over questions of discipline. Cole sought to recognize this change and to substitute direct control over discipline for the wasteful, negative use of the strike.

Political leaders found another sort of difficulty with Cole's proposals. Kingsley Martin expressed it well: 'The trouble is that this sort of Socialist way of life is best practised by small groups; it can't be legislated into existence or formulated as an election programme.'[2] This objection is too timorous, in view of the crucial importance of creating 'democratic ways of living for little men in big societies'. Certainly one could legislate works councils into existence. If the natural leaders are there, and if the workers can choose the men who will supervise well, then the policy will work, as long as the unions support the works councils, and the management really negotiates in good faith over the introduction of new machinery. The reason for this timorousness, of course, was the Labour Party's inevitable absorption in political calculations. There was little expressed demand for this sort of democracy which could be translated into votes – and little hope of rewards for attempting to stimulate it.

The same sort of unwillingness to take bold democratic departures met Cole's other suggestions. He joined his voice to those who had been seeking to develop forms of social ownership which did not involve nationalization.[3] He wanted to see local consumers' councils entrusted with the task of safeguarding consumer interests and wrote a lengthy report for the Co-operatives, sketching a variety of services

[1] G. D. H. Cole, 'Wages and Production', *New Statesman and Nation*, XLIV (18 October 1952), 440–1.
[2] 'London Diary', *New Statesman and Nation*, XLI (12 May 1951), 525.
[3] 'World Socialism Restated', p. 27. See also Crosland, chapter XVII; Paul Derrick, *The Company and the Community* (Fabian Research Series No. 238, London, 1964); R. H. S. Crossman (ed.), *New Fabian Essays* (London, Turnstile Press, 1952).

they could perform.[1] Pointing out that traditional staples now consume a smaller portion of a family's expenditure, he suggested that the co-operatives construct their own cinemas, restaurants, and bowling alleys. But suggestions like these ran up against the traditionalism of the Co-operative movement, based upon the maintenance of the 'divi'.[2] The Co-operative movement had lost its idealism, the urge of the founders to create a new form of commercial relationships which would replace capitalism. An historian writing at a later date will perhaps go on to say that the whole Labour and working-class movement had developed its own forms of conservatism which no amount of writing and propaganda on the part of Cole and people like him could have broken down.

Cole gradually came to feel that the democratic and socialist cause was being abandoned, in little things as in major ones. When Attlee accepted an earldom, Cole wrote: 'I used to have some respect for Mr Attlee; but he forfeited it all . . . How on earth could he wish to be degraded in these ways? I do not know the answer; but I am grieved and hurt, even more than I am angry, for he has brought discredit on the Socialist cause.'[3] To combat his growing dissatisfaction with the state of the Labour movement, Cole turned to his customary policy of creating unofficial but not disloyal research and agitation. However, his return to independent socialist research was more drastic than before, a sign of an uneasiness bordering on desperation. It imperilled his strong loyalty to the Labour Party; it involved admitting that the work of the previous years had brought him no closer to socialism, even though it had done many good things along the way. He was returning to the political wilderness in a more drastic form than his earlier experiments with pressure-groups designed to influence Labour. The N.G.L. and L.R.D. had taken place within what seemed to be the growing edge of socialism, as had the N.F.R.B. and S.S.I.P.; the efforts of the latter groups had been welcomed by the Party's leaders. Now he

---

[1] G. D. H. Cole, *The British Co-operative Movement in a Socialist Society* (London, Allen & Unwin, 1951). He had been making similar suggestions for years; see in particular G. D. H. Cole, 'The Future of British Co-operation', *Co-operative Productive Review* (February 1944), pp. 28–9.

[2] See Tom Williams, 'A Voice of Prophecy', *New Statesman and Nation*, XLII (18 August 1951), 188; articles discussing Cole's *British Co-operative Movement in a Socialist Society* in *Co-operative Productive Review* (February 1952).

[3] 'World Socialism Restated', p. 29.

entered upon pressure group activity in a position more like that of the early Fabians, seeking to create an organization which could state the whole case for socialism in light of changed circumstances. Semi-official organizations such as the Fabian Society could no longer really serve his purpose, for they had become too involved in the Labour Party's short-run policy and recruitment.

In the important pamphlet in which he appealed for a restatement of socialism, Cole emphasized two points that indicate the directions in which he had continued to grow. Over the years he had grown much more aware of the sheer obstacles which poverty created, so that he virtually reversed his Guild Socialist dictum that 'Poverty is the symptom: slavery the disease'. He called for

... a concerted effort to put an end to primary poverty in every country, to open to all peoples the means of taking advantage of knowledge and of what we are coming to call 'scientific know-how'. It involves a world war of mankind against want and ignorance, against squalor and disease, waged with all the constructive weapons men possess or can devise to serve the purposes of this great crusade.[1]

The magnitude of this battle would postpone the full coming of socialism; but one of the conditions for waging it was the revival of socialist idealism. And so he called for 'a World Order of Socialists individually pledged to put first their duty to Socialism as a world-wide cause, and offering the working-class and Socialist movements of their own countries no more than a secondary loyalty'.[2] He admitted that he would even be willing to defy the national Labour organizations to which he belonged. However, he muted his internationalism by asserting that 'I do feel a much greater responsibility for helping to put things right in the country of which I am a citizen than in the world as a whole ...'[3]

The author of the *Manchester Guardian* obituary asserted, wrongly, that Cole had grown increasingly less concerned with other countries since his Guild Socialist days. In *The World of Labour*, Cole had looked

[1] 'World Socialism Restated', p. 33.
[2] G. D. H. Cole, 'The Future of Socialism', *New Statesman and Nation*, IL (23 January 1955), 92–3.
[3] 'The World Socialist Movement News Bulletin', No. 4 (October 1955), p. 3. Cole is answering a member who asserted a form of internationalism that he felt would have denied all such loyalties.

at foreign labour movements to see if he could draw any conclusions that would help British Labour. In the 1930s, the problems of international trade and the rise of Hitler helped bring him out of exclusive concentration on British problems; at the end of the 1930s, he made the liberation of colonies one of his 'war aims'. Gradually he had outgrown his implicit faith in creating socialism in Britain alone.

. . . it is essential that this levelling shall be achieved, not merely within each Socialist society, but all over the world. Socialism cannot be fully achieved in one country irrespective of what is happening elsewhere.[1]

True socialism – fellowship – could not exist in a world of international trade rivalries and cold war. Cole realized that a socialism that did not meet the needs of the whole world – a socialism that concentrated only on improving the European Welfare State – was in serious danger of becoming irrelevant.

Organizing such an international movement would be even more difficult than organizing a national one. Cole, ageing and in need of frequent periods of hospital treatment, knew that he could not undertake it. But when the World Socialist Movement was formed in answer to his articles in the *New Statesman*, Cole consented to speak to their inaugural meeting, and could not help but play a prominent part. A parallel movement at Oxford, organized by Clovis Maksoud, a Lebanese graduate student, similarly attracted him. This effort was the first to bear fruit internationally. In March 1956, Cole attended, together with Kingsley Martin and William Warbey, M.P., a conference in Paris, out of which arose the International Society for Socialist Studies. The World Socialist Movement became the United Kingdom section of the I.S.S.S., and Cole became the President of the Society. Prominent British left-wingers such as Fenner Brockway, leaders of the left wing of the French Socialists and the 'nouvelle gauche', and a scattering of men from the United States, Italy, Yugoslavia, Israel, and other nations showed interest in the new organization.[2]

---

[1] 'World Socialism Restated', p. 33. See also G. D. H. Cole, 'Socialism and the Welfare State', *New Statesman and Nation*, L (23 July 1955), 88–9.

[2] I am grateful to John Papworth, the secretary of the London branch of I.S.S.S. until its demise, for letting me see the Society's records and for talking with me. There is also a box, 'International Society for Socialist Studies', Cole Papers, Nuffield College. Three journals were published at various times: *The World Socialist Movement News Bulletin*, *The World Socialist*, and *I.S.S.S. Information*.

Since he believed so strongly that such an international body must be formed, to unite warring socialist factions, Cole could not avoid becoming more of a leader than his health could really afford. Naturally he could not run the day-to-day organization of the society, although a good portion of the correspondence passed through his hands. But he prepared a speech on 'How Current Trends in Capitalism Influence Socialist Policies' for a conference in September 1957, and drafted a memorandum on the research which the United Kingdom section could undertake.[1] This memorandum did not give any shape to the society's efforts; it reveals only too clearly the difficulties of starting to rethink socialism completely, in world terms rather than in national terms. The questions Cole jotted down ranged from some of the most difficult perennial problems concerning freedom to economic and social problems affecting several societies in different ways, such as the best ways of developing new technological processes and the impact of social change on the family. The memorandum did not impose an order of priorities on problems, or present a meaning of socialism that could reduce several problems to a common starting-point. Small wonder that the members of I.S.S.S. found it too broad and diffuse. The Research Sub-Committee set up to make proposals from Cole's memorandum found a polite way of rejecting it:

We believe that Cole's document is an essential element in the training of Socialists in research and that it should be read by everyone who wishes to study the problems of socialism. But in its existing form it does not provide any integrated programme for the Society's activities, and we do not propose to discuss it further. We have however been much influenced by it in framing our proposals.[2]

Very little came of the society's research activities; the likelihood of returning to socialist fundamentalism or discussions of socialist moral values was too great. Nor did the society succeed in keeping inter-national socialists in contact with each other; immediate national problems in each country proved distracting. In Britain, I.S.S.S. failed to attract the intellectuals who left the Communist Party after Hungary

---

[1] G. D. H. Cole, 'Suggestions for a Research Programme', in 'International Society for Socialist Studies', Cole Papers, Nuffield College; 'How Current Trends in Capitalism Influence Socialist Policies', Papworth MSS. The latter article was mimeographed for members attending a Conference, 20–2 September 1957.
[2] Research Sub-Committee, 'First Report', Papworth MSS. (c. February 1957).

and formed the *Universities and Left Review;* the better known of the society's members, including Kingsley Martin, John Freeman, and T. B. Bottomore, drifted away. The remaining members had difficulty obtaining speakers for the conferences which came to be the society's main activity. Individual contributions to *I.S.S.S. Information* remained lively enough, but often repeated traditional socialist rivalries. The Hungarian revolution, Algeria, and Suez all dampened Cole's hopes for frank, unprejudiced research and exchange of opinion; research gave way to routine discussions of international politics. Meanwhile Marxists and Social Democrats of varying shades aimed articles at one another, exchanging blame for the parlous state of socialism in their countries.

Cole had not expected great success; he had felt that the purely technical problems of translation and the cost of communications were virtually insuperable. At the same time, he had hoped for a stronger spirit of fellowship among socialists. In the midst of partisan bickering and lack of interest, his dream of international socialist co-operation withered. Certainly I.S.S.S. failed to provide him with the sort of criticism and help which he could have used in rethinking his own position. In the autumn of 1958, just a few months before his death, Cole resigned as president, too late to save his own health.

CHAPTER 7

AUDIENCES, VALUES AND IMPORTANCE

So far, I have examined Cole's writings as they relate to socialism, trade unionism, and contemporary problems. These were the areas of thought and life on which Cole made the great impact. His primary audience consisted of the alert citizen, the active young trade unionist, the student of the W.E.A. or of Ruskin College, the socialist intellectual or Labour militant.[1] They provided the audience for the Left Book Club, the *New Statesman*, and Cole's *Intelligent Man's Guides*. They translated this ferment into a variety of progressive political activities. They made Labour's minimum political and economic programme into 'practical politics', changing the tone of British politics. They were most numerous and lively in the 1930s, but Cole had been speaking and writing for them for years; he had helped to create them.

Cole developed his basic literary and mental style for this audience. He concentrated upon being lucid rather than elegant. He simplified subjects without patronizing his audience; he had a real gift for untangling difficult subjects to create a clear narrative description. Cole covered a wide range of subjects, without pretending to give the last word on any; he acknowledged difficulties candidly, rather than resolving them fully. The frankness of his mode of expression meant he never disguised his personal opinions; yet he always sought to elucidate problems rather than to indoctrinate. Cole's style invited the reader to think with him, and provided him with the facts he might want to use. In short, Cole developed the mental and literary style of a great and original popularizer, one who administered 'truth serum' rather than opiates.

The mental skills which made Cole a great popularizer also shaped his most fruitful educational roles. He often treated students as a special

---

[1] Cole delineated his audience carefully in editing *New Standards*, the journal which succeeded the *Guild Socialist* in 1923; he tried to merge its audience with the W.E.A.'s students. G. D. N. Worswick discussed Cole's audience briefly in his contribution to *Essays in Labour History*.

segment of the audience for his popular and political books; his success at Oxford came, to a fair degree, from the continued use of practices he had learned in adult education. Early in his tutorial days, he turned to the production of study guides, and then to writing textbooks, continually expanding his contributions to democratic education. Three of his textbooks filled notably large gaps in social and political education: *An Introduction to Trade Unionism* (1918), *A Short History of the British Working-Class Movement* (1925–7), and *The Common People* (1938). Cole revised each book periodically; all three are still read widely, while his more ambitious political and economic works are often ignored.

At Oxford, too, Cole pressed for a socially aware, humanitarian education that would retain intellectual rigour. His greatest successes in these directions occurred during his period of relative political quiescence after 1945. Quietly and institutionally, he contributed to the development of the social sciences, although he had not taken part in the first step, the formation of the P.P.E. Honours Schools in 1924. When he returned to Oxford in 1925, he began to participate in the variety of extension and delegacy activities which culminated in the broadening of the social sciences and the eventual acceptance of sociology. Individual steps are hidden in terse committee minutes, but the basic mechanism of change is clear. External developments forced new subjects upon Oxford, with Cole playing an important catalytic role. Lord Nuffield and the adult education movement were the two most important external influences. Nuffield provided the most dramatic opportunity, a new home for the social studies, when he endowed Nuffield College just before the Second World War. Cole was one of the first Fellows appointed; the Social Reconstruction Survey was the College's first important activity. But he was unable to make his idea of what the College should be dominant. He wanted something other than the traditional Oxford collection of strong, disparate individuals, each going his own way; he wanted Nuffield College to have a basic plan of research, resembling the Survey (or the New Fabian Research Bureau, without its partisan overtones).[1]

[1] G. D. N. Worswick, 'Cole and Oxford, 1938–1958', in Asa Briggs and John Saville (eds.), *Essays in Labour History in Memory of G. D. H. Cole* (London, Macmillan, 1960), p. 34.

Nuffield College took the traditional Oxford form, and so it was less of a break with the past than if Cole had become Warden. Consequently the changes in the content of the social studies came through Rewley House (later the Delegacy for Extramural Studies) and Barnett House (later the Delegacy for Social Administration). Cole, holding important positions on the Board for the Faculty of Social Studies and on the various delegacies, served as a link between the two. He had been appointed to these positions in the late 1930s, but the war postponed many developments. In 1945, he became an intellectual adviser to Ruskin College, and helped communicate its needs to the University. After the war, the Faculty of Social Studies was permitted to institute a B.Phil. degree, and the delegacies were reorganized. Cole pushed strongly for more tutors in industrial and sociological subjects. The fruits of his agitation were Lectureships in Industrial Relations, Criminology, Social Psychology, and finally one in Sociology. Some of these lectureships were connected to the delegacies, but undergraduates could attend the lectures; the subjects tended to enter the Honours Schools as optional special subjects. Cole's approach to the new subjects was permissive; he supported the new lecturers, but they had to demonstrate the worth of their topics. As they did so, Oxford finally came to accept sociology.[1]

But Cole did not think of social studies as a simple series of specialized disciplines, to be introduced to Oxford by their practitioners alone. Well before he succeeded in broadening the P.P.E. Honours Schools to include various sociological studies, he had taught and analysed sociological theories. He also felt strongly that excessive specialization was a fault of much British sociology, and combated it by teaching an awareness of the moral assumptions and interrelations of the social studies. Both tasks formed part of his interpretation of the chair to which he was elected in 1944, the Chichele Professorship of Social and Political Theory.

The chair suited him perfectly; he probably had a hand in deciding

[1] A. H. Halsey first called this subject to my attention; R. B. McCallum and John Mogey discussed it with me. Mr Mogey lectured in Sociology from 1951 to 1959. I have consulted the records at Barnett House, thanks to Mr Halsey; both Mr McCallum and Mr Herbert Nicholas assured me that the records of the Faculty of Social Studies were too terse and too anonymous to be of any real use. Part of the story may be gleaned from the spare pages of the *University Gazette* and by comparing the requirements for the P.P.E. Honours Schools in back issues of the *Oxford University Examination Statutes*.

its subject-matter through his seat on the Board for the Faculty of Social Studies. Two words in the title pleased him considerably: 'social' and 'theory'. He insisted that social theory had to study all social institutions, not separate politics from the rest of society. In this way he escaped the artificiality of much political theory, which could only answer questions in terms of a dichotomy between individuals and the state. His definition of social theory introduced instead the pluralistic conception of society which had always seemed more plausible and more desirable to him as a socialist popularizer.

This broad definition of the nature of social and political theory served, in Cole's mind, to make it a focal point for the undergraduate study of all the social studies. He argued that it was stupid to isolate political science from psychology, economics from sociology, and any of them from philosophy and history. Both the student who would specialize in one social science and the student who would go no further needed a broad, liberal grounding in the various disciplines that discussed human society. The battle for this 'liberal arts' approach, against more technical definitions, often has to be refought in most Universities. The forcefulness with which Cole had made his point appears in his successor's inaugural lecture. Sir Isaiah Berlin indicated that he would preserve Cole's liberal approach, while paying more attention to technical philosophical questions.[1]

Cole did not intend to discuss the full subject matter of each of the social studies; much of the material could be more adequately covered by the Chichele Professor of Social Institutions. He used the second important word in the title of his chair, 'theory', as his way of unifying the social studies. Instead of developing a common logic and methodology, Cole emphasized theoreticians of society such as Marx, Weber and Pareto. At their worst, these lectures degenerated into potted biographies of these theoreticians.[2] At his best, Cole added something to the professional, academic study of social theory – his own ethical concern. '"Social Theory", then, I regard as an essentially normative

[1] Isaiah Berlin, *Two Concepts of Liberty* (Oxford, 1958), pp. 5–7.
[2] Several boxes of Cole's lectures are preserved at Nuffield College; four lectures are reprinted in *Essays in Social Theory*. H. D. Hughes commented that it often was hard to find a point on which to ask a question; since he wrapped things up so neatly, one could only quarrel with his whole interpretation of a person.

study, of which the purpose is to tell people how to be socially good, and to aim at social goods and avoid social evils.'[1]

He did not interpret his instructions as crudely in practice, but his concern for 'the good life' was generally present as he explored the assumptions and conclusions of social theorists. He insisted upon his obligation to judge theories and institutions by his basic values and the needs of Western society.

Cole's lectures as a professor were always well attended, but they probably came to have less impact on the students of the 1950s than his lectures had had in the 1930s. The difference lay in the development of his audience, as J. F. C. Harrison points out in his study of adult education:

By the mid-fifties a generation had arisen which knew nothing of the Great Slump, the Spanish Civil War, and the People's Front, except by hearsay ... Within the Universities the mood of the fifties was very different from that pre-war; among the new generation of intellectual leaders the preoccupation with left-wing politics, and movements for social reform was much less marked; they did not, like their predecessors, draw their inspiration from R. H. Tawney and G. D. H. Cole.[2]

Even the waning of Cole's educational importance mirrored his career as a socialist intellectual and popularizer.

Cole's style and success as a popularizer and his political influence made it difficult for him to communicate as successfully with the academics, his secondary audience. The virtues of his egalitarian popular style were often handicaps to scholarly readers of his works – works which, even when written largely for a mass audience, had potential importance for the professional economist, sociologist and historian. Cole's most academic books retained annoying popularizing traits. His refusal to use the formal language of mathematics set him aside from the academic development of economic unorthodoxy. Cole could use this language, and was adept at statistical analysis,[3] but he maintained that putting a thought into a formula added nothing. In one pungent review, he accused Pigou of 'writing Choctaw', but saying

[1] G. D. H. Cole, *Essays in Social Theory* (London, Macmillan, 1950), p. 10.
[2] J. F. C. Harrison, *Learning and Living 1790–1960* (London, Routledge & Kegan Paul, 1961), p. 336.
[3] See G. D. H. Cole, 'The Social Structure of England', *Studies in Class Structure* (London, Routledge & Kegan Paul, 1955).

nothing that he could not have put into English.[1] Yet as mathematical economics grew, Cole's economic theories remained qualitative advice rather than academic demonstrations. He habitually used the language of practical ethics and politics, which many intellectuals by virtue of their training find vague. Cole thus had much to say about the goals and presuppositions of economics, yet could be ignored by those who had most to learn.

Cole's concentration upon posing problems irritated scholars who wanted solutions. Cole's more academic books were always useful contributions to a subject. They never transcended the status of contributions, however, to become definitive works. Maurice Dobb, himself a fine socialist scholar, brilliantly diagnosed the dissatisfaction many a scholar felt after reading Cole's books:

> ... why is it that so frequently one lays down a book by Mr Cole with something of an unsatisfied feeling, pondering whether it is a merit or a demerit that a book should leave one's appetite more whetted than appeased? One has a sense that one has listened to someone thinking aloud, with the charm and sometimes the irritation which such listening entails. One feels eminently informed yet unsufficiently enlightened. One feels stimulated to thought yet let with concepts which are vague and imperfectly defined. One feels that the commentary has been, perhaps, too facile; that the ideas discussed have been rendered in the process rather less interesting than their authors intended and a trifle pedestrian, and the final conclusions, in the desire to make them plausible, rather too eclectic to have a quite satisfactory ring.[2]

One feels that Cole could have made his academic books truly satisfying. He had the intellectual power and the factual information to do something definitive. And so, the critic often concludes, his crucial failing was simply attempting too much. He wrote too many books, and too quickly, to make any one of them a masterpiece. This criticism grasps a corner of the truth, but it comes at it from the wrong side. Cole did not want to write a masterpiece; he had decided at the outset to follow his master Morris in doing everything well, rather than one thing superbly. He wanted to change the world – and he wanted to do it democratically, by showing people the problems and making them think along with him about what they could do.

[1] G. D. H. Cole, 'To-Day's Economists', *New Statesman and Nation*, II (17 October 1931), 488.
[2] Maurice Dobb, *Economic Journal*, XXXXV (June 1935), 296.

Thus academic writing was a secondary way of expressing himself on the things which mattered to him – economic policy, trade unions, and the nature of a good society. And Cole, in writing for an academic audience, lost many of the virtues of his less formal writings – probably because he found less enjoyment in this sort of writing. His academic books are heavier. Seeking academic objectivity, he often became very passive towards the facts; at his best, he sought objectivity not by repressing his opinions, but by expressing them along with the facts and with indications of where opposing opinions could be found.

At the same time, Cole's success as a socialist and as a popularizer distorted the reactions of academic audiences. Invariably reviewers in the *Times Literary Supplement* in the 1930s criticized him for lack of 'impartiality'. Some challenged him with his own words, trying to defend capitalism by Cole's admissions that the general standard of living had risen under capitalist modes of production.[1] These reviewers sought to force most of what he wrote on to the defensive for political reasons, and, in doing so, underestimated the intellectual basis for his political opinions. Equally important, the responses of his readers confirmed that his primary influence would be political rather than academic.

There was one field in which academic readers could admit Cole's scholarly ability, and in which his literary talents could often find expression: Labour history. Several of his books on Labour history are recognized as classics; undoubtedly they will remain the most widely read of all his books. Currently scholars appear to favour Cole's encyclopaedic works, especially *A History of Socialist Thought*. It is especially valuable as a record of Cole's vast knowledge of the subject, combining erudition with intelligent judgment of his socialist predecessors and contemporaries. None the less, one would wish that Cole had written a less encyclopaedic and more analytic history of socialist thought, asking the sorts of questions that would have related changes in thought to changes in industry and society. His encyclopaedic histories are overwhelming in their detail, and thus obscure his perceptions of essential ideas and events in Labour history. Despite the drawbacks of its approach, *A History of Socialist Thought* remains

[1] *Times Literary Supplement* (26 April 1934), 292.

indispensable; but its reputation has the effect of unjustly discrediting many of his earlier books.

At least four of his other historical works more ably combine his scholarly ability with good judgment and good writing. One, *The Common People*, he wrote with Raymond Postgate; Postgate wrote most of the text, and to him must go much of the credit for making the book more than simply a normal narrative history. From his earliest days as a W.E.A. tutor, Cole had understood the importance of making history the study of the development of society rather than a mere record of the successes of the articulate. However, he usually found the working class and socialist movements so attractive and so complex that he treated them as ends in themselves. One reviewer of *A History of Socialist Thought* objected to

... the vacuum in which Professor Cole's Socialists move and live and have their being ... he lacks altogether the curiosity to discover why they thought and acted as they did.[1]

Cole usually retorted that integrating the socialist movement into the rest of history was beyond any one person.[2] Writing with Postgate, he was able to transcend this limitation.

Cole wrote *Chartist Portraits*, another of his best books on Labour history, in 1940, shortly after *The Common People*. In it he brilliantly used the device of interlocking portraits of twelve Chartist leaders to illustrate the variety of motives and local circumstances which shaped the movement. His work on Chartism stimulated a new, more professional concern with it and with parallel events in the early history of the working class. Others, notably Asa Briggs, have taken up his suggestion that 'there is room for a dozen local studies in Chartism'. Such local studies, written with a more sociological approach, have inevitably modified Cole's conclusions in some respects, but they have not supplanted his book. Professor Briggs concludes that '... Cole's *Chartist Portraits* needs to be treated as an introduction to be followed up by other books, some of which have not yet been written.'[3]

[1] *Times Literary Supplement* (15 June 1956), 364.
[2] G. D. H. Cole, *A History of Socialist Thought*, I: *The Forerunners 1789–1850* (London, Macmillan, 1953), p. v.
[3] Asa Briggs, 'Introduction', in G. D. H. Cole, *Chartist Portraits* (London, Macmillan, 1965), p. xiv. Cole's *Attempts at General Union* (London, Allen & Unwin, 1953, first published in 1939) was perhaps the first of these local studies, for it dealt with union

Two other books which have gained the status of standard works are his biographies of Cobbett and Owen. Cole wrote them in 1924 and 1925, a difficult time for him because of the collapse of the Guilds movement; they were written before his return to academic life from teaching for the W.E.A. Although in discussing these biographies I shall draw examples from *The Life of William Cobbett*, they have the same virtue. Cole arrived at a deep personal understanding of the subjects through sympathy with their personalities and roles. He appreciated Cobbett's energy; he respected the simplicity and freshness of his life, and shared his instinctive love of Britain. He had the good sense to let Cobbett speak for himself about these things, preserving Cobbett's strength and humanity within the framework of his interpretation. He relished Cobbett's battles with 'the Botley parson', and endorsed his reaction against unduly formal education.

Cole respected his subjects as persons; but equally he sympathized with the people for whom they had affection and sympathy. Cole set the background carefully in his *Life of William Cobbett*: The dislocation of rural England, the rise of new industry, hunger, dirt, political corruption – and the vigorous response of some men to these things. Cole saw Cobbett and the Industrial Revolution together; his theme was how Cobbett developed from being a defender of a dying way of life to the radical 'tribune of the people'. He wrote with a trace of nostalgia for the days of the scurrillous pamphleteer, speaking to an active citizenry:

These were the great days of the political pamphlet – squibs, lampoons, mere scurrility, party controversialists at it hammer and tongs, serious and philosophical arguments making its topical appeal ... Elections were more amusing when all the rival candidates and their supporters gathered to a single meeting than in these days when, for the most part, political speeches are spoken only to the faithful.[1]

Cobbett and Owen were his political ancestors, speaking out against the human effects of industrialization. He had no higher praise: 'No man helped more to build up the confidence of the workers in their own power ...'[2]

[1] G. D. H. Cole, *The Life of William Cobbett* (London, Collins, 1924), pp. 61, 126.
[2] *The Life of William Cobbett*, p. 432.

---

activity in Lancashire and Yorkshire in the 1830s, when earlier historians had attempted to discuss Owenite unions simply on a national basis.

Although he saw Cobbett as a forerunner of the socialist movement, Cole did not write what one could call a recognizably Marxist, or notably socialist, history. He did not reduce history to the story of class-struggles, or judge his subjects simply by the way they fitted into the development of classes. Part of the answer lies in Cole's empiricist traits, which led him to develop a broad understanding of the processes of industrialization. The rest of the answer lies in the sort of socialist he was. He belonged to the democratic and libertarian wing of the socialist movement; he had a strong sympathy for his radical and democratic forebears, and he suspected the more facile versions of Marxism.

Cole found Marx's historical method more useful than any of his specific conclusions or predictions. But he sought to bring it into line with English empiricist and democratic theories:

A Realist Conception of History, closely akin to Marx's, may be universally valid without Marx's statement of it in terms of class-struggles possessing the same validity.[1]

He found Marx's comments about 'the preponderant influence of the powers of production' more fundamental. His interpretation of the 'powers of production' was pluralistic rather than monistic:

The 'powers of production', which Marx makes his independent variable, are in fact a highly complex set of phenomena, arising out of the interaction between the natural and social environment and the contemporary activity of the human mind in devising new ways of exploiting it.[2]

Cole's analysis of the 'powers of production' tended to make them not a purely independent variable, for human choices shaped both the natural and social environment. He seized on the remarks which Marx made late in his life indicating that human creations, such as law and art, could develop a large degree of independence from human events. For Cole, men were more nearly the independent variable, conditioned by their environment but able to manipulate it through their knowledge. His conception clearly restored freedom and importance to human wills and minds:

What this conception does assert is that mind, as a formative force in history, works by embodying itself in things, changing their shape and potency, and

---

[1] G. D. H. Cole, *The Meaning of Marxism* (London, Gollancz, 1948), p. 48.
[2] Ibid., pp. 79–80.

combining them into relations and systems whose changing phases are the basis of the history of mankind.[1]

As a result, Cole emphatically denied any fatalistic inferences or assertions that historical progress had to follow a set path. He could not write a dogmatic sort of history; what he found valuable in Marx's theory of history were Marx's emphases. Marx emphasized the dynamic, changing aspects of history; he also wrote history 'not only to understand, but to make out of understanding a basis for action'.[2] In acting upon these precepts, Cole interpreted them more broadly than Marx. One of his purposes in writing biographies of Cobbett and Owen was to convey their humane feelings, their belief in the working class and their egalitarian concepts of education.

Part of Cole's importance as an educator was that he kept people from seeing Marx in an exclusively Communist light. He usually preferred to say that he was 'Marx influenced'[3] rather than Marxist. In the period from 1932 to 1935, when he wrote the first version of *What Marx Really Meant*, he occasionally called himself a Marxist, within this humanistic, empiricist interpretation. Cole could accept this kind of Marxism because Marx's philosophy of history contains basic insights reached independently by libertarian British socialists from their own experience. The Marxism he set forth in *The Meaning of Marxism* was really the common sense of the British Labour movement. The socialist – and the non-socialist – who tries to change his society inevitably discovers that economic power often bars his way, and often needs to be conquered for him to make progress. But at the same time Cole refused to make economic power a unitary explanation. Cole's *The Meaning of Marxism* is one of the ablest expositions of this practical, liberal kind of Marxism. It shares the virtues of his other successful books. It incorporates academic arguments into material useful to the general reader who is interested in understanding his society, creating a unity useful both to an academic audience and to the active sections of the working class movement.

The Marx Cole expounded in *The Meaning of Marxism* was a Marx humanized by Cole's basic beliefs in individual creativity, fellowship,

[1] Ibid., p. 18.
[2] Ibid., p. 18.
[3] Ibid., pp. 11–12.

equality, and liberty. One cannot understand Cole without seeing how these beliefs provided a foundation for his thought and his importance. Cole imbibed them in his youth; he could be converted to socialism because William Morris appealed to them, showing that socialism would create a free society in which men would enjoy fellowship and creativity. His beliefs created guide lines for Cole's actions and thoughts. They gave him an intuitive perception of what a good society would feel like; he devoted his life to converting this feeling into reality.

Among the most important services Cole offered the Labour movement was that of analysing and clarifying its ethical values. Reuniting Cole's most careful discussions of his values can contribute to our understanding of the common sense of the Labour movement. Cole's treatment of these values stands out above scores of treatises that try to express 'the Socialist idea'. He showed that freedom, individuality, equality, democracy, and fellowship, when worked out carefully, created a web of values rather than standing alone. When audiences responded to Cole, they responded to this Labour humanism.

The contribution made by clear expressions of socialist ideals to Labour's growth can be demonstrated indirectly by the weakness caused by slovenly moralizing. By amassing examples of imprecise and conflicting moral language, C. A. R. Crosland was able to argue that ritualistic invocation of socialist ideals prevented the rethinking of policies in the 1950s. Several of his most telling quotations came from Cole's works of the mid 1930s, in which he frequently became less precise as he sought to reach a larger uncommitted audience. But the sheer volume of vague appeals to socialist ideals, by Cole and by others, must not be allowed to obscure the carefulness and attractiveness of Cole's ethical thinking at its best, and Labour's dependance upon ethical values for a portion of its persuasiveness.

The obvious invocation of moral values to criticize capitalism and the Tories also can obscure the more creative roles that ethical criticism played in Cole's life. Cole's values were 'sticking-points', establishing limits that he would not allow practical political activities to violate. When he felt that one form of political activity was not serving these values, he shifted to another form. In this way Cole's ideals lay behind the formation of the New Fabian Research Bureau and the International

Society for Socialist Studies, as well as behind his Guild Socialism. Nor were Cole's beliefs merely a guide to what the world should eventually be like. He lived according to them, maintaining egalitarian relationships with those with whom he worked. One can sense the pervasiveness of Cole's belief in fellowship in the reminiscences of his friends, in the closeness of the Guild Socialist movement and in the Cole group at Oxford.

Cole's deepest social principles remained static; their content and nature changed little after 1915. By then he had developed his basic values adequately enough for his purposes as a radical social reformer, and had stopped worrying about value problems that did not affect the way he treated human beings.[1] Even the catastrophic events of the 1920s and 1930s only led him to alter the relative importance he attributed to specific basic values within his complex of values, and to re-evaluate the policies and institutions which were corollaries or partial manifestations of his ideals. In the 1930s he put less weight on functional organization and limited the sphere of workers' control. Other middle-level concepts, such as the idea of a self-acting society and the protection of the realm of personal liberties, then made up a larger proportion of his theory of democracy. These changes in emphasis corresponded to changes of mood within the Labour movement itself. When Cole became Chichele Professor of Social and Political Theory, he re-stated his basic ideals, trying to express them clearly and to solve some of the epistemological problems that had become obvious because of the threat of Fascism and because of his presence in an academic environment. The ideals themselves constituted a source of unity, a stable centre in the midst of unprecedented changes.

Cole felt deeply that his values were objective. 'They are *good*, in a thoroughly and finally objective sense.'[2] This is not a trivial point. Cole's strength as a moral force in politics rested upon this certitude. He knew what was good, in a confident way that made his knowledge something he could build upon. He was so sure of what was good that he could be flexible in his choice of means without losing sight of the 'good life' which he sought to realize.

---

[1] 'What I Believe', p. 128. A proof, dated March 1953, in 'Manuscripts and Proofs', Box 8, Cole Papers, Nuffield College.
[2] *Essays in Social Theory*, p. 250.

Cole found his beliefs so obviously correct that 'anyone who denies their truth is blind, or mad, or wicked, or at least purblind'.[1] Many people who believe so firmly in a set of values are potentially totalitarian. Cole was not. He managed to give a libertarian interpretation to his values without losing his certitude. He introduced flexibility into his values by admitting that they could be affected by facts, and by asserting that values evolved socially. The result was a rare mixture of moral strength and tolerance. He realized that others would feel as strongly about their beliefs, and that ultimately one could not settle a conflict of beliefs by argument. Where Cole knew a fundamental difference of principle was involved, he stated his belief, gave the partial justifications he could, and then left the subject.

The result was that while his ideals were objective to him, Cole recognized the subjectivity of the act of belief. 'I at any rate am not prepared to allow any really important question to be decided for me by authority ...'[2] Cole's social theory was basically libertarian, in claiming the individual's right and duty to assent to the objectivity of social principles; and it was democratic, in extending the right to everyone. Here again Cole walked the tight-rope between relativism and absolutism in ethics. The greatest danger was that of an ethical *laissez faire*, in which Cole would have hidden behind his own right to his own values and would have been unable to discuss problems relating to them with his opponents.

The complex of empiricist and pragmatic traits that Maurice Reckitt labelled Cole's 'Fabian muzzle' prevented him from becoming an isolated, abstract moralist. Cole knew, as a socialist and as an historian, that his principles could not vanquish many facts, and that it was absurd to act as if they could. Implicitly, Cole set himself the task of overcoming the purist distinction between values and facts that G. E. Moore had just struggled to establish in *Principia Ethica*. The two realms were distinct in theory, yet confounded in practice; social theory had to treat them as confounded. Cole made this clear in 1920 in *Social Theory*:

My object in this book is primarily philosophical. I am concerned principally with social theory as the social complement of ethics, with 'ought' rather

[1] *Essays in Social Theory*, p. 251.
[2] 'What I Believe', p. 127.

than with 'is', with questions of right rather than of fact. But this does not mean that it is desirable or possible to extrude from consideration the other forms of social study . . . Social psychology . . . offers, in particular, indispensable material for any study of social conduct. The difference is that, in relation to the particular inquiry upon which we are setting out, it forms part, not of the ultimate interest or object before us, but of the material on which we have to work. We must know how associations and institutions actually work, what human motives and distortions of human motive are actually present in them, before we can form any philosophical conception of the principles on which they rest. We therefore cannot quite say, like Rousseau, 'Away with all the facts!' although in our conclusions the facts drop away and only questions of right remain.[1]

In this way, Cole's major beliefs were residues left when facts had dropped away. He insisted that facts were a major ingredient in forming beliefs. 'Belief, in the sense here relevant, is a compound of factual judgments and of value judgments, in such a way that the two are merged into a single act of faith.'[2] This important role for facts in the formation of beliefs kept Cole's beliefs realistic; it kept Cole's beliefs oriented towards the objective conditions of his society.

Cole was protected from the isolation which ethical relativism can impose by the fact that his values were objective in yet another sense. They were socially objective, the beliefs of his society. They were the values of the great Victorians which more contemporary liberals such as Hobhouse had reshaped into a critique of Victorian society. Cole extended the language of the advanced liberals; he did not have to create a new set of values, but simply to demand a fuller acceptance of concepts in which people claimed to believe. Both the defenders and the challengers of the *status quo* spoke the language of liberty and the individual.

This formal continuity of language, of course, concealed radical differences of meaning and interpretation. For this reason, we must look very closely at what Cole meant by his major beliefs – the individual, freedom, fellowship, and democracy. We cannot separate them fully from their manifestations, from corollaries such as workers' control or industrial democracy. Nor can one major value be dissoci-

---

[1] G. D. H. Cole, *Social Theory* (London, Methuen, 1920), p. 21.
[2] 'What I Believe', p. 116.

ated from the others. Cole's conceptions of the nature of the individual, freedom, and democracy intertwine to form an impressive complex of values that defined the 'good life' he sought to realize.

Cole started from a libertarian concept of human nature. This statement is true on several levels. The nature of the human being was the problem he set for philosophy in a paper written in December 1912, as he was beginning his public intellectual career with *The World of Labour*.

The problem of matter and mind, closely linked with that of individuality, is the central problem of the immediate future . . . Before we can talk sense about any concrete political question, we want some means of deciding upon our view of the political individual, some principle to apply in a rough and ready location of actual and imperfect political individuality.[1]

Often Cole's books open with a discussion of the nature of humanity or individuality. He began *Labour in the Commonwealth*, for example with a strong attack on the commodity theory of labour as a violation of 'The Humanity of Labour'. Given the rapidity and ease with which Cole wrote, it is clear that this sort of beginning is no accident, but instead revealed his mental process of creation and his foundation of values.

Raised in the liberal tradition, Cole equated humanity and individuality. The Idealism taught at Oxford made him suspicious; he rejected it, as he rejected a literal use of the idea of the general will, by insisting that people were individuals. Individuals were the ultimate reality. Life was individual life; 'phenomena must be of someone; an appearance must appear to somebody.'[2] Cole's conviction that individuals were the ultimate reality was a major source of the tolerant and empirical tendencies in his social theory – as it was for the Labour movement as a whole. If people were the ultimate reality, one had to know the sorts of people they were. This, of course, did not mean that one took them at face value; facts about them were the beginning, not the end of social theory. Social theory was essentially normative; but the norms it recommended had to fall within limits established by people as they were. The capacities of human beings created certain definite

[1] G. D. H. Cole, 'What Philosophy Is: A Plea for a Revised Metaphysic', in 'Manuscripts and Proofs', Box 7, folder 92, Cole Papers, Nuffield College. Dated 18/12/12.
[2] G. D. H. Cole, 'Personality', *The Highway* (May 1913), p. 153.

limits for a theorist; so did people's moods and interests. Ideas, institutions, and obligations had to be evaluated as they affected individuals.

Only individuals could be ethical ends; other things were means. An individual was ethically prior to his actions, to the functions he performed and the purposes he had. 'Every individual is in his nature universal; his actions and courses of action, his purposes and desires, are specific because he makes them so; but he himself is not, and cannot be, made specific . . .'[1] Social theory concerned itself with these specific things about individuals. Talk about people was inevitably talk about their activities and functions, not about their essences. There was no one language which would suit all human functions and actions. Cole thus instinctively insisted upon a pluralistic approach to social theory which sought to separate the ways in which individuals worked out different purposes.

In his social theories, Cole excluded any direct consideration of unorganized, personal action by individuals. This did not mean that he ignored direct individual action in thinking of the 'good life'; he kept it in mind as the background to social activity. But he did not try to account for it in his social theories. He retained a traditional liberal attitude towards private life: 'As long as human life remains, most of the best things in it will remain outside the bounds and scope of organization, and it will be the chief function of Society so to organize these parts of human life which respond to organization as to afford the fullest opportunity for the development of those human experiences to which organisation is the cold touch of death.'[2] There was little he cared to say beyond this; it would be safe to say that private life did not present major problems to him, at least not problems that demanded philosophical exploration after his school days.

Cole thus chose to think about human beings in their social relations. He drew a careful distinction between acts that were social and those that escaped social theorising. He did not make the distinction the crude one of individual and society which earlier liberals made. Cole treated individuals in treating society. The individual was a social creation; the distinction lay not between individual and social content, but between

[1] *Social Theory*, p. 49.
[2] Ibid., pp. 31–2.

individual ways of acting personally and socially. 'Of course, the act of an individual may be just as "social" in its content and purpose as the act of a society or group.'[1] But if one construed 'social' in this broad way, it would absorb almost all the acts which Cole chose to view as personal. Cole therefore made his essential distinction that between individual actions and actions demanding group participation and organization. He realized that the distinction was not absolute; it was only a working distinction, which was all it had to be. It allowed him to recognize the value of personal activity and to try to safeguard it, while concentrating on opportunities for and threats to individuality that arose when individuals in a society had to organize their essential collective activities.

Cole felt strongly that the existence of classes created the greatest threats to individuality. He hated capitalism for creating a class structure that denied most people their full individuality. Capitalism claimed the right to treat people as machines or 'hands', discarding them as they wore out. Where capitalism did offer a person a chance, it perverted his individuality and called upon the wrong motives. 'The "gambling instinct", as we sometimes call it, is simply a perversion of man's natural vitality that might go into the creation of the good things of life into unprofitable channels, by an economic system which has, broadly speaking, no use for humanity.'[2] More often, the necessity of surviving in a class society simply destroyed individual abilities. Thus, while an individual was inherently social, his individuality was not inherently the forms which it took in a class society. The sort of individuality Cole presupposed and built upon did not include classes; rather, it presupposed the creation of a classless economic and social system for its full realization. In social theory, many of the facts pertaining to man living in capitalist society had to 'drop away'.

The true individual, freed from class barriers, would not be identified with any single function or ability; he had many aspects for which Cole provided in his social theory and practical policies. Of these, Cole placed the greatest emphasis on will. In an undergraduate paper, Cole wrote: 'We are confronted in our inner experience with two

[1] Ibid., p. 7.
[2] *Labour in the Commonwealth*, p. 120.

great facts – will and existence. We will, and, *a fortiori*, we exist . . . The first and greatest characteristics of ourselves and subjects . . . [are] our autonomy, our freedom to will, to initiate, to create and to act.'[1] The emphasis on will had important implications for social theory and policies. For Cole, man was inherently a creative organism, in all his varied activities. Art was not a special preserve set aside to absorb man's creativity; creativity should be exercised everywhere and by everyone. Cole responded to this point in William Morris. As a Guild Socialist particularly he sought to bring creativity into work. In the 1920s, he reluctantly decided that the average person's work would not be artistic. However, he did not retreat to locating creativity in a special artistic enclave, but continued to urge self-government in all aspects of life.[2] In effect, self-government became his model of creative self-expression. Secondly, by emphasizing will, Cole emphasized the decision-making nature of individuals. Through their choices, men shaped themselves and their society. Their decisions were real choices: in this sense, they had free will. 'I do not believe that it is somehow settled what I am going to do before I have done it – and I believe that free will applies to history as well as to the behaviour of individual men.'[3]

Cole's position on free will was libertarian, resembling John Stuart Mill's formulation. The presence of social causation did not necessarily destroy free will, except when causation took the form of coercion in a class society; rather, causation made free will more intelligible. And, of course, the right to choose entailed the right to choose wrongly. Thus, in picturing the individual as a willing creature, Cole based his political and social policies on a dynamic model of humanity, in which individuals grew and changed through their own choices, instead of being static or being passive towards choices made for them.

While Cole emphasized the role that will be played in determining an individual's actions, he was largely untouched by the growing under-

---

[1] G. D. H. Cole, 'Theism and Freedom, or The One and the Many', in 'Manuscripts and Proofs', Box 7, folder 92, Cole Papers, Nuffield College. Not dated, but clearly 1911 or 1912.

[2] For the Guild Socialist period, see his papers on Morris and in *Labour in the Commonwealth*, pp. 220 ff; also in 'Art and Socialism: A Forgotten Incident of the Paris Commune', in 'Manuscripts and Proofs', Box 7, folder 93, Cole Papers, Nuffield College, probably written in 1911. For his later position see 'William Morris and the Modern World', in *Persons and Periods* (London, Macmillan, 1938).

[3] 'What I Believe', p. 118.

standing of irrationality which developed before the First World War.
Cole was a rationalist, in the sense that he believed

that the rational elements in men ought to be encouraged, and their reasoning
faculties developed to the fullest possible extent. This is not to say that all the
irrational elements in humanity are evil – far from it. But it is to recognize
reason as the human quality which, as civilization advances, ought more and
more to exercise a paramount and coordinating control.[1]

The development of reason did not mean to Cole a simple expansion of
book-learning and formal reasoning. It meant above all good judgment – both the common-sense judgment of what was feasible and the
intelligent choice of means, and the sort of moral vision the objectivity
of which has already been discussed. Both these abilities were present
in individuals at any particular stage of social development, partially
in actuality and partially in potentiality. '[For the average man] ...
individuality and initiative are not of a kind that will burst the bonds
of circumstance; they need to be called forth, stimulated by circumstances, and given every chance to develop.'[2] They could not be called
forth simply by formal education. One would have to change the
whole social environment which discouraged individual development.
Because man's individuality was such a social creation, 'it follows that
men's greatest task is the making of good societies'.[3] This was Cole's
injunction to himself and to others; his concept of individuality entailed
the general considerations which guided his hands as he sought to
remodel society.

The concept of full individuality led him in two important directions.
First, it led him to political pluralism and to the principle of function.
Society should be organized around the essential functions which men
performed; it should not try to organize the individual as a whole. The
principle of function was most important to Cole during his Guild
Socialist period, when it led him to deny the principle of the sovereign
state.

Secondly, any basic social organization and the social structure as a
whole must 'everywhere express the personality of those who compose

[1] *Essays in Social Theory*, p. 76.
[2] G. D. H. Cole, *Labour in the Commonwealth: A Book for the Younger Generation* (n.p.
and n.d.), p. 119.
[3] 'What I Believe', p. 123.

it'.[1] For social organization, the individual was the end rather than the means; institutions were only projections of individuality. The individual took precedence over all rules and commandments one might wish to impose. 'All such particular commandments or laws are abstractions made by the mind for its own convenience. They are the scaffolding of human freedom; but they are not part of the building.'[2]

The moral pre-eminence which Cole gave to the human will thus led him to a firm commitment to freedom. Freedom was not an abstract right; it was a demand, virtually an instinctive demand, which the individual had to make in order to attain individuality. Cole never forgot that liberty derived its meaning from individuals. Freedom had value because of

the qualities which only flourish freely among free men – the willingness to experiment, to take risks, the desire to do things well for the sake of doing them well, the desire to cooperate with one's fellows which is implanted in every political animal ... free man is man adventurous, mobile and progressive; it is the man in chains who is conservative, timid and stationary.[3]

Freedom was a means to the development of the individual; but its role in that development was so important that Cole did not hesitate to make freedom an essential moral and social value. 'I know that in saying this I am erecting freedom into an end, and attributing to it an absolute value. That is what I mean to do.'[4]

So far we have talked about freedom without distinguishing between freedoms. Cole, however, concentrated on the multiple ways in which liberty entered individual lives. He divided freedom into two basic manifestations, in the way that the most advanced liberals did before the First World War.

The first thing we have to do is to get clear in our minds a distinction between two senses in which the word is used – liberty attaching to the individual qua individual, and liberty attaching to associations and institutions with which the individual is concerned. This is not the familiar distinction between 'civil' and 'political', or even 'social', liberty as it is ordinarily drawn; for a

---

[1] G. D. H. Cole, *Self-Government in Industry* (London, G. Bell & Sons, 1917), p. 30.
[2] *Labour in the Commonwealth*, p. 197.
[3] *Labour in the Commonwealth*, p. 125; *Self-Government in Industry*, p. 297.
[4] G. D. H. Cole, 'Freedom in Danger', *Middlesex County Times* (16 June 1934); clipping in 'Manuscripts and Proofs', Box 4, folder 59, Cole Papers, Nuffield College.

liberty attaching to the individual qua individual may be political or economic in its content as well as civil. It is a distinction, not in the *content* of the liberty, but in its form of expression, between the liberty of personal freedom and the liberty of free and self-governing association.[1]

The quality which separates Cole from advanced liberals such as Hobhouse or de Ruggiero who used a similar distinction was their greater perception of the potential and actual conflicts between the manifestations of the two concepts of liberty. Advanced liberals especially feared a decision by a self-governing group to limit personal liberty. Cole shows much less fear of this; two of his mental characteristics help account for his confidence that self-government would not circumscribe personal liberty. First, Cole was wholeheartedly a democrat, whereas, as Collingwood said, the advanced liberals were 'something between' democrats and authoritarians.[2] Cole's belief in democracy actively affected the development of his policies. When one of his ideas failed to attract the support of the working class, which Cole considered the essential part of the British people, he treated this as a democratic verdict against those ideas. Secondly, Cole reduced potential conflicts between the two meanings of liberty by defining his terms more carefully than they did. He defined democracy in terms of equality, fellowship, and self-government, rather than in terms of majority rule or electoral procedures. Again, Cole defined the area of personal freedom more narrowly than they did, and hence there was less room for mutual infringements and conflicts. He did not see personal freedom as the right to private property, in the traditional manner; this removed a whole sphere of conflicting rights and obligations which concerned more traditional liberals.

The result was that Cole was able to treat the two concepts of liberty as fundamentally complementary, where de Ruggiero saw them as dialectically opposed as well as complementary. In *Social Theory*, Cole said that 'to treat these two forms of liberty separately leads us nowhere. They acquire a real meaning only when they are brought into relation and when their complementary character is fully revealed. Until that is done they remain abstractions'.[3] The danger of making either personal

[1] *Labour in the Commonwealth*, p. 181.
[2] R. G. Collingwood, 'Translator's Preface', Guido de Ruggiero, *The History of European Liberalism* (Boston, Beacon, 1959), p. viii.
[3] *Social Theory*, p. 184.

or social liberty an abstraction lay in the destruction of the complementary relation between the two, which would limit the individual's total liberty. Cole sought to design a society which would preserve the varying forms of both liberties and give the individual the greatest chance for self-determination.

When, therefore, we seek to bring personal and social liberty into a complementary relation, what we are really doing is to seek that relation between them which will secure the greatest liberty for all the individuals in a community, both severally and in association. It is not a question of striking a balance between the claims and counter-claims of the individual and of Society, but of determining what amount of organization and what absence of organization will secure to the individual the greatest liberty as the result of a blending of personal and social liberties.[1]

The two types of liberty thus were half-dependent. Neither needed to be subordinated to the other one, but neither could exist fully without the other one. For analytical purposes, Cole, like de Ruggiero, distinguished between them as human creations, going into their histories to find their essences and to prove their complementarity. Personal liberty was the earlier concept, with social liberty arising as a correction of faults inherent in the simple notion of personal liberty. For Cole, 'personal liberty is so simple an idea in itself as to need no detailed separate treatment. It is simply the freedom of the individual to express without external hindrance his "personality" – his likes and dislikes, desires and aversions, hopes and fears, his sense of right and wrong, beauty and ugliness, and so on.'[2] Aspects of the important civil liberties fell within the sphere of personal liberty; Cole firmly supported the freedom of speech, of conscience, and of taste. As the tide of events turned against socialists in the 1930s, he became more adamant in defending these liberties. But even then he argued that the idea of personal liberty taken by itself had a major flaw, especially in a class society. It was so negative as to be unable by itself to provide actual liberty. 'If every individual is left absolutely free and unrestricted, the result, taken as a whole, is not liberty but anarchy. Nominally free, in such circumstances, the individual has really no freedom because he has no security or safeguard, and no certainty of the way in which other

[1] Ibid., pp. 184–5.
[2] Ibid., p. 184.

people will behave towards him.'[1] Cole was well aware that personal liberty as it existed was a class-privilege. 'Money brings with it ... freedom to do a great many things which poorer people cannot afford, freedom to refuse to be ordered about or treated like dirt, even freedom, up to a point, to choose work that is a real pleasure and refuse work that is mere drudgery.'[2] But Cole, unlike some of the Idealist and Marxist thinkers of the times, did not let these arguments discredit the whole notion of personal liberty. Instead of being destroyed, these freedoms had to be removed from the sphere of class privilege and given to everyone; abstract, negative personal liberty had to be paired with complementary social liberties. His defence of negative liberties was as significant as his criticism of them; it placed Cole firmly on the anarchist or libertarian wing of socialism.

Cole agreed with the nineteenth century critics of *laissez-faire* that freedom meant a positive condition of man, not a mere negation of social controls. Freedom was generally the freedom to do something, and especially the right to join with others to create collective ways of developing and expressing their personalities and wishes. The majority of civil liberties necessarily took this social form to make the personal form of liberty real where it would otherwise remain abstract. But Cole did not accept the whole argument of Idealists who argued that liberty was positive. 'They go wrong when they leap from this affirmation to the paradox of freedom as restraint ... In this view freedom is conceived not as the absence of restraint but as the presence of law.' Cole retorted that the position was carried to extremes. 'It is not true either that the individual is more free in proportion as he imposes upon himself more moral laws, or that the Society becomes more free in proportion as it imposes upon itself further laws.'[3] Cole's strong attachment to personal liberty led him to hope for a minimum of laws. In his Guild Socialist days, this hope carried strong anarchist overtones. Later, his libertarian temper found expression in the milder wish for a self-acting society in which few public decisions would have to be

[1] Ibid., p. 181.
[2] G. D. H. Cole, 'Another Sort of Freedom', published in: *The Worksop Guardian*, 1 March 1940; *The Dumfries Standard*, 28 October 1939; *The Blackley Guardian*, 28 October 1939; clippings in 'Manuscripts and Proofs', Box 4, folder 59, Cole Papers, Nuffield College.
[3] *Labour in the Commonwealth*, pp. 194–5.

taken. Throughout his career, his belief in a balance between positive and negative liberties made him suspicious of those whose socialism stressed collectivism.

What made self-government or social liberty positive was not law, but the participation of the individual in the making of the decisions that affected him in a society or group. Where the early liberals had modelled their conception of freedom on the right to own property, Cole made self-government his fundamental right.

Freedom is not merely the absence of restraint; it assumes a higher form when it becomes self-government. A man is not free in himself while he allows himself to remain at the mercy of every idle whim; he is free when he governs his own life according to a dominant purpose or system of purposes. In just the same way, man in Society is not free where there is no law; he is most free where he co-operates best with his equals in the making of laws.[1]

Self-government, the positive liberty of a man in Society, entailed three demands. First, the individual had to be free to create and join associations to express particular purpose of his will. Secondly, an association founded in this way had to be free *'from external dictation in respect of its manner of performing its function'*.[2]

Here liberty intersected the functional principle, which left its impact especially on Guild Socialism. Briefly, a function was an essential individual purpose, such as the production of a useful object, which required social organization. Cole insisted that each function should be organized separately; when this was done, he asserted, conflicts between various liberties would largely be removed.[3] The independence of functional organizations would also further self-government by allowing the individual to choose specific tools for his needs; he would be represented with respect to a particular need on which he could validly choose, whether as a consumer or as a producer. And finally, the functional associations thus created had to be internally democratic. Only then could the individual determine his own fortune by determining the future of the social forces which weighed upon him.

Freedom, and the idea of self-government which lay at the centre of

[1] *Self-Government in Industry*, p. 227.
[2] *Social Theory*, p. 182.
[3] *Labour in the Commonwealth*, p. 191; *Social Theory*, pp. 57 ff.

positive freedom, thus led Cole directly to democracy. For Cole, the two concepts were practically inseparable; each created the other. Freedom demanded democracy for its realization. Conversely, Cole would not accept a so-called democracy which did not call forth a maximum of individuality and responsibility and create a sense of free will in industry. Democracy had to be judged by the freedoms it created; conversely, the complementary nature of democracy and freedom meant that democracy could not function without particular freedoms, both personal and social: Free speech, freedom to organize, freedom to develop one's personality in many directions.

The essential unity of freedom and democracy derived from their common basis in human will. 'Democracy rests essentially on a trust in human nature. It asserts, if it asserts anything, that man is capable to govern himself.'[1] This capacity entailed the fundamental human right to help decide how society should be organized. Cole also justified democracy by relating it to another characteristic of the individual, his creativity, and the corresponding need to exercise creativity. He defined democracy as a system which met these basic needs and rights. 'It follows that I mean by democracy ... an arrangement of public affairs which is designed to give every man and woman the best possible chance of finding out what they really want, of persuading others to accept their point of view, and of playing an active part in the working of a system thus responsive to their needs.'[2]

Cole relied upon certain formal principles – pluralism, function, and small groups – to bring problems within the reach of those who were affected by them. He sought to assign decisions to the smallest, most precise units possible, favouring what sociologists would call a face-to-face community. Cole was deeply contemptuous of those would-be democrats who could not see that one vote every five years gave the individual no control over his destiny. In *Self-Government in Industry*, he wrote:

Make a man a voter among voters in a democratic community; it is at least a half-truth that the measure of control he will have will vary inversely to the total number of votes.[3]

[1] *Self-Government in Industry*, p. 230.
[2] *Essays in Social Theory*, pp. 97–8.
[3] *Self-Government in Industry*, p. 279.

'One man, one vote' was at best a half-truth to a man who felt that each person should be represented in each area of organized life that concerned him. But his contempt for the pretensions of formally democratic institutions did not lead him all the way to Rousseau's conviction that democracy was only possible in city-states. Instead, Cole held that following democratic procedures on the lowest levels would make a large-scale democratic society possible. '[Men] can control great affairs only by acting together in the control of small affairs, and finding, throughout the experience of neighbourhood, men whom they can entrust with larger decisions than they can take rationally for themselves.'[1]

Cole thus explicitly accepted a representative model of democracy, and sought ways of reducing the imperfections in the representation of individual desires. The essential principle was that of reducing decisions to the level which the individual could handle. Devolution and decentralization were only one stage of the battle. If one merely decentralized decisions, all the confusion that prevailed on a national level would simply be recreated on the local level. It was more essential to separate problems from each other and to encourage direct representation of each of a man's relevant interests. At his most optimistic, in *Guild Socialism Re-Stated* (1920), Cole sought to design a society in which functional associations would take over all those tasks which states usually performed or could be asked to peform. Cole had a strong faith in functional representation as the most necessary and most practicable way of giving individuals intelligent control over their lives.

Functionalism depended on pluralism, the analysis of man as a subject having various purposes and activities. It led directly to a powerful criticism of commonly accepted notions of sovereignty and representation which were normally called democratic. Cole insisted that it was impossible to design a sovereign body that could represent the whole of a man. This did not lead him to insist upon pure, direct democracy; instead, it led him to a more democratic and libertarian theory of representation. What could be represented was a particular purpose, a function.

Men group themselves in different ways for the doing of different things – for the execution of different sets of purposes. They cannot find full com-

[1] *Essays in Social Theory*, p. 94.

munal expression for their personalities through a single form of organization.[1]

Since men naturally organized themselves around their functions, the social theorist could reconstruct society around them. In order to maximize their control over their lives, men could organize each of their major purposes and interests separately. Within a limited functional sphere, Cole believed that the 'general will' could really operate. The concept of the general will both attracted and repelled him. Clearly there was something to it. Certain solutions to problems were objectively better, in that they fulfilled purposes which were inherent in belonging to a group. Talk about the interest of a group or a community was not mere cant devised to conceal selfish interests. When the purpose, need, or function of a group was defined clearly, it would be possible for members of the group to recognize an objectively valid solution.[2] However, Cole continued to distrust Rousseau's effort to apply the concept of general will to nations. It led easily to the substitution of the state for individuals, making the state the ethical end and the citizens means to that end. Cole insisted that only individuals, not states, had real wills, which they could express democratically through functional organizations.

Institutions which exist for specific purposes can be truly representative of the common purposes of their members. There is ... in these cases, no question of one man taking the place of many; for what the representative professes to represent is not the whole will and personalities of his constituents, but merely so much of them as they have put into the association, and as is concerned with the purpose which the association exists to fulfill.[3]

Cole felt that a theory of functional representation would eliminate the dangers of leadership to democracy. 'It enables us to provide representation with constant counsel from the constituents, and thus makes it possible to abandon the theory of delegation without imperilling democratic control.'[4] In a functional system, the constituents would know the purposes for which they had chosen their representative.

[1] *Labour in the Commonwealth*, p. 188.
[2] *Social Theory*, p. 51; G. D. H. Cole, 'Introduction', Jean Jacques Rousseau, *The Social Contract and Discourses*, trans. G. D. H. Cole, rev. ed. (London and New York, Everyman, n.d.), p. xxxvi, first edition, p. xxxix.
[3] *Social Theory*, p. 105.
[4] Ibid., p. 110.

They could give him valid, specific advice and criticism, and recall him if necessary. At the same time, the representative need not be passive; he could become a real leader, given constituents who could assess what he was doing. However, he would have to lead by influence and cooperation, not by imposing his will. This kind of democratic leadership, by men who rose out of the ranks for specific purposes rather than seeking power for its own sake, was essential to the success of a functional system.

Cole found it easiest to envisage a functional society when trade union militance called forth his faith in workers' control. A complementary principle, which came to overshadow function in the 1920s and 1930s when Cole realized how a-political most people were, was the creation of a 'self-acting' society. One had to restrict democratic decisions to the issues which really required a statement of opinion by some element in the community, to avoid destroying democracy by internal friction.

> ... any healthy society in the future, like all the social forms that have preceded it, must be largely self-acting. It must be based itself, as it must base its methods of production, on the principle of the economy of effort. It must not, in the name of democracy, multiply unnecessarily committees and representative bodies, or consider that a job is being done the better because a lot of people are engaged in what one man could do by himself ... It must not ask its citizens to make the affairs of society the chief pre-occupation of their lives ...[1]

That is, society should ask the citizen to take an interest in each of these affairs about which he could know enough to make a decent decision or which might affect his life radically: otherwise society should seek to run smoothly. Cole argued that a society in which few decisions were required because matters ran without turmoil and injustice would be more democratic than one which applied democratic procedures to an unnecessarily large number of problems.[2] This argument mattered most to Cole during the 1930s, when he sought to justify a concept of planning that allowed less scope for direct individual participation.

Even in a planned economy, he looked to unions and to other volun-

---

[1] G. D. H. Cole, *The Next Ten Years in British Social and Economic Policy* (London, Macmillan, 1929), pp. 18–19.
[2] *The Next Ten Years*, p. 171.

tary associations to express human desires, rather than simply relying upon the Parliamentary mechanism. The concept of a self-acting society was one expression of his acute awareness that democracy was not to be equated with any political machinery – even with functional representation and the leadership style that he considered most democratic. No formally democratic structure could act democratically unless a large number of people became active in the politics of economic and social decisions. Any political mechanism would have to be judged by the public interest and activity that took place within it. Applying this criterion seriously to Guild Socialism resulted in the self-criticisms we have seen in earlier chapters. After Guild Socialism, Cole reduced his expectations concerning the direct control that a citizen could exert over his life through representative machinery. He refused to return to the formal shibboleths of other democrats. He refused to equate democracy with a Parliament or with a system of direct elections. 'Representative institutions are good, not in themselves, but for their effects; and, applied inappropriately, they may become thoroughly undemocratic in their working. For democracy implies, not that the whole body administers, or even appoints delegates to administer, but that it has effective means of insisting on the sort of administration that meets its needs.'[1] Getting beyond this perception, however, proved difficult. Neither various forms of indirect representation, nor the concept of planning for needs, nor a traditional Fabian reliance on publicity and professionalism, ever fully solved the problem of ensuring a responsive administration.

He also disputed the prevailing definition of democracy as majority rule. Democracy was not majority rule, if that meant denying the humanity of the minority. '. . . In the vast majority of decisions, it is not essential that the will of the minority should be merely effaced. Majority and minority can both be, if not satisfied, at all events left with a sense that life is still worth living, and the road to creative satisfaction can be kept open to men of diverse aspirations and values.'[2] In attacking these shibboleths, Cole may seem to be raising obvious quibbles that are hard to act on; but an important point lay behind them. Democracy meant something much greater than assenting to the right

[1] Ibid., pp. 168–9.
[2] 'For Democracy', *Rotary Service* (August 1941), p. 2.

of the majority to make decisions. It meant a particular sort of society, permeated by fellowship. Some formal democratic procedures were an inherent part of such a society; but Cole recognized that formal democracy might even be undemocratic.

I am on the side of the common people, in the sense that I want *all* men to have an equal chance of the good life and of living it in the ways that suit them best. This does not mean that I want all men to have everything the majority of them would vote for now, if they were asked. I do not stand for that kind of democracy.[1]

To a limited extent, Cole was prepared to tell men what they should want, and to recommend giving it to them even if they did not want it. But this did not have a totalitarian ring. At most, it echoes the self-assurance displayed by earlier aristocratic reformers. Cole was insisting that men be given the conditions which would allow them to exercise freedom.

I want people to have good nutrition, good housing, good education, freedom of speech, writing and association, self-government, peaceful relations with their neighbours, sound moral notions, whether they would vote for having them or not. To this extent, but no further, I am prepared to assert that I know better what is good for people than many of them can know for themselves, being less well informed and more held in mental subjection. By the democracy I stand for I mean making the people really free and self-governing, not the votes they record when they are neither. Voting is merely a handy device; it is not to be identified with democracy, which is a mental and moral relation of man to man.[2]

This 'mental and moral relation of man to man' was fellowship; fellowship was one of the elements that attracted Cole to Morris. He was fond of quoting from Morris's *Dream of John Ball*: 'Fellowship is heaven, and lack of fellowship is hell.' Cole's notion of fellowship was far from abstract; it meant literal personal comradeship in a small group, such as he found at Oxford and in the National Guilds League.

Furthermore, my notion of democracy is that it involves a sense of comradeship, friendliness, brotherhood – call it what you like. I mean a warm sense – not a mere recognition, cold as a fish. I mean that democracy means loving your neighbours, or at any rate being ready to love them when you do not happen to dislike them too much – and even then, when they are in trouble,

[1] *Essays in Social Theory*, p. 247.
[2] Ibid., p. 247.

and come to you looking for help and sympathy. A democrat is someone who has a physical glow of sympathy and love for anyone who comes to him honestly, looking for help or sympathy; a man is not a democrat, however justly he may try to behave to his fellow-man, unless he feels like that.[1]

In this personal way, fellowship meant the recognition of each person as an individual. 'Fellowship involves, above all, treating men as ends and not means . . . Fellowship does not count heads, or, if it does, it counts everyone as more than one – in fact, as infinite.'[2]

This ideal of fellowship may look like cant to a world which has not even achieved 'one man, one vote'.[3] Making a genuine ideal sound like cant is one of the dangers involved in writing about a person whose ideals surpassed the compromises we have accepted as ideals. But Cole understood fellowship not as cant but as something he could realize in his own life. His students and associates testify to that. Maurice Reckitt reports one incident which stands for many:

. . . I have known him cut a whole week out of a holiday to stay behind and look after an invalid, taken ill at a conference, towards whom he had no obligation whatsoever.[4]

Characteristically, he made no show of what he was going to do and refused to apply high-flown language to his behaviour.

Cole extended this sort of consideration towards all sorts of people. Some relationships went much further, developed into a real fellowship. The ordinary person who came in contact with Cole, however, never got beyond the stage of kindness. Cole was awkward about offering full fellowship to a person, and he often over-awed people. Consequently, he appeared aloof to most people. Reckitt recalls that the first time he met Cole

. . . I was as much impressed as I expected to be, but rather less attracted; he was never at his best, I think, at a first meeting. He told me some while after

[1] Ibid., p. 98.
[2] G. D. H. Cole, *Economic Tracts for the Times* (London, Macmillan, 1932), p. 323.
[3] Cole's more basic principle was to give each person as many votes as he had interests; see *Social Theory*, p. 115. In the 1930s, he accepted 'one man, one vote', but made it clear that he still intended to apply this to industry; see G. D. H. Cole, *The Simple Case for Socialism* (London, Gollancz, 1935), p. 179.
[4] Maurice B. Reckitt, *As It Happened* (London, Dent, 1941), p. 122.

that he 'wondered what had happened to your voice' which was, in fact, exactly what I wondered about his![1]

Fellowship entailed accepting another person as a real equal. 'Equality is but the political and social expression of the idea of fellowship,' he wrote in 1931. Cole interpreted equality in a libertarian way. He did not deny differences between men, although he implicitly sought to minimize them. 'Those who value equality as a political concept do not mean that all men are really equal, in any mathematical sense, or that all differences between them are due to differences of education and environment, or to remediable physical or inherited defects.' Nor did he desire uniformity in opinions, habits, and participation in functional bodies. He wanted 'to abolish only those differences which stand in the way of fellowship'.[2] Thus Cole was a leveller, but only a leveller of what he considered unnatural distinctions between men.

Effectively, Cole asserted a man's right to equality of opportunity. But he guarded against a threat to equality that has absorbed interest recently – the danger of the creation of a 'meritocracy' which would make equality of opportunity the basis of a new, more rigid class system. Cole demanded equality of status as well as equality of opportunity. The basic requirement was sufficient economic equality to prevent the formation of classes. Classlessness was not negative; it was part of the essential spirit of democracy. When equality of status had been established, it would be possible to run society according to the motives of fellowship and service. There would be no artificial barriers to prevent intelligent opinions from being voiced and followed. One could count on the participation of every individual in the formulation of the decisions that affected him.

There must be, in every group, close and constant consultation upon policy, a constant sharing-out of tasks, a constant willingness to help one another – or, in other words, the spirit of democracy must be continually evoked.[3]

Fellowship, democracy, freedom, and the 'universality' of the indi-

---

[1] Maurice B. Reckitt, 'G. D. H. Cole, the N.G.L. and the L.R.D.', unpublished manuscript written in 1961.
[2] *Economic Tracts*, p. 326.
[3] *Essays in Social Theory*, p. 104.

vidual – these were 'the articles of my social faith'.[1] Added together, they were socialism. 'By socialism I mean fundamentally, not a particular economic arrangement by which the State owns and runs industry, but the entire body of principles . . .' which he professed.[2] He was a socialist because of them. 'I am and have always been a Socialist *because* I believe profoundly in the ultimate value of the individual human spirit.'[3] His ultimate values were tightly woven together; in discussing one we often ran across the tracks of the others. Individuality leads to freedom and to democracy; each of them is defined in terms of individuality and by its relations with the other. The corollaries and expansions of the meanings of the key words – secondary words such as pluralism, workers' control, self-government in industry, the exercise of creativity and will – came into the argument at many different points. The ideals hang together; they gave Cole a harmonious, attractive sense of what a good society would feel like. Cole perhaps went the furthest of all the classic socialists in defining the nature of a good society, and his ideals undoubtedly gave him strength in the terrifying years after 1914.

The fact that Cole's life and work depended so much on his ideals raises difficulties in assessing his importance. It is easy to be contemptuous of his values, or to denigrate him for working within the liberal, Social Democratic language that he accepted and extended. To many, Cole's beliefs will appear too tidy and too rationalistic. Others, will have difficulty understanding his emphasis on individuality in work rather than in leisure; his concern for self-expression in work and politics can easily be made to sound prudish. Cole's values were not unique to him; consequently, many will find them commonplace and not see how seriously he tried to act upon them. It may be difficult to appreciate the reforms that came from this framework of values; it may be hard to see that for many these were practical values to which people responded.

Ten years after a man's death often finds his reputation at a low ebb, and G. D. H. Cole is no exception. Much of what he sought has been partially accomplished, with compromises and unforeseen side effects; other dreams and efforts failed to penetrate the public consciousness.

[1] Ibid., p. v.
[2] Ibid., p. 250. Interestingly enough, Cole refused to draw the conclusion that a 'socialism' that denied these liberal values was not a true socialism.
[3] 'For Democracy', *Rotary Service* (August 1941), p. 2.

Both the partial successes and the dreams are too close to be history, too distant to be the stuff of current politics. Cole's reputation currently survives most strongly in circles where his books on Labour history are still widely used. Some of these books are both well-written and illuminating, such as *Chartist Portraits* and his biographies of Cobbett and Owen, while others are more encyclopaedic. Despite their continued usefulness, our evaluation of Cole should not rest upon these contributions to Labour history. They were by-products of his more basic work for the Labour movement. Some of Cole's work still bears on the problems of living well in an industrial society, while other parts of his life's work need to be examined for the role that Cole and other thinkers played in the development of the Labour movement as it became able to reshape society.

What is the basis for arguing that Cole was important, and at times influential? One answer would be to look for his relationship to those who held power. Cole is scarcely visible from this perspective. He did not seek power, even the sorts of power intellectuals can aspire to. When he and some of his friends launched the New Fabian Research Bureau in the 1930s, they insisted upon a 'self-denying ordinance' in its rules barring them from making the N.F.R.B., and later the Fabian Society, a power base for candidates or ideological lines within the Labour movement. Yet this refusal to seek power may have been a strength, not a weakness. It allowed Cole and the N.F.R.B. to pursue important questions of goals and policies without contributing to the divisions and strains within the Labour movement. It allowed them to serve as propagandists and as educators for the Labour movement as a whole.

Cole's importance as an intellectual adviser and Labour theorist is subtle and diffuse rather than dramatic. He could not have been an *eminence grise;* to have claimed that role would have brought numbing distrust from within the Labour Party. Both Cole and Keynes served on the Economic Advisory Committee established by the second Labour Government – without making any impact on policy. Similarly, Cole's independent writing and arguing did not produce formulae that were taken over directly by the decision-makers. When Cole produced his most far-reaching ideas about workers' control, Guild Socialism, and a planned economy, both the Party leaders and the

G. D. H. COLE

public could not embrace them. On the other hand, when Cole worked within the framework of accepted Labour policies, his comments on Labour's choices, prospects, and values drew attention. Combined with the work of others, his less original work had a cumulative effect.

Cole's importance thus is an amalgam, and each element of the amalgam required a different treatment. When Cole's work yielded an original, comprehensive picture of what Britain might have become, that picture required a straight forward development. At other points in his career, Cole's importance depended upon the ways he reached a wide variety of people through research and propaganda for the Labour movement, through education, and even through the murder mysteries he and his wife wrote in their 'leisure time'. It would be simpler to argue for Cole's importance if it were to rest upon one brilliant book, one major new idea that gained instantaneous acceptance, or one dramatic irruption into politics. Instead, our argument will have to parallel Cole's own defence of William Morris:

... though a man's work may fall short of greatness if he attempts too many things, it does not at all follow that he would do better in attempting less. For the truth may be that he wants to do and say so much that he is much more concerned to get it done and said than to do one thing, or a few things, supremely well. He may have the power of expressing himself, and of serving his fellow-men, rather in many things than in a few; and though no one thing mark him out as master, his mastery may appear none the less plainly in them all. This, I think, is true of William Morris. He is greater as a man and as an influence than in any one part of his work.[1]

Part of our argument will have to be that there are important political roles other than those of decision-maker and *eminence grise*. political scientists have long been aware of the importance of unofficial leaders and moulders of opinion, recruiters and researchers. These less noticeable persons do the important work of testing ideas and converting both leaders and followers to them. They make a movement out of an idea and force it on the attention of society; they take the intellectual offensive, forcing other interest groups to defend themselves against the new conception of society.

Nowhere have these unofficial leaders been more influential than in the long process of political change that was registered in the 1945

[1] 'William Morris and the Modern World', *Persons and Periods*, pp. 288–9.

British election. The official leadership of the Labour Party had been discredited in 1931. The unofficial leadership helped overcome the contempt of the electorate by elaborating the concepts of full employment and social services. Through a horde of solid pamphlets and books, they made these concepts known to the general public. In the 1930s they attracted new active workers to the Labour movement. During the Second World War, the official leaders were politically hamstrung by accepting office in the Churchill coalition. Their experience helped dispel the feeling that Labour was not competent to handle power; but the electoral truce put the responsibility for propaganda squarely on the shoulders of the unofficial leaders. They kept their ideas alive and found new opportunities for spreading them. In the process, they changed the political atmosphere of Great Britain. They destroyed the limits that had been placed on the activity of the state and re-wrote the economic rules the state had followed. This change in political morality is fully as important as the laws that ultimately codified it.

In order to understand this basic change of opinion, it is important to bring Cole out of the background. Cole helped educate a whole generation politically. He influenced many of the past and current leaders of the Labour Party at Oxford. Others he reached through the Workers' Educational Association, Ruskin College, radio talks, public lectures, and, above all, his countless articles and books. His audience was not simply the Labour militant, the reader of the *New Statesman*, or the W.E.A. student; Cole also sought ways of reaching people outside the Labour movement. He taught them many things, most of which they have now forgotten;[1] but above all, he led them to think for themselves, and to repudiate the belief that politics could do nothing to cure the problems of depression and poverty. His influence as a political popularizer, like that of any good educator, was diffuse rather than dogmatic.

Cole's influence as a propagandist is thus inseparable from the service he gave to the Labour movement as an educator. Often he found that 'being influential' did not mean forcing his opinions upon

[1] R. H. S. Crossman, 'John Strachey and the Left Book Club', *The Charms of Politics* (London, Hamish Hamilton, 1958), pp. 140–1. Crossman points out how the specific assumptions and advice of the left-wingers was irrelevant in many cases after the war, while the broad influence of Strachey and others on the left still made an impact.

those he was influencing, but meant instead helping sections of the Labour movement find their tongues. In his Guild Socialist period, between 1913 and 1920, Cole and his friends established closer connections with British trade unionism than any previous Labour intellectuals since the Webbs. These close connections led to union use of the Labour Research Department for ammunition in industrial disputes. The intellectuals also found themselves helping publicize and defend strikes in pamphlets and through the *Herald*. After 1920, Cole had fewer direct relationships with the trade unions, but was still available to write a pamphlet with Ernest Bevin on the Labour Party crisis of 1931, to call a conference composed largely of trade union leaders to rethink workers' control in 1932, and to write a history and a report on the future for the Co-operative movement in 1944.

Cole's career spanned the rise, the flowering, and perhaps the decline of a powerful tradition of public service. J. F. C. Harrison suggests that this concept of service has declined, perhaps permanently, since the success of the Labour government of 1945.[1] Similar traditions of service survive outside of the Labour movement, but they too have been undercut by the professional provision of services and the decline of an earnest yet leisured élite. Cole's career has an interest as an embodiment of this tradition that gives an added dimension to his own service for the Labour movement. For Cole, as a Labour intellectual, service meant loyalty to the Labour movement as a whole, trying to avoid attacking any segment of the movement unless more basic loyalties made it inevitable. Service meant being available for the kind of tasks that required an intellectual's abilities. It meant a sacrifice of time travelling in trains to hold a W.E.A. tutorial class, or a heavy expenditure of energy putting out a magazine. It meant doing research into the wide variety of problems that affected the working class condition, getting the facts before one presumed to give advice. It entailed a kind of asceticism and hard work, without being joyless; the Guild Socialist movement and the Cole group at Oxford both brought out the songwriter and the parodist in Cole.

On his death in January 1959, Cole was remembered by friends and students as a moral force, the embodiment of a conception of the

[1] J. F. C. Harrison, *Learning and Living 1790–1960* (London, Routledge & Kegan Paul, 1961), p. 336.

'good life'.[1] As G. D. N. Worswick wrote, 'ironically, perhaps, for one who had such a profound belief in principle and the power of reason, his greatest influence may prove to have been through his own goodness'.[2] Born late in the Victorian period, he imbibed the Victorian concepts of service and liberty, but not the Victorian idea of democracy. Cole played an important role as a curator of those values and as a thinker who worked creatively with them, extending them to new problems such as man's relationship to work. As a social theorist, Cole spent much of his time working on the common-sense problems that arose in trying to live by this concept of the good life. The moral viciousness of many twentieth-century events, and a growing awareness of the subjectivity of values, forced Cole into an interesting attempt to vindicate his belief that his values were objective. Similarly, the growth of the social sciences challenged him to think about the relationship between values and facts. Despite these incursions into epistemological territory, Cole found little cause to do more than change the emphases he placed on particular values within the frame of reference he had developed before 1914. For Cole, these values were a basis for action; and much of our interest in Cole's life comes from his efforts to make his values permeate the whole of society. His beliefs flowered briefly in the atmosphere of reconstruction after the First World War, yielding an attractive form of Guild Socialism. The depression gave a new urgency to his brand of public service and to his concept of democracy; the 1930s, with the agitation for jobs, planning, and social services, Spain and the Popular Front, was the heyday of Cole's brand of active citizenship. Throughout this period there runs the strand of intelligent moral response to new problems; and Cole had both practical and symbolic importance as a Labour moralist.

Another strand that makes Cole interesting and important is closely related – his role as an intelligent observer of his society. From *The World of Labour* in 1913 to 'World Socialism Restated' in 1956, Cole examined the new currents in socialism and in socialism's relationship

[1] See the many obituaries written by Cole's friends and students, among them Kingsley Martin, 'G. D. H. Cole', *New Statesman*, LVII (17 January 1959), 63; A. J. P. Taylor, 'His Socialism was Pure', *Tribune* (23 January 1959), pp. 6–7; H. L. Beales, 'G. D. H. Cole', *The Highway* (March 1959), pp. 147–8; letters in the *Manchester Guardian* from Naomi Mitchison and Royden Harrison (19 January 1959) and from Benedict Meynell (17 January 1959).
[2] G. D. N. Worswick, 'Cole and Oxford, 1938–1958', *Essays in Labour History*.

to the world. At each point he had something interesting to say; he worked with the new ideas and new facts, instead of simply reporting them. His clear but undogmatic set of values helped him observe; he gauged the impact of events and changes on the basic values he hoped to realize. His responses to the rise of British Communism, the collapse of post-World War optimism, the defections of Mosley and MacDonald in 1931, the idea of a Popular Front, and the results of the Welfare State programme enacted by Labour in 1945 all stand out beyond most contemporary political analysis.

Historians do not simply rake over the past to discover what happened; they try to rescue from anonymity the persons who, in retrospect, had something worthwhile to say which did not receive adequate attention at the time and which remains unknown at the present. Cole's earliest writings fall into this category. His Guild Socialist speculations have something important to say to the person who senses alienation in modern ways of producing and living. Cole thought seriously of possible ways of giving men more meaning in their lives and a greater sense of control and belonging. His concepts of industrial democracy claim to do both of these things, by restoring meaning to work and control to the worker. It is possible that men will return to these speculations as they realize the incompleteness of political democracy without industrial democracy and as they wrestle with problems of decentralization and democratic participation.

Cole's importance is the sum of these various contributions, and the sum total of people he affected and will affect. Some people he served directly, as trade unionists or students at Oxford or in the Workers' Educational Association. Others he influenced as a propagandist and popularizer in the period of agitation that led up to the Labour victory of 1945. Some responded to the values he discussed and exemplified, others to the policies he recommended and the comments he offered on current problems. To a more recent generation, Cole has a historical interest, both for what he did and for the tradition of service and the conception of the good life he symbolized. His work as a Labour historian still has significance to scholars and students. And Cole may have a further importance yet to come, as increasing affluence once more poses the problem of how to live freely and creatively in an industrial society.

SELECT BIBLIOGRAPHY

I. *Some of Cole's more important books and pamphlets, arranged in order of their first publication*

1913: (with William Mellor) 'The Greater Unionism'.
   The World of Labour: A Discussion of the Present and Future of Trade Unionism.
1914: 'Conflicting Social Obligations', *Proceedings of the Aristotelian Society*, New Series, XV (1914–15), 140–59.
1915: *Labour in War-Time.*
1916: (with Robin Page Arnot) *Trade Unionism on the Railways.* (Labour Research Department Trade Union Series.)
1917: *Self-Government in Industry.*
1918: *An Introduction to Trade Unionism* (Labour Research Department Trade Union Series).
   (with William Mellor) 'The Meaning of Industrial Freedom'.
   The Payment of Wages (Labour Research Department Trade Union Series).
1919: *Labour in the Commonwealth: A Book for the Younger Generation.*
1920: *Chaos and Order in Industry.*
   Guild Socialism Re-stated.
   Social Theory.
1924: *The Life of William Cobbett. With a Chapter on 'Rural Rides' by the Late F. E. Green.*
1925: *A Short History of the British Working-Class Movement.*
   Robert Owen.
1929: *The Next Ten Years in British Social and Economic Policy.*
1931: (with Ernest Bevin) 'The Crisis' (*New Statesman* Pamphlet).
   'The Essentials of Socialization' (New Fabian Research Bureau Research Pamphlets No. 1).
   'A Plan for Britain' (*Clarion* Texts).
1932: *Economic Tracts for the Times.*
   The Intelligent Man's Guide Through World Chaos.
1933: 'Saving or Spending; Or, The Economics of "Economy"' (*New Statesman* Pamphlet).
   (with William Mellor) 'Workers' Control and Self-Government in Industry' (New Fabian Research Bureau Research Pamphlets No. 9).
1934: *Studies in World Economics.*
   What Marx Really Meant.
1935: *Principles of Economic Planning.*
1937: (with Margaret Cole) *The Condition of Britain.*
   The People's Front.

1938: (with Raymond Postgate) *The Common People 1746–1938.*
The Machinery of Socialist Planning.
1939: *A Plan for Democratic Britain.* Labour Book Service.
'War Aims.' (*New Statesman* Pamphlet).
'The War on the Home Front' (Fabian Tract No. 247).
1941: *British Working-Class Politics 1832–1914.*
Chartist Portraits.
Europe, Russia and the Future.
1942: 'The Fabian Society, Past and Present' (Fabian Tract No. 258).
Great Britain in the Post-war World.
1943: *Fabian Socialism.*
The Means to Full Employment.
1944: *A Century of Co-Operation.*
Money: Its Present and Future.
1945: 'Scope and Method in Social and Political Theory. An Inaugural Lecture Delivered Before the University of Oxford.'
1946: *Labour's Foreign Policy* (*New Statesman* Pamphlet).
1947: *The Intelligent Man's Guide to the Post-War World.*
1948: *The Meaning of Marxism.*
1949: 'Labour's Second Term' (Fabian Tract No. 273).
1950: *Essays in Social Theory.*
Socialist Economics.
1951: *The British Co-operative Movement in a Socialist Society.*
1953: *A History of Socialist Thought.* I: *The Forerunners 1789–1850.*
An Introduction to Trade Unionism.
1954: *A History of Socialist Thought.* II: *Marxism and Anarchism 1850–1890.*
'Is This Socialism?' (*New Statesman* Pamphlet).
1955: *Studies in Class Structure* (International Library of Sociology and Social Reconstruction).
1956: *A History of Socialist Thought.* III: *The Second International 1889–1914* (2 parts).
'World Socialism Restated' (*New Statesman* Pamphlet).
1957: *The Case for Industrial Partnership.*
1958: *A History of Socialist Thought.* IV: *Communism and Social Democracy 1914–1931.*
1960: *A History of Socialist Thought.* V: *Socialism and Fascism 1931–1939.*

II. *A List of Cole's books and pamphlets, arranged topically*
A. *Guild Socialism, Workers' Control, and Industrial Democracy*

Chalmers, J. M., Ian Mikardo, M.P. and G. D. H. Cole. 'Consultation or Joint Management?' (Fabian Tract No. 277). London, 1949.

Cole, G. D. H. *The Case for Industrial Partnership.* Macmillan, London, 1957.

Chaos and Order in Industry. Methuen, London, 1920. 2nd edition, 1921.

Cole, G. D. H. and William Mellor. 'The Greater Unionism' (*Daily Herald.* Manchester and London, 1913).

Cole, G. D. H. 'Guild Socialism' (Fabian Tract No. 192. London, 1919).

Guild Socialism Re-stated. Leonard Parsons, London, 1920. 2nd edition, 1921.

Labour in the Commonwealth: A Book for the Younger Generation. Headley Bros, London, 1918.

Cole, G. D. H. and William Mellor. 'The Meaning of Industrial Freedom.' Allen & Unwin, London, 1918.

Cole, G. D. H. *Self-Government in Industry.* G. Bell & Sons, London, 1917. Subsequent editions in 1918, 1919, 1920.

Cole, G. D. H. and William Mellor. 'Workers' Control and Self-Government in Industry' (New Fabian Research Bureau Research Pamphlets No. 9, London, 1933).

Cole, G. D. H. *The World of Labour: A Discussion of the Present and Future of Trade Unionism.* G. Bell & Sons, London, 1913. Subsequent editions in 1815, 1917, 1919, 1920, 1928.

B. *Socialism and Public Problems, 1921–56*

Cole, G. D. H. 'Beveridge Explained' (*New Statesman* Pamphlet. London, 1943).

The British Co-Operative Movement in a Socialist Society. Allen & Unwin, London, 1951.

Building and Planning. Cassell London, 1945.

Cole, G. D. H. and Ernest Bevin. 'The Crisis' (*New Statesman* Pamphlet, London, 1931). Reprinted in G. D. H. Cole, *Economic Tracts for the Times.* Macmillan, London, 1932.

Cole, G. D. H. 'Co-Operation, Labour and Socialism' (6th Thomas Blandford Memorial Lecture. Manchester, 1946).

'Economic Prospects: 1938 and After' (*Fact* No. 11. London, 1938).

Economic Tracts for the Times. Macmillan, London, 1932.

'The Essentials of Socialization' (New Fabian Research Bureau Research Pamphlets No. 1. London, 1931).

Europe, Russia and the Future. Gollancz, London, 1941.

Fabian Socialism. Allen & Unwin. London, 1943.

'The Fabian Soc ety, Past and Present' (Fabian Tract No. 258. London, 1942. Revised edition by Margaret Cole, 1952).

The Future of Local Government. Cassell, London, 1921.

'A Guide to the Elements of Socialism' (Labour Party Pamphlet, London, 1947.)

Cole, G. D. H. and Margaret I. Cole. *A Guide to Modern Politics.* Gollancz, London, 1934.

Cole, G. D. H. *Great Britain in the Post-War World.* Gollancz, London, 1942.

'How to Obtain Full Employment' (Post War Discussion Pamphlets No. 4 Odhams Press, London, 1944).

The Intelligent Man's Guide to the Post-War World. Gollancz, London, 1947.

The Intelligent Man's Guide Through World Chaos. Gollancz, London, 1932.

The Intelligent Man's Review of Europe To-day. Gollancz, London, 1933.

'Is This Socialism?' (*New Statesman* Pamphlet. London, 1954).

'Labour's Foreign Policy' (*New Statesman* Pamphlet. London, 1946).

'Labour's Second Term' (Fabian Tract No. 273. London, 1949).

'Living Wages: The Case for a New Minimum Wages Act' (New Fabian Research Bureau Research Pamphlets No. 42. London, 1938).

The Means to Full Employment. Gollancz, London, 1943.

'The National Coal Board. Its Tasks, its Organization, and its Prospects' (Fabian Research Series No. 129, London, 1948).

Cole, G. D. H. and G. R. Mitchison. 'The Need for a Socialist Programme' (Socialist League, London, 1933).

Cole, G. D. H. *The Next Ten Years in British Social and Economic Policy.* Macmillan, London, 1929.

The People's Front. Gollancz and Left Book Club, London, 1937.

A Plan for Democratic Britain. Labour Book Service, London, 1939.

'A Plan for Britain' (*Clarion* Texts, London, 1931).

'The Planning of World Trade' (Post War Discussion Pamphlets No. 3, Odhams Press, London, 1944).

'Saving and Spending; Or, The Economics of "Economy"' (*New Statesman* Pamphlet, London, 1933).

The Simple Case for Socialism. Gollancz, London, 1935.

Socialism in Evolution. Penguin, Harmondsworth Middlesex, 1938.

'Some Essentials of Socialist Propaganda' (Fabian Tract No. 238. London, 1932).

'War Aims' (*New Statesman* Pamphlet, London, 1939).

Cole, G. D. H. and Raymond Postgate. 'War Debts and Reparations. What They Are; Why They Must be Cancelled' (*New Statesman* Pamphlet. London, 1932).

Cole, G. D. H. 'The War on the Home Front' (Fabian Tract No. 247. London, 1939).

'When The Fighting Stops' (*Peace Aims* Pamphlet No. 18. National Peace Council). London, 1943.

'What is Wrong With the Trade Unions' (Fabian Tract No. 301. London, 1956).

'Why Nationalise Steel?' (*New Statesman* Pamphlet, London, 1948).
'World Socialism Restated' (*New Statesman* Pamphlet, London, 1956).

C. *Economics*

Cole, G. D. H. *British Trade and Industry: Past and Future*. Macmillan London, 1932.

(ed.). *British Trade-Unionism To-day*. Gollancz, London, 1939.

Cole, G. D. H. and Margaret Cole. *The Condition of Britain*. Gollancz, London, 1937.

Cole, G. D. H. 'The Economic System' (W.E.A. Outlines, London, 1927).

'Fifty Propositions About Money and Production' (Pamphlets on the New Economics No. 18, S. Nott. London, 1936). Reprinted as an appendix to Cole, G. D. H. *Money, Its Present and Future*. Cassell, London, 1944.

Gold, Credit and Employment, Four Essays for Laymen. Allen & Unwin, London, 1930.

An Introduction to Trade Unionism (Labour Research Department Trade Union Series No. 4. London, 1918). See also Cole, G. D. H. *Organized Labour. An Introduction to Trade Unionism*. Allen & Unwin, London, 1924; Cole, G. D. H. *An Introduction to Trade Unionism*. Allen & Unwin, London, 1953, which are later revised versions of this work.

An Introduction to Trade Unionism. Allen & Unwin, London, 1953.

The Machinery of Socialist Planning. Hogarth Press, London, 1938.

Modern Theories and Forms of Industrial Organization. Gollancz, London, 1932.

Money, Its Present and Future. Cassell, London, 1944, revised editions in 1945 and 1947. See also Cole, G. D. H. *Money, Trade and Investment*. Cassell, London, 1954, which was based upon this work.

Organized Labour. An Introduction to Trade Unionism. Allen & Unwin, London, 1924.

Out of Work. An Introduction to the Study of Unemployment. Labour Publishing Co, London, 1923.

The Payment of Wages. (Labour Research Department Trade Union Series No. 5. Allen & Unwin, London, 1918). Revised edition, 1928.

The Post-War Condition of Britain. Routledge & Kegan Paul, London, 1956.

Practical Economics. Penguin, Harmondsworth Middlesex, 1937.

Principles of Economic Planning. Macmillan, London, 1935.

Cole, G. D. H. and Margaret Cole. *Rents, Rings and Houses*. Labour Publishing Co., London, 1923.

Cole, G. D. H. 'Socialist Control of Industry' (Forum Lecture Series No. 6. Socialist League. London, 1933).

Socialist Economics. Gollancz, London, 1950.

(ed.). *Studies in Capital and Investment*. New Fabian Research Bureau, London, 1935.
Studies in Class Structure. Routledge & Kegan Paul (International Library of Sociology and Social Reconstruction). London, 1955.
Studies in World Economics. Macmillan, London, 1934.
(ed.). *What Everybody Wants to Know About Money: A Planned Outline of Monetary Problems by Nine Economists From Oxford*. Gollancz, London, 1933.

D. *Social Theory*

Cole, G. D. H. 'Conflicting Social Obligations'. *Proceedings of the Aristotelian Society, New Series*, XV (1914–15), 140–59.
Essays in Social Theory. Macmillan, London, 1950.
The Meaning of Marxism. Gollancz, London, 1948.
'Scope and Method in Social and Political Theory. An Inaugural Lecture Delivered Before the University of Oxford'. Clarendon Press, Oxford, 1945. Reprinted in Cole, G. D. H. *Essays in Social Theory*. Macmillan, London, 1950.
Social Theory, Methuen, London, 1920. Fourth edition, 1930.
Some Relations Between Political and Economic Theory. Macmillan, London, 1934.
Theories and Forms of Political Organization. Gollancz, London, 1932.
What Marx Really Meant. Gollancz, London, 1934.

E. *Labour History*

Cole, G. D. H. *Attempts at General Union 1829–34. A Study in British Trade Union History*. Macmillan, London, 1953. First published as Cole, G. D. H. 'A Study in British Trade Union History. Attempts at "General Union", 1829–1834', *International Review for Social History*, IV (1939), 359–462.
'Beatrice Webb as an Economist', in Cole, Margaret (ed.). *The Webbs and Their Work*. Frederick Muller, London, 1949.
'British Labour Movement – Retrospect and Prospect' (Ralph Fox Memorial Lecture, April 1951. Fabian Special No. 8. London, 1951).
British Working-Class Politics 1832–1914. Routledge, London, 1941.
Cole, G. D. H. and A. W. Filson. *British Working Class Movements. Select Documents 1789–1875*. Macmillan, London, 1951.
Cole, G. D. H. *A Century of Co-operation*. Co-operative Union Ltd, Manchester, 1944.
Chartist Portraits. Macmillan, London, 1941. Reissued 1965.
Cole, G. D. H. and Raymond Postgate. *The Common People 1746–1938*. Methuen, London, 1938. Subsequent editions 1946, 1949, 1956, 1961.
Cole, G. D. H. 'The Development of Socialism During the Last Fifty Years'

(Webb Memorial Lecture, 30 October 1951. Athlone Press, London, 1952).

A History of the Labour Party from 1914. Routledge & Kegan Paul, London, 1948.

A History of Socialist Thought. 5 vols. Macmillan, London, 1953–1960.
  I. *The Forerunners 1789–1850.* 1953.
  II. *Marxism and Anarchism 1850–1890.* 1954.
  III. *The Second International 1889–1914.* 2 parts. 1956.
  IV. *Communism and Social Democracy 1914–1931.* 2 parts. 1958.
  V. *Socialism and Fascism 1931–1939.* 1960.

Introduction to Economic History 1750–1950. Macmillan. London, 1952.

'James Keir Hardie' (Fabian Biographical Series No. 12, London, 1941).

'John Burns' (Fabian Biographical Series No. 14, London, 1943).

Labour in the Coal-Mining Industry (Carnegie Endowment for International Peace. Division of Economics and History. Economic and Social History of the World War. British Series. Clarendon Press, Oxford, 1923).

The Life of William Cobbett. With a Chapter on 'Rural Rides' by the late F. E. Green. Collins, London, 1924. 3rd edition, Home & Van Thal, London, 1947.

'Richard Carlile' (Fabian Biographical Series No. 13, London, 1943).

'Robert Owen. Benn. London, 1925. 2nd edition Cole, G. D. H. *The Life of Robert Owen.* Macmillan, London, 1930. Reissued (London) 1965 as a 'Cass reprint'.

'Safeguards for Dilution: What Circulars L2 and L3 Mean'. London, 1915.

A Short History of the British Working-Class Movement 1789–1927. 3 vols. Allen & Unwin, London, 1925–7. New edition in one volume, 1932; complete edition in one volume with a supplementary chapter, 1937; *A Short History of the British Working-Class Movement 1789–1947.* Allen & Unwin, London, 1947; and subsequent reprints.

Trade Unionism and Munitions (Carnegie Endowment for International Peace. Division of Economics and History. Economic and Social History of the World War. British Series. Clarendon Press, Oxford, 1923).

Cole, G. D. H. and Robin Page Arnot. *Trade Unionism on the Railways* (Labour Research Department Trade Union Series No. 2, London, 1916).

Cole, G. D. H. 'William Cobbett' (Fabian Tract No. 215. London, 1925).

'William Morris as a Socialist. A Lecture Given on 16th January 1957 to the William Morris Society at the Art Workers' Guild by G. D. H. Cole.' Privately printed at the Leicester College of Art for the William Morris Society, Leicester, 1960.

Workshop Organization (Carnegie Endowment for International Peace.

Division of Economics and History. Economic and Social History of the World War. British Series. Clarendon Press, Oxford, 1923).

F. *Education and Literature*

Cole, G. D. H. and Margaret Cole (eds.). *The Bolo Book.* Labour Publishing Co, London, 1921.

Cole, G. D. H. *The Crooked World.* Gollancz, London, 1933.

'Hints on Reading and Writing. A Guide for W.E.A. Students'. London, n.d., Reprinted 1966.

New Beginnings and The Record. B. H. Blackwell, Oxford, 1914.

Persons and Periods. Macmillan, London, 1938. The first nine essays were reprinted under the same title (Penguin, Harmondsworth Middlesex, 1945).

Politics and Literature (Hogarth Lectures on Literature No. 11. L. & V. Woolf, London, 1929).

Samuel Butler and The Way of All Flesh. Home and Van Thal, London, 1947.

'Samuel Butler' (Bibliographical Series of Supplements to British Book News No. 30. London, 1952.)

'The Tutor's Manual, Prepared by Members of the Association of Tutorial Class Tutors, and Edited for the Association by G. D. H. Cole.' London, n.d. (1923?).

III. *Materials in the Cole Papers, Nuffield College, Oxford*

A. 'Manuscripts and Proofs'. Eight boxes of papers; materials in the first seven boxes are sorted into folders.

B. 'National Guilds League: Various Papers'. One box.

C. 'Society for Socialist Inquiry and Propaganda'. One box.

D. 'International Society for Socialist Studies'. One box.

E. 'Lectures'. Five boxes.

F. Materials kept in the Manuscript Cupboard. Most prominent among them are:

    1. Cole, G. D. H. 'The Striker Stricken'. His operatta on the General Strike, written in 1926.

    2. Complete editions of *The Guildsman* and *The Guild Socialist* (1918–23), *New Standards* (1923–4), *The Octopus* (1906–7), *The Oxford Socialist* and *The Oxford Reformer* (1908–10).

    3. A scrapbook containing articles by Cole and Mellor published in the *Daily Herald* and the *Herald* (1914–16).

G. Materials shelved in the general stacks of the Nuffield College library. In addition to Cole's published works, there are several bound volumes of Cole's most important articles from 1913 to 1953, and a useful collection of materials related to the Nuffield College Social Reconstruction Survey.

IV. *Works by other authors*

Arnot, Robin Page. *History of the Labour Research Department.* Labour Research Department, London, 1926.

Barry, E. Eldon. *Nationalization in British Politics.* Jonathan Cape, London, 1965.

Bechhofer, C. E. and Maurice B. Reckitt. *The Meaning of National Guilds.* Cecil Palmer & Hayward, London, 1918. 2nd ed. 1920.

Beer, Samuel H. *British Politics in the Collectivist Age.* Alfred A. Knopf, New York, 1965.

Berlin, Sir Isaiah. *Two Concepts of Liberty.* Clarendon Press, Oxford, 1958.

Briggs, Asa, and John Saville (eds.). *Essays in Labour History in Honour of G. D. H. Cole.* Macmillan, London, 1960.

Briggs, Asa. 'Social Welfare, Past and Present.' *Rewley House Papers,* IV, No. III (1964–5), p. 13–35.

Brockway, A. Fenner. *Inside the Left.* Allen & Unwin, London, 1942.

Bullock, Alan. *The Life and Times of Ernest Bevin.* I: *Trade Union Leader 1881–1940.* Heinemann, London, 1960.

Carpenter, Niles. *Guild Socialism. An Historical and Critical Analysis.* Appleton, New York, 1921.

Clegg, H. A. *Industrial Democracy and Nationalization.* Blackwell, Oxford, 1955.

A New Approach to Industrial Democracy. Blackwell, Oxford, 1963.

Coal Inquiry Commission. *Reports and Minutes of Evidence on the Second Stage of the Inquiry.* H.M.S.O., London, 1919.

Cole, Margaret I. *Growing Up Into Revolution.* Longmans Green, London, 1949.

The Story of Fabian Socialism. Heinemann, London, 1961.

(ed.). *The Webbs and Their Work.* Frederick Muller, London, 1949.

Cooke, Colin. *The Life of Richard Stafford Cripps.* Hodder & Stoughton, London, 1957.

Crosland, C. A. R. *The Future of Socialism.* Cape, London, 1956.

Crossman, R. H. S. (ed.). *New Fabian Essays.* Turnstile Press, London, 1952.

Dangerfield, George. *The Strange Death of Liberal England.* H. Smith and R. Haas. New York, 1935.

Estorick, Eric. *Stafford Cripps: A Biography.* Heinemann, London, 1949.

Glass, S. T. *The Responsible Society: The Ideas of the English Guild Socialists.* Longmans Green, London, 1966.

Goodrich, Carter. *The Frontier of Control: A Study in British Workshop Politics.* Harcourt Brace & Howe, New York, 1920.

Graubard, Stephen Richards. *British Labour and The Russian Revolution 1917–1924.* Harvard University Press, Cambridge, Mass., 1956.

Harris, Seymour E. (ed.). *The New Economics: Keynes' Influence on Theory and Public Policy.* Alfred A. Knopf, New York, 1947.

Harrison, J. F. C. *Learning and Living 1790–1960.* Routledge & Kegan Paul, London, 1961.

Harrod, Sir Roy. *The Life of John Maynard Keynes.* Macmillan, London, 1951.

Hobson, S. G. *Guild Principles in War and Peace.* Bell, London, 1917.

National Guilds: An Inquiry into the Wage System and the Way Out. Bell, London, 1914.

Pilgrim to the Left: Memoirs of a Modern Revolutionist. E. Arnold, London, 1938.

Hyams, Edward. *The New Statesman: The History of the First Fifty Years.* Longmans Green, London, 1963.

Kellogg, Paul U., and Arthur Gleason. *British Labour and the War.* Boni & Liveright, New York, 1919.

Keynes, John Maynard. *The General Theory of Employment, Interest and Money.* Macmillan, London, 1936.

Lansbury, George. *The Miracle of Fleet Street: The Story of the Daily Herald.* Victoria House Printing Co, London, 1925.

Lipset, Seymour Martin, Martin Trow, and James Coleman. *Union Democracy.* Free Press, Glencoe, Ill., 1956.

McBriar, A. M. *Fabian Socialism and British Politics 1884–1918.* Cambridge University Press, Cambridge, 1962.

McCallum, R. B. and Alison Readman. *The British General Election of 1945.* Oxford University Press, London, 1947.

Mackenzie, Compton. *Sinister Street* 1. M. Secker, London, 1913.

Magid, Henry Meyer. *English Political Pluralism: The Problem of Freedom and Organization.* Columbia Studies in Philosophy No. 11. Columbia University Press, New York, 1941.

Mairet, Philip. *A. R. Orage.* J. M. Dent, London, 1936.

Martin, Kingsley. *Editor.* Hutchinson, London, 1968.

Father Figures. Hutchinson, London, 1966.

Marwick, Arthur. *Clifford Allen: The Open Conspirator.* Oliver & Boyd, Edinburgh, 1964.

Miliband, Ralph. *Parliamentary Socialism: A Study in the Politics of Labour.* Allen & Unwin, London, 1961.

Mogey, John. *Family and Neighbourhood: Two Studies in Oxford.* Oxford Pilot Social Survey Committee. Oxford University Press, London, 1956.

Morris, William. *Stories in Prose. Stories in Verse. Shorter Poems. Lectures and Essays.* G. D. H. Cole (ed.), Nonesuch Press. London, 1948.

Nuffield College Social Reconstruction Survey. General Editors G. D. H. Cole and A. D. Lindsay. Individual volumes:

Bourdillon, A. F. C. (ed.). *Voluntary Social Services: Their Place in the Modern State.* Methuen, London, 1945.

Fogarty, M. P. *Prospects of the Industrial Areas of Great Britain.* Methuen, London, 1945.

Silverman, H. A. (ed.). *Studies in Industrial Organization.* Methuen, London, 1946.

Pease, Edward R. *The History of the Fabian Society.* New ed., Intro. by Margaret Cole, Methuen, London, 1946.

Pelling, Henry. *The British Communist Party: A Historical Profile.* Black, London, 1958.

A History of British Trade Unionism. Penguin, Harmondsworth, Middlesex, 1963.

Pribicevic, Branko. 'The Demand for Workers' Control in the Railway, Mining and Engineering Industries, 1910–1922.' D.Phil. Thesis, Nuffield College, Oxford.

The Shop-Stewards' Movement and Workers' Control. Blackwell, Oxford, 1959.

Pritt, D. N. *The Labour Government 1945–51.* Lawrence & Wishart, London, 1963.

Reckitt, Maurice B. *As It Happened.* J. M. Dent, London, 1941.

'G. D. H. Cole, the N.G.L. and the L.R.D.' (unpublished MSS. kindly lent me by Mr Reckitt.)

Robson, W. A. *Nationalized Industry and Public Ownership.* Rev. ed. Allen & Unwin, London, 1962.

(ed.). *Public Enterprise: Developments in Social ownership and Control in Great Britain.* Allen & Unwin, London, 1937.

Rousseau, Jean Jacques. *The Social Contract and Discourses.* Trans. G. D. H. Cole. Everyman, London, n.d.

Ruggiero, Guide de. *The History of European Liberalism.* Trans. R. G. Collingwood. Oxford University Press, Oxford, 1927.

Russell, Bertrand. *Roads to Freedom.* Allen & Unwin, London, 1918.

Shaw, George Bernard (ed.). *Fabian Essays in Socialism.* 6th. ed., Allen & Unwin, London, 1962.

Skidelsky, Robert. *Politicians and the Slump: The Labour Government of 1929–31.* Macmillan, London, 1967.

Stocks, Mary. *The Workers' Educational Association: The First Fifty Years.* Allen & Unwin, London, 1953.

Sturmthal, Adolf. *Workers' Councils: A Study of Workplace Organization on Both Sides of the Iron Curtain.* Harvard University Press, Cambridge, Mass., 1964.

Symons, Julian. *The Thirties: A Dream Revolved.* Cresset Press, London, 1960.

Ulam, Adam B. *The Philosophical Origins of British Socialism.* Harvard University Press, Cambridge, Mass., 1951.

Webb, Beatrice. *Diaries 1912–24.* Ed. Margaret I. Cole. Longmans Green, London, 1952.

Webb, Sidney and Beatrice. *A Constitution for the Socialist Commonwealth of Great Britain.* Longmans Green, London, 1920.

The History of Trade Unionism. 1666–1920. Printed privately, London, 1920.

Industrial Democracy. Printed privately, London, 1944.

Williams, Raymond. *Culture and Society 1780–1950.* Chatto & Windus, London, 1958.

Wood, Neal. *Communism and British Intellectuals.* Gollancz, London, 1959.

INDEX